Women's Political Participation

Researching the Past and Designing the Future

Women's Political Participation

Researching the Past and Designing the Future

Alok Kumar Gupta
Asha Bhandari

AUTHORSPRESS
Publishers of Scholarly Books

Worldwide Circulation through Authorspress Global Network
First Published 2010
by
Authorspress
E-35/103, Jawahar Park
Laxmi Nagar, Delhi-110 092
e-mail: authorspress@yahoo.com

Women's Political Participation:
Researching the Past and Designing the Future
ISBN 978-81-7273-544-9

Printed in India at Tarun Offset, Delhi.

Preface

Should the Father of the Nation, Mahatma Gandhi, or Raja Ram Mohan Roy be alive today, they would have died a million deaths out of the national shame that is meted out to women in India. It is not a satirical statement. Hardly are there days when one does not get to read or listen to news related to atrocities on women in one or another part of the country. A number of movies have been made to bring the issue to the fore. Hundreds of books have been written to draw the attention of the policy makers. Laws have been enacted and implemented to control crime against women. Many women have made it to the central and state legislators and now the panchayti raj institutions (local self-government) as well. However, at the micro level of Indian society it seems things have not changed much. It appears that there is no effective legislation against the horrific torture that goes on in the garb of religious practices, rituals, traditions and customs in different parts of the country. Possibly the existing legislations are either not adequate, or are ill conceived, or it is marred by tardy implementation. There seems to be serious lack of awareness about the role and relevance of women in society as well as in the life of a person.

Erstwhile initiatives have failed to initiate a process of women emancipation. It is puzzling how the existing laws against immoral trafficking, flesh trade, domestic violence, dowry deaths, molestation, rape, gang rape, servitude cannot be used by the very same state which has made it to put an end to such inhuman slavery on one or another pretext. Several literature have been produced on the gory tales of torture inflicted on voiceless women in different parts of India; how even little girls are not spared by the sadistic and perverted men in India who at times are socially powerful.

Education seems to have failed to broaden our outlook. Having been denied the basic right to education and a means to decent and honourable living, women are forced into conditions of life which by all means are inhuman. There are colossal indifferences on the part of official machinery designated to provide aid and, plan and work for appropriate help and emancipation of women. It is a great irony that even after over 60 years of independence, we have failed to liberate half of our own population which seems to have been suffering on different accounts that depicts a situation like internal colonialism, where one gender is the colony of the other.

It is in this backdrop that an initiative has been made to enhance the level of women's political participation. Political participation should be taken as an all-encompassing word. It should not mean merely representation in central and state legislatures, rather it should mean ensuring adequate space for women in the process of decisionmaking within the lowest form of social organisation, i.e., family to the highest form of social organisation, i.e., state. The Women's Reservation Bill in legislatures seems to have shown some light at the end of the dark tunnel that they have been pushed into since time immemorial. Merely lamenting upon the state would not lead us anywhere. The movement for creating adequate space for half of our own population in the process of decisionmaking, right from within the home to the state and national legislature is required to be taken to its logical end.

This book is an endeavour to present a cross-section of opinions related to the need and imperatives towards enhancing women's political participation. An attempt has also been made to peep into the history of political participation, and also as to how Indian and Western philosophers have viewed the necessity of women's political participation. The book also presents an analysis of constitutional and other legal provisions towards enhancing women's political participation. Last, and the most important, there are articles which suggest: How the goal and objective of providing women their due space can be achieved.

I am extremely thankful to all the contributors for withstanding my comments from time to time during the course of editing their piece. I also owe gratitude to them for cooperating with me. I owe a special note of thanks and a deep sense of gratitude to my Vice Chancellor, Justice N.N. Mathur, for his constant support and pressure but for which the book would not have seen the light of day. I owe a special word of thanks to Prof. K.K. Bannerji for his moral support and encouragements during the course of the work. I am grateful to my co-editor, Dr. Asha Bhandari, for her faith and trust in me and help extended. I would like to acknowledge the tremendous help extended by my colleague, Om Prakash, for reading through the texts. I also thank my other colleagues, Rashmi Mathur, Maneesha Mirdha, Kranti Kapoor and Chitra Saruparia, in the Faculty of Policy Science. Last, and the most important, I profusely thank the researchers and authors whose works have been quoted in different articles and also to those whose works we may have used but unknowingly missed to acknowledge.

Alok Kumar Gupta

List of Contributors

Abhilasha Kataria is an Assistant Professor in the Faculty of Law at National Law University, Jodhpur.

Alok Kumar Gupta is an Associate Professor in the Faculty of Policy Science at National Law University, Jodhpur

Aman is a third year student of Law at National Law University, Jodhpur.

Amar Pal Singh is an Associate Professor in the Faculty of Law at National Law University, Jodhpur.

Anand Mathur is Professor and former Head of the Department of Political Science at Jai Narain Vyas University, Jodhpur.

Asha Bhandari is an Assistant Professor of Philosophy in the Faculty of Policy Science at National Law University, Jodhpur.

Baserat Fatima is a research scholar at Symbiosis Law School, Pune.

Geetanjali Sharma is a second year student of Law at National Law University, Jodhpur.

Iswarya Balakrishnan is a third year student of Law at National Law University, Jadhpur.

Jagruti Upadhyaya is an Associate Professor and Head in the Department of English and Humanities at Jodhpur National University.

Kamla Kumari is a Research Scholar at Jawaharlal Nehru University, New Delhi.

Manorma Upadhyaya is a Senior Assistant Professor and Head of the Department of History at Mahila Post-Graduate Mahavidyalaya, Jodhpur.

Mushtaq Ahmad is Sr. Assistant Professor (Law), Directorate of Distance Education, University of Kashmir, Srinagar.

Nayantika R. is a third year student of Law at National Law University, Jodhpur.

Nirupma Prakash is Chairperson of Women Studies and Social Development, and Coordinator of UGC Centre for Women at BITS Pilani, Rajasthan.

Om Prakash is an Assistant Professor of History in the Faculty of Policy Science at National Law University, Jodhpur.

Pradnya Satish Talekar Patil is a second year student of Law at National Law University, Jodhpur.

Prateek Bhattacharya is a third year student of Law at National Law University, Jodhpur.

Saumya Sharma is a third year student of Law at National Law University, Jodhpur.

Shreya Garg is a third year student of Law at National Law University, Jodhpur.

Shubhadha Pednekar is an Assistant Professor at Symbiosis Law School, Pune.

Sindhu V. Reddy is a third year student of Law and Public Policy at National Law University, Jodhpur.

Contents

1

Women Empowerment through Equal Political Participation: A Global Perspective with Special Reference to India

— Anand Mathur

Introduction

"Politics" always remained the men's domain. Jean Jacques Rousseau, whose ideas inspired the French Revolution, advocated women's exclusion from politics in 1762. The American Declaration of Independence also denied the right of equal participation of women in politics. After one century, thinkers like J.S. Mill advocated gender equality in every field including politics. He observed in 1869:

> That the principle which regulates the existing social relations between the two sexes – the legal subordination of one sex to the other—is wrong in itself, and now one of the chief hindrances to human improvement; and that it ought to be replaced by a principle of perfect equality, admitting no power or privilege on the one side, nor disability on the other.[1]

In post-World War II, the sensitivity about equality of sexes gained ground. The UN Charter and the Universal Declaration of Human Rights highlighted equality between men and women. But women are still marginalised in political field and are victims of masculine prejudices towards their participation in politics.

Not to talk of developing countries, women's participation in politics remained limited even in most developed and democratised countries. The average representation of women worldwide presently stands at 16.08 per cent. In Switzerland, known for its deep-rooted democratic traditions, women were given voting right at the federal level only in 1971, after 123 years of male suffrage, while at the local level, women were allowed to vote in every canton only by 1990. The first country where women were allowed to stand for election was the United States in the year 1788. Women were granted the right to vote in US only in 1920. The first three countries where women received the right to vote and right to stand for elections simultaneously were Finland (1906), Denmark and Iceland (both 1915). Very rarely did countries grant these rights at the same time, and many countries which introduced either one or the other in the first half of the Twentieth Century did so with some restrictions or conditions.[2]

Thus, the women had to struggle hard to attain basic political rights. By contrast, many newly independent countries in the later half of the twentieth century took the opportunity in the aftermath of de-colonisation to introduce suffrage simultaneously for men and women.[3]

Only Scandinavian countries have more than 40 per cent representation of women in their legislature, the rest of the world has marginal representation of women in parliaments. Sweden in 1999 became the first country to have more female ministers than male ones in its government. In 2002, women constituted over 42 per cent of the members of parliament in Sweden, 38 per cent in Denmark, and 36 per cent in Norway. Except these Nordic countries, the slow pace of women's participation in the larger arena of political life is a sad feature in the history of women's empowerment. A careful study undertaken by the International Labour Organisation indicates that at this rate, women will take five centuries to have equality with men in political life.

The Inter-Parliamentary Union has compiled the list of women in national parliaments as on May 31, 2009,[4] providing the classified list of 187 countries in descending order of the percentage of women in the lower or single house. If Rwanda is on the top of the list with 56.3 per cent women in its parliament,

Qatar, Saudi Arabia, Oman, Nauru, etc., did not have any women in their national parliaments.

STATUS OF INDIAN WOMEN'S POLITICAL PARTICIPATION

The Indian women were gifted with the equal right to vote and contest immediately after independence (Article 326). But constitutional provisions of universal suffrage could not change their status or mindset and attitude of men-dominated society. The table below shows the thin representation of women in the Lok Sabha (House of People).

Table 1: Women Parliamentarians in Lok Sabha

S.No.	*Year*	*Total Seats*	*Women*	*Percentage*
1.	1952	449	22	4.8
2.	1957	500	27	5.4
3.	1962	503	34	6.8
4.	1967	523	31	5.9
5.	1971	521	22	4.2
6.	1977	544	19	3.4
7.	1980	544	28	5.1
8.	1984	544	44	8.1
9.	1989	517	27	5.22
10.	1991	544	39	7.18
11.	1996	543	40	7.3
12.	1998	543	43	7.9
13.	1999	543	48	8.8
14.	2004	543	46	8.4
15.	2009	543	59	10.9

It is evident from the above table that women's participation in parliament has never gone beyond per cent, and the average representation remained a mere 7.1 per cent. Similarly, in state assemblies, it has never crossed 10 per cent, though Indian womenfolk had actively participated in the freedom struggle and other movements for their rights.

The grim situation indicates that women's representation in politics requires special consideration. Mahatma Gandhi believed that without equal participation of women, the politics would partially remain paralysed. The factual position of women's political participation clearly indicates that India as well as the world is suffering from such partial paralysis.

In support of equal participation, two arguments are being advanced; first, the human rights-based democratic argument and second, the efficiency-based pragmatic argument. It is a basic principle of democracy that adult citizens from all walks of life should have equal right to political participation. It is advocated that women's participation would result in better decision making, with broader perspectives and in congruence of the needs of society.

Why are Women Marginalised?

The developing countries of the world are facing the problems of poverty, ignorance, illiteracy, deprivation and exploitation. It is obvious that women are facing the brunt of problems more than men. Disparity in the developed world takes the form of women being an unequal partner in the progress while in the developing world it takes an additional dimension in the form of ignominies and atrocities on women.

The traditional role of women in society is an obstacle to their participation on equal terms with men in political life. Their primary role confined to household activities only. This mindset is so deeply imbibed that women's participation in the political field on an equal footing with men is not easily accepted by society. Domestic responsibilities, lack of financial clout, the ever growing criminalisation of politics and the threat of character assassination[6] are making it increasingly difficult for women to be part of the political framework.

Julie Ballington, Gender-Project Manager at the Stockholm based Institute for Democracy and Electoral Assistance says, there are many obstacles that continue to hinder women's advancement to parliament. The obstacles include factors such as the strength of the women's movement, patriarchy, discrimination, illiteracy and poverty, and a host of other socio-economic problems that have a direct impact on women. However, the key obstacle is the nature of the political party system and the commitment of political parties to gender equality.

The obstacles include factors, such as the strength of the women's movement, patriarchy, discrimination, illiteracy and poverty, and a host of other socio-economic problems that have a direct impact on women. However, the key obstacle is the nature of the party political system and the commitment of political parties to gender equality.

What can be done?

This analysis of the reasons for women's marginalisation from politics suggests a number of strategies for equal participation of both sexes. The Beijing platform for action calls on actors to: create a gender balance in government and administration; integrate women into political parties; recognise that shared work and parental responsibilities promote women's increased participation in public life; promote gender balance within the UN system; work towards equality between women and men in the private sector; establish equal access for women to training; increase women's capacity to participate in decision making and leadership; and increase women's participation in the electoral process and political activities.[7]

The introduction of the quota system is an efficient and effective means of addressing the problem. The quota system takes different forms in different countries. The most common forms are those that are introduced through constitutional or national legislation, and those that are adopted voluntarily by political parties. In 1994, the social democratic party of Sweden introduced the principle of Zipper or Zebra. According to this, the principle male and female candidates be placed alternately on list of contestants, in order to have 50 per cent quota for women. The labour party of Norway introduced 40 per cent quota for women in 1983 whereas the social democratic party fixed 40 per cent quota in Denmark in 1988. But there is no constitutional clause in these countries fixing the quota for women in their parliaments. It is the political parties that have adopted their own informal quota mechanism to ensure certain minimum representation of women. The quota system needs to be well articulated and women Organisations with their coordinated efforts should lobby for implementation, only them the desired goal may be achieved.

What is being done?

The countries of world, individually and collectively, are taking measures for promoting women's equal participation in the political field. The United Nations (UN) and various governmental and non-governmental organisations are preparing the ground for a more active political role for women at the local, regional and global levels.

India is working for a quota system through Constitutional legislation and also at the political party level. The Committee on the Status of Women in India (CSWI) suggested that women's representation in political institutions, especially at the grass-roots level, needed to be increased through a policy of reservation of seats for women. In 1988, the National Perspective Plan for Women suggested that a 30 per cent quota for women be introduced at all levels of elective bodies. This demand translated into reality by the adoption of the 73rd and 74th Amendments to the Indian Constitution in 1993. A provision for 33.3 per cent quota for women at the local level bodies like panchayats, blocks and municipalities, has been made by these amendments. Now, there are nearly one million women in such democratic bodies. Such large-scale women's participation in public life is very encouraging trend for women's empowerment. This has provided a grooming ground for prospective candidates for parliament. However, the 81st Constitutional Amendment Bill for reserving one-third seats for women in parliament and state legislature is pending since 1997. Although all political parties showed their commitment to 33 per cent reservation for women in their manifestos yet till date this has not be translated into legislation. If this amendment is adopted by the Indian parliament, India will set an example before the world.

The World Classification of Women in National Parliament has put India on 99 position out of 187 countries. There is a slight improvement of its position from 104 out of 189 countries in July 2006.

Conclusion

To secure women's rightful place in society and to enable them to decide their own destiny, and for the growth of genuine and sustainable democracy, women's participation in politics is essential. This will not only uplift their personality but will open the way for their social and economic empowerment. Their participation in public life will solve many problems of society. Gandhiji had written in 1929: "Woman is the embodiment of sacrifice and suffering, and her advent into public life should, therefore, result in purifying it, in restraining unbridled ambition and accumulation of property."[8]

It is supposed that women's participation will clean the politics and bring more transparency in administration. More women representation would expand areas of cooperation, reduce unnecessary irritants, and develop reciprocity in goodwill and mutual confidence. Equal participation of women would change the political face of the globe, and will also open a new vista of co-operation, amity and growth. Swami Vivekananda rightly observed: a civilisation could be judged by the way it treats its women. If a true democratic and equitable society is to be created then women from all segments, including the less privileged, must be given a voice in decisions that affected their lives and that of their family.

References

1. "On Liberty, Representative Government, The Subjection of Women—Three Essays by John Stuart Mill," Oxford University Press, 1960, p. 427.
2. International IDEA Sweden.
3. Joni Saeger & Inter Parliamentary Union, *The State of Women in the World Atlas*, Penguin Books, 1997.
4. Annex. 1.

5. Umesh Chandra Agarwal, "Rajniti Aur Prashasan mein Mahila!," *Yojna,* December 2000, p.17.
6. *Times of India,* February, 1998
7. Dr. Lorraine Corner, "Women's participation in decision making and leadership—A Global Perspective."
8. K.R. Narayanan, "Human Rights and Empowerment of Women." Justice Sunanda Bhandari Memorial Lecture, *Mainstream,* Dec. 21, 2002.

2

Women's Status and Political Participation: The South Asian Perspective

— *Alok Kumar Gupta*

Alongside several movements and struggles that ensued to mitigate the class distinction prevailing in the society, the other prominent struggle that has been waged in the South Asian region is the movement for women's emancipation. The South Asian region that consists of seven countries, i.e., India, Pakistan, Bangladesh, Sri Lanka, Bhutan, Nepal and the Maldives are largely the traditional societies with several pockets of modernised groups scattered within these societies. Mostly the centres or the urban and semi-urban areas in these countries have experienced doses of modernisation but they are largely cultural modernisation which is, put precisely, a Western influence rather than modernisation in real sense of the term.

Modernisation in fact is a developmental concept. Modernisation means economic, social, political and cultural development. The economic development is the key to development in the rest of the other field. It means that economic development would automatically trigger political, social and cultural modernisation. The growth of economy and development in the field of science and technology is bound to trigger a chain reaction in all other walks of life. It is bound to change the very outlook of individual in society. Such a modernisation shall be sustainable and would have a momentum of its own. However, in the South Asian region it is cultural modernisation which has invaded the society first and then modernisation in all other walks of life. This has also precipitated many problems. Cultural modernisation in most cases leads to a generation gap where one generation is more akin to Western lifestyles, clothes, food habits, practices, etc., and the other generation is still rooted in the traditions of society. This leads to a generation gap where practices on younger generation often become a bone of contention between the younger and the older generations.

Precisely, this is what has happened in most of the South Asian societies, though many scholars brand these societies as a society with 'modernity in traditions.' Nevertheless, the fact remains that these societies are suffering some kind of anomalies which require to be addressed with due care and perseverance. The most vulnerable section of such an anomaly happens to be women and children, and the status of South Asian women is no exception to this rule. Though the conditions of South Asian women has improved remarkably in the recent past, still a very large section of the women population in this region are writhing under the burden of traditional society which is largely a male-dominated society, where a large section of the women are still treated as personal property of the men, and all norms that a society evolves are required to be observed by the women, and in case of failure, are punished by men. Punishment varies from domestic violence, beating, mental and physical torture, and rape to murder.

Therefore, a study of the status of women in South Asia is both interesting as well as disturbing. Interesting because it provides a unique mix of traditions and modernity which can not be readily observed in any other part of the world. Disturbing because the kind of challenges that the women of this region face are at times heart-rending and is also unique as it cannot be seen in any other part of the world. Some of these challenges can be enumerated as follows:

- This is a region where women are treated as personal property of men, as mentioned above.
- This is a region where women are sold and bought for purposes varying from marriage to serve as maid-servant as also to work in brothels and flesh trade.

- This is a region where women are burnt alive for want of dowry or for any other dispute, including issues like virginity.
- This is a region where women in the rural areas suffer from acute poverty, with no access to food, shelter and education, i.e., the basic necessities of life.
- This is a region where women's are made to fight guerrilla war as part of insurgent groups in the zones of conflict.
- This is a region where a women's lives are terminated before they arrive in this world, i.e., during the phase of pregnancy itself.
- This is a region where a mother (who is a woman herself) discriminates between a male and a female child.
- This is a region where acute poverty forces families to sell their women for flesh trade.

These are challenges to name but a few that the South Asian region as a whole is suffering from. However, it should not be misunderstood that the governments of the region are not doing anything about it. Undoubtedly, each of the governments of the seven South Asian countries have initiated several programmes to emancipate women from the shackles of the traditional practices, to uplift the status of women through women empowerment programmes. However, the fact remains that these governments have initiated many programmes for women empowerment and to uplift the status of women but still the rate of success has been considerably less. Therefore, it makes it imperative to explore the reason as to why the status of women in South Asian region has continued to be largely deplorable. It is in this backdrop that the political empowerment of women is observed, discussed and analysed. India is the dominant culture of the region and modernisation trickles through from this country to the other countries of the region. Therefore, it makes and imperative to address the issues such as: the present status of women in India *vis-à-vis* different countries of South Asian region; the possible reasons for their status; the major initiatives taken by the governmental and non-governmental organisations in different countries of the region; and why the conditions of women continue to be deplorable even today. Could it be improved upon by enhancing women's political participation? What are the ways and means through which women's political participations can be enhanced?

DEMOGRAPHY OF SOUTH ASIA

South Asia is roughly inhabited by more than 1.5 billion[1] people of which India has a major share with over one billion of the total population of South Asia. The total area of the South Asian region is about 4.4 million[2] square kilometres. Table 1 provides the details of population in the South Asian countries.

Table 1
Population of South Asian Countries

S.No	*Country*	*Area (Sq. Kms)*	*Population*	*Census Year*
1	India	3,166,414	1,028,610,328	March 1, 2001
2	Pakistan	796,095	132,352,279	March 2, 1998
3	Bangladesh	143,998	130,522,598	March 22, 2001
4	Sri Lanka	65,525	16,864,544	July 17, 2001
5	Nepal	147,181	23,151,423	June 22, 2001
6	Bhutan	38,364	672,425	May 30-31, 2005
7	Maldives	298	298,968	March 21-28, 2006

Source: The Population Data have been compiled from *The Europa World Year Book 2008* (London & New York: Routeledge, Taylor and Francis Group, 2008).

Out of the total population of 1.5 billion in South Asia nearly half of the population is women. Except for Sri Lanka and Nepal where the population of women is slightly higher than the male population, rest of the South Asian countries have less population of women *vis-à-vis* the population of male. Gender discrimination and violence against women are the major reasons for the decline of female population in these countries over the years. Table 2 below provides a comprehensive picture of female population in different South Asian countries.

Thus, it is quite evident that South Asia consists of a major part of the world population. India is a dominant country both in terms of geographical area as well as population in the region. However, the region is not rich in terms of resources as it is rich in population compared to many other regions of the world. There are several reasons for the same and the most remarkable feature of the South Asian region is that in this part of the world, the population is hardly considered as a resource, rather it is considered as a burden unlike China, the most populated country of the world. The lack of resources and other means has been a great limitation towards transforming the population into a resource. Consequently, nearly half of the South Asian population, i.e., women, have remained a neglected lot. Nevertheless, economic, social and political developments in South Asia have brought with them profound changes in the status of women. In general, women's conditions have improved with economic development and social and political change that favours equality and individual rights. At the same time, cultural traditions, especially those related to family life, continue to have a strong influence on the status of women in the region.

Table 2

Female Population and Their Percentage of Total Population

SN	*Country*	*Male*	*Female*	*Percentage of Female Population*	*Census Year*
1	India	532,156,772	496,453,556	48.3%	March 1, 2001
2	Pakistan	68,873,686	63,478,593	48%	March 2, 1998
3	Bangladesh	67,731,320	62,791,278	48%	March 22, 2001
4	Sri Lanka	8,343,964	8,520,580	50%	July 17, 2001
5	Nepal	11,563,921	11,587,502	50%	June 22, 2001
6	Bhutan	364,482	307,943	48%	May 30-31, 2005
7	Maldives	151,459	147,509	49.3%	March 21-28, 2006

Source: The Population Data have been compiled from *The Europa World Year Book 2008* (London & New York: Routeledge, Taylor and Francis Group, 2008).

Until recently in most South Asian countries, few women attended secondary school or university, and few worked outside the home. Over the past 50 years, larger and larger proportions of women have completed primary and secondary school. The proportion of women attending university, although much smaller, is also growing. More recently, women have started taking up paid employment in greater numbers, particularly in the manufacturing, clerical and service sectors. Rural women too have been working in the unorganised sector as wage labourers on daily basis. Over the past 50 years, women's life expectancy has improved across the region, overtaking men's life expectancy in nearly all countries. Yet during early childhood, girls are still more likely to die than boys in South Asian countries, as also in these countries, unusual birth rates for boys and girls in recent years point to the prevalence of sex-selective abortion.

Another remarkable feature of the region is the feudal mindset of the male community, and this is why the South Asian society is sometimes called as a male-dominated society. This is starkly evident in Pakistan and Bangladesh followed by India. The other major reason for the suffering of the women of South Asian region is the prevalence of the Zone of Conflicts in the region. South Asia is rampant with numerous conflicts such as Maoist and Naxalbari movement in Nepal and India, atrocities of Taliban in Pakistan, Tamil separatist movement under the aegis of Liberation Tigers of Tamil Elam (LTTE) in Sri Lanka, insurgency movement in Kashmir valley and Northeast India, political volatility in Bangladesh, Loathsampas problem in Bhutan to name but a few. The plight of women in any area of conflict nappens to be extremely painful, and it is often the women who have to bear the brunt of violence and conflict. The most heinous of the crime against women is committed against women in Pakistan. The way the young women were being caned and beaten by the Taliban militia in Swat of Pakistan which was shown on various news channels was really a shame on humanity. The incident speaks volumes about the feudal mindset of the South Asian male community. The worst stories of crime against women must have been well beyond the reach of media and the investigative journalists in the region or the world, and whatever have been revealed through media may just be the tip of the iceberg.

Thus, the status of women in South Asia presents a complex mix of growth and backwardness. Growth is very limited whereas backwardness and suffering are widely prevalent. It is this complex mix that makes the study of the status of South Asian women an interesting one. It is also difficult to reach at any kind of further generalisation in terms of growth, development and empowerment of South Asian women. The United Nations has defined the status of women in the context of their access to knowledge, economic resources and political power, as well as their personal autonomy in the process of decision making.

Empowerment of Women: Predicament or Affirmative Action

The political participation of women in the world seems relatively low and it is duly because of the existence of the patriarchal mindset even in the political parties in almost all countries in the world. The participation of women in the parliament of Japan and USA is only 7.1 per cent and 17 per cent respectively, while in the countries like Rwanda it is 49 per cent and in Sweden, 46 per cent. The status of women in the developed countries is also lower in all sectors. Barring some exceptions of European, American and Asian countries, women in the world are socially, economically, culturally and politically dominated and they are excluded from the opportunities.

The ability of women in politics is found in many South Asian countries to alacrity. History bears witness that South Asia has been a region where various faces of women have been revealed from time to time, like Aung Sang Suu Kyi of Mayanmar, politically shrewd like most of the women parliamentarians as Jayalalitha, Uma Bharti, Mayawati, Mamatha Bannerjee to name but a few, development-oriented like Siriavo Bandarnayike and Chandrika Kumaratunga of Sri Lanka. Benazir Bhutto was the first Prime Minister of an Islamic state. Interestingly women's participation in politics has been found increasingly more in a number in South Asian in countires spite of the fact that the sex-ratio is the least and female infanticide is widely rampant, it is far more than any other region of the world. It becomes clear that, like some thinkers point out, these are the sporadic cases of women's power. This becomes evident from the fact that political participation of women in South Asia is in general quite pathetic. The number of countries that belong to the low human development are four out of seven, namely, Pakistan, Nepal, Bhutan and Bangladesh. One-third reservation has been given to women in the Union Parishad of Bangladesh. Most of the cases regarding violence against women occur during the election time. Though women in these areas have the right to franchise yet most often they are not allowed to use their franchise due to religious fundamentalism and also due to patriarchal structure, military regime, etc. In the Indian parliament there are a mere 9.1 per cent women. The UNDP report shows that in 2001 the women's representation in the Lower House is extremely low.

Table 3

Representation of Women in South Asia

S.No.	*Country*	*Year Women Received Rights Appointed in Parliament*	*Year First elected or*	*Lower House as in 2002*
1	India	1950	1952	8.8 %
2	Pakistan	1947	1973	Nil
3	Nepal	1951	1952	5.9
4	Bhutan	1953	1975	9.3
5	Sri Lanka	1931	1947	4.0
6	Bangladesh	1972	1973	9.1
7	Maldives	1932	1979	6.0

Source: UNDP Report 2001 (As quoted in an Article by Shubhamitra Das, titled "Women and Empowerment: Predicament or Affirmative Action" *The Indian Journal of Political Science*, vol.LXVIII, No.1, Jan-March 2007, p.127.)

The pattern masquerading under the guise of equity shows that the women's representation did not even cross the 10 per cent margin. The talk of empowerment doesn't seem complete if 50 per cent of the population is not given enough representation. For the process of democratising the region and for political development, women entering politics is imperative.

The section of society most notably excluded from the process of all-round development of the South Asian region in terms of both the beneficiaries and the contributors is women. Casting a cursory glance, or to put it more precisely, a macro level analysis of the status of women in South Asia reveals that economic development and social modernisation have benefited women in South Asia. Shrinking gender gaps in enrolment at schools and employment in South Asian countries suggest that the status of women is improving. Women's increasing life expectancy at birth also points to advances in nutrition and heathcare. Yet significant improvements in women's status require changes in attitudes that are embedded in centuries of traditional culture and feudal mindset.

Detailed studies often show that high levels of education and household income do not necessarily assure a better women's status in societies with strong traditions of male domination. At times it has come to the notice that, relatively wealthy, educated women may be more restricted within the household than poor, uneducated women who are forced to play a stronger, more independent role by economic necessity. In India, the influence of son preference on fertility is stronger among women who are literate and who live in urban areas than among other women. On this pretext in countries like India it has been the practice that the biggest hurdle in the progress and emancipation of women is women itself. At times the voice of a feminist and a progressive male is subdued by the mother and other older women in the family.

What does the future hold? Advances in women's education can be expected to continue, although in some countries of South Asia, like Bangladesh, Nepal and Bhutan, the pace of change is slow. A shrinking proportion of working-age men in some South Asian populations combined with continuing reductions in hours worked will exert pressure on employers to hire women and to encourage them to remain in the workforce. In the process, employers will have to accommodate women's needs to manage both work and family responsibilities, and husbands will have to provide more help at home. Lingering problems of son preference and the advent of sex-selective abortion pose a dilemma for South Asian policymakers. Evidence suggests that social and economic development alone may not fully counteract these manifestations of women's low status in a patriarchal society—at least not right away. Given the existing gender differences in earnings in the marketplace, parents or parents-in-law may perceive long-run returns from sons to be substantially higher than from daughters. Social development for men and women—in the form of education, media exposure, and opportunities to work outside the home—can provide access to new ideas and, with time, a transformation of cultural values. In South Asia's developing countries and advanced economies alike, hiring practices and employment conditions need to be reviewed to reduce gender discrimination and to make it easier for parents—both men and women—to balance work and family obligations. Both men and women are expected to broaden their thinking pattern and be increasingly more accommodative of the aspiration of daughters and daughters-in-law, and promote them to join the mainstream of education and employment opportunities. They must try to groom more and more of Kalpana Chawlas and Sunita Williams.

Although it has proven difficult to end gender discrimination by government legislations alone, specific issues—such as sex-selective abortion, and care and support for elderly women—require immediate policy attention. Education could be the right panacea of such ills in post-colonial societies. Law has its own limitations, and legal obligations alone would not lead to a drastic change in the mindset and the society as a whole, it can only check the growth of violence against women to an extent. Education would make the women aware about their rights, and would broaden the perspective of men to accept the individuality of women, and provide the space that she rightfully deserves as an equal partner in the home, society and the country.

Even though women are the major founders of the society, yet they have not achieved equality with men. Of the world's 1.3 billion poor people, it is estimated that nearly 70 per cent are women. Between 75 and 80 per cent of the world's 27 million refugees are women. There are many countries where women are second-class citizens. No matter how talented they are, they never get a chance to develop. There are lot of countries where women are treated as subordinate and second-class citizens, though the 'equal rights' is preserved in the Constitution. The status of women in South Asia is no exception to the status of women in most other parts of the world.

Women in India enjoy far more freedom as per the Constitution of India. Law in most cases is tilted in favour of women, including the family and divorce laws. However, in terms of practical implementation of such laws, a lot depends upon the socio-economic conditions of women, and their caste and class. India is a society where tradition and modernity exist side by side. A number of public policies have been initiated towards women's upliftment and empowerment. The status of women in India has improved remarkably and there are also growth and development of feminist organisations of different hues. NGOs, National Women Commissions, Independent Women Organisations, are working along with governmental organisations to improve the status of women and strengthen their socio-economic conditions. Such initiatives have really come a long way in India. However, there still remains a tremendous lot to achieve in this direction especially in case of rural India. Therefore, this book is an attempt to continue the ongoing debate about women's empowerment in India by creating a political space for them within the Legislatures across the country. The title of the book is suggestive enough of the theme. The book aims at researching the past to reshape the future. The past helps us to learn about the mistakes and opportunities. A nation-state is required to learn from its mistakes so that it should not keep repeating the same. Similarly, it requires taking note of the opportunities and marching forward. Both are essential if India aspires to have a strong international personality among the comity of nations, as it cannot achieve the same by neglecting nearly half its population.

References

1. The exact total population of South Asia as compiled from *Europa Year Book 2008* is 1,332,472,565 which is based on the figure mostly belonging to the Census data of 2001 to 2005. Therefore, the official update for the year 2009 may exceed 1.5 billion mark.
2. The exact area as compiled from *Europa Year Book 2008* is 4,357,875 square kilometres. However, some part of the territory stands

disputed between neighbours in the region. For example, the 11,639 square kilometre of Azad Kashmir and the Northern Areas (including Gilgit and Baltistan) with an area of 28,000 square kilometres both currently in possession of Pakistan, remains a disputed territory and is claimed by India. On the other hand, some parts of Jammu and Kashmir are claimed by Pakistan.

3

Political Philosophy of Women's Political Participation

— *Alok Kumar Gupta & Geetanjali Sharma*

Should women be allowed to participate in the decision-making process or political process within a state? This has always remained a matter of debate. The debate that has ensued in India on account of reserving 33 per cent of the seats in the Indian legislatures is not a new debate, rather the whole of political philosophy is replete with this debate. Therefore, to widen the perspectives of the Indian policy makers in particular and the policy makers of other parts of the world in general, a thorough perusal of the political philosophy would never be out of place. Therefore, this article makes it imperative to provide a stock of the status of women's political participation according to the Western political philosophy.

Political philosophy of Plato: Strong Case for Women's Political Participation

Plato's *Republic* seems to be the first written account wherein the philosopher has made a strong case for women's political participation. Plato writes in *Republic*:

> We must select women of the necessary character to share the life of men of like character and guard the city along with them, in as much as they are capable and of a kindred nature.[1]

An indepth analysis of the text of *Republic* reveals that Plato recognised the presence of women, and viewed their potential contributions in a positive light for the betterment of the *polis* (City-State). He was concerned with the usefulness of the rights possessed by the women[2], equality of men and women, and in certain cases, women being better than men[3], the opportunities to hone their skills in terms of education and gymnasium for becoming a guardian being given to both men and women.[4] Thus he successfully articulates that differentiation in treatment between one guardian and another should be based on difference of talent, not on difference of sex[5]. He clearly mentions:

> That if women are to become fit to be guardians, we shall not have one education to make guardians out of men and another for the women, especially when education will have the same nature to work upon.[6]

Plato, thus, strongly advocates that women have all rights to become guardians and rule the *polis* if they are so suited for it, and merely their biological make-up should not be a hindrance towards their becoming the rulers.

Therefore, in order to substantiate his views, Plato presents a simple analogy of a watchdog, and says that both the he-dog and she-dog possess equal capacity and perform equally well when it comes to performing the job of a watchdog. It is not that one entrusts males to take exclusive care of the flocks and leave females at home under the idea that bearing and suckling of puppies is just enough labour for them.[7] Similarly the job of guardianship within a state shall be performed equally well by men and women. Thus he clearly denied that there is any systematic difference between men and women with respect to the abilities relevant to guardianship—the capacity to understand reality and make reasonable judgements about it.[8]

Thus the two basic arguments on which Plato's feministic views get their support are:

1. Woman's biology ought not to settle the question of her destiny;
2. Women's intelligence and reason ought to be called upon in the running of the state.

From his *Republic,* we derive the true nature of a ruler and its determination being done by one's soul and clearly not by one's gender. Thus the soul is an innate aspect of the person, one which is not dictated upon by society or gender but by the individual inclinations or the manifestations of the soul. The person is born with the kind of soul he or she has, and his/her amount of responsibility depends on the type of soul he/she has whether ruler, auxiliary or multitude. Thus more emphasis is on the principle of "different pursuits to different natures and the same to the same."[9]

It is the equality of some men in the context of some women who have similar pursuits which is being talked about. Hence Plato's assertion is derived from two metaphysical arguments that emphasize inequality:

1) People are by nature different and because of that they should be educated separately to be able to assume different roles in the *polis.*
2) People with special skills can spot particular talents or skills that are vital in a specific pursuit these people should become leaders.

Thus Plato articulately concludes by saying: "We have, without being swamped, managed to reach the conclusion that our men and women guardians must follow all pursuits in common: rather the argument somehow comes to an agreement with itself that its proposals are practical and advantageous."[10]

These ideas are viewed as extremely radical to the ancient Greek society where Plato lived in. Plato gave rights to women guardians which were otherwise denied to Athenian women—rights being that of education, vocation opportunity, unimpeded social intercourse, equal legal status, sexual choice, own and dispose of property, and equal political participation. The liberalist definition of feminism which promotes equality of sexes traces its origin in Platonic thoughts.[11]On similar lines the post-modern liberalism advocates the actual presence of women in the political space, her bodies, works, labours and voices to be recognised in the political front, which is very similar to what Plato advocated in *Republic.*

On the grounds of differences between men and women being the reason for women's exclusion, we again see the refutation of this argument in Plato's *Republic*. Plato advocates that pleasure and pain are vital principles of a *polis*, and citizens must share them in common. In order for that to be possible, both men and women should hold political offices in common, work in tandem to neutralise the "differences" between them when male "begets" and female "bears." Thus his eugenics programme solves the problem of differences. Therefore, by depicting women as guardians, Plato elevates them to a level where they are no longer a desired object nor desire themselves.[12]

The critics of Plato might articulate that his actions were intended towards the strengthening of *polis* and not women per se. His rationale of bringing women to the political front was to ensure that more than half the talent of the city does not get wasted, and hence for the sake of *polis*, the potential of women needs to be exploited as well. But this too favours the side of women as by this mechanism women are being given opportunities which they were otherwise denied by other philosophers in several different eras either in pre-Socratic or post-Socratic political philosophy.

Political Philosophy of Aristotle: Antifeminist or Equally Feminist as Plato?

Aristotle was the disciple of Plato, yet he goes on to refute most of the philosophies that Plato supported. Plato's work is a compilation of several unique and radical ideas that aim to establish an ideal state. Aristotle, on the other hand, explains the political situation prevalent during his time, and his work is just a compilation of the ideas and views from different constitutions and government. Thus quite evident is the fact that unlike Plato, Aristotle accepted the customary subordination of women to men, which was the common idea prevalent in ancient Greek society. In his philosophy women are portrayed inferior to men and their place in the social ladder was more than slaves but less than men.

In his book, the *Generation of Animals,* Aristotle says that male and female are different on the grounds that the male is better and more divine than the female.[13] The female is weaker and colder in her nature and she should be looked upon as a deformity though present in the ordinary state of nature. In his book *Nichomachean Ethics,* Aristotle points out that man is the master, right and proper, and manages everything that falls within him as the head of the house. If the wife takes charge of some matters in certain situations, it is not by virtue of merit but by money and influence.[14] Aristotle explains that the relationship between husband and wife is just like that of the government and the governed in an aristocracy. Therefore he claims that justice is to be distributed in such a way that the male who is superior in merit receives the larger share of affection than his female counterpart.[15]

Aristotle in his book, *Politics,* has discussed relationship and the status of male and female more elaborately. He writes that in the relationship of male and female, the inequality is permanent.[16] The woman is described as "an infertile male" and also "a male is a male in virtue of a particular ability and a female in virtue of a particular inability."[17] In comparison between the slave and women he says that a slave has no deliberative authority at all, however the woman has it but without authority.[18] Though the moral virtues belong to all, the temperance, courage and justice of a man and a woman are not the same. The courage of a man is shown in commanding and that of a woman is shown in obeying.[19] According to Aristotle a man would be a coward if he has no more courage than a courageous woman, and the woman would be thought as loquacious if she imposed no more restraint on her conversation than a good man.[20] This would be opposed to the basic attribute, which she has been depicted with as: *Silence is a women's glory.*[21]

Thus his opinion of women is seen in a negative light where they have no authority and hence should give in to the commands of the men. By depicting them in a stereotypical manner he disapproves of any political liberty given to women in terms of speech, expression and decision making. However it is vital to remember that Aristotle can be justly called as the founder of essentialism and one of his themes—women's essence—is seen with metaphysics, biology and politics. Aristotle said that women have a biologically based essence that is distinct and inferior to that of men, and thus they deserve a subordinate status. Such essentialism is rejected today as an illegitimate kind of naturalism that ignores the differences among women or the diverse facts of women's experiences.[22] Further, Aristotle's views can be seen in the light of certain ideas which support the cause of his feminism, though it is not overtly mentioned anywhere.

Firstly, he offers an ideal for women that include active participation in political life. He rejects the views that political life involves the irrational use of force to control others but argues that a life of virtue involves statesmanship. He says that happiness requires activity, and such an ideal would require proper restructuring of society. If human life acquires active and social engagements, then social structures that prevent particular groups from engagement would automatically become morally wrong, and thus subjugation of women would not hold any justification. Thus his concept of ethics can serve as a basis for social change.[23]

Secondly, females have been relegated to a subordinate position by virtue of them being influenced by emotions, and as emotions are associated with lack of reason their actions are considered less moral. However, Aristotle too is trying to project that rationality requires appropriate emotions. His discussion on anger, when he says that the extent to which it is to be displayed should neither be too much nor too less, clearly shows that he recognises the value of emotions. Hence women being emotional in nature cannot be a basis for classifying them to be low on morals.[24]

Thirdly, Aristotle says that humans by themselves do not produce true excellence. They rely on parents to bring them up; a social structure where parents are protected is thus emphasized in Aristotle's projected state. Therefore he is an opponent of the principle of virility. Caring thus becomes a trait, which helps to promote, encourage and develop human excellence in others.[25] Thus opposing Ethics of Care as being responsible to the subdued role of women may not be completely justified.[26]

Based on the above-mentioned arguments it is clear that Aristotle's subjugation of women and their denial to enter into political foray was based on certain premises which either are flawed or else could be interpreted in a better manner to facilitate their increasing role in society and *polis*. Moreover, one may also argue that in his urge to oppose Plato, may have thought of keeping women in perpetual conditions of subjugation as opposed to the idea of emancipation of women as argued by Plato. On the other hand, on most occasions he has ended up being the greatest of Platonists, hence to he should not be treated as being anti-feminist.

Political Philosophy of Stoics: Championed the Cause of Women's Equality

Stoics viewed that both men and women have an equal capacity for virtue, so both should philosophize.[27] Women have an important role to play in progression. Since they are equals as human beings, they are alike capable in wisdom and temperance, and should have an equal share in courage and justice as well. According to Musanius, since men and women differ in physical strength, some jobs are more suitable to one sex than to the other. But all jobs can be done by either sex and women who have the worth should not be prevented from a particular job by unequal distribution so as to not to attain equal virtue.

On the question of citizenship, Stoics demarcated between citizens and inhabitants, thereby excluding foreigners and slaves as citizens. However there is no explicit mention about the women. Further it is to be noted that the Stoics spoke in terms of a cosmic city which is governed with universal law that applies rationally to all human beings.[28] Therefore, Stoics could be considered as champions for women's equality and granting them equal political rights such as right to become citizens and thereby chose whom to be governed by.

Political Philosophy of St. Augustine: Recognition to Women's Intellectual Worth

St. Augustine was a prominent medieval philosopher whose ideals were modelled on the Platonic ideas. As per the role of women, he is one philosopher whom the feminists love to hate. He refused to believe the fact that women are made in the image of God. In the complex issue of human sexuality, he relied on language of hierarchy, control and subordination of women to men.[29] It is interesting to note that in, "Augustine's Letters to Women"[30], a wide range of issues have been discussed. As a church leader in Hippo, Augustine discussed issues like disposition of property disputes, church rituals and administration. Though the women did not loom in the public sphere their views were called for in case of advice and adjudication. Thus whatever Augustine thought about women's body, he did not discount their intellectual powers. Hence even though the medieval era championed the suppression of women, especially in church, thereby demeaning their importance in both temporal and spiritual world, yet the scope for appreciation of their intellectual powers by great philosophers like Augustine, shows that women's intellect was respected, and this could be a ground to accept their abilities to govern and rule.

Political Philosophy of John Locke: Women and Law Making

Prior to Locke, the early liberal root of feminism emerged as an opposition to the patriarchal theory where English Law permitted women to rule as sole monarchs. Locke, a social contractualist, while formulating his principles, firstly destructed the patriarchal paradigm (established by Robert Filmer) and elaborated the concept of power by recognising parental and conjugal authority to show the status of women in Lockean society. From enjoying these powers, the source of political participation can be traced.[31] John Locke believed in individual rights, and his liberalism envisioned a civil society that included rather than excluded women. He opened new places for women by granting them property rights, whether married or unmarried, as well as shared responsibility with the husband and father in raising children. However the husband's superior decision-making power in a marriage questions his feminist bent. Locke describes the husband as "abler and stronger" when making decisions about the family, but feminist interpretations of Locke's conjugal relationship between a husband and wife accuses him of supporting the natural subordination of the wife and mother in marriage and family life. Critics argue that the equality promised in his civil society is thus compromised, because women as a consequence of being unequal to the men in their lives are prevented from participating in politics.

However, it is important to take into account that the authority of husband over wife tells more about the conditions of seventeenth-century feudal England that confirms a natural inferiority of women. Further Locke's conjugal authority for the husband extends mainly to common interests and property of husband and wife. Locke recognises that a husband and wife have "one common concern," but have "different understandings" and "different wills." Assigning "the last Determination" or "the Rule" to "the abler and stronger" man though weakens the idea of equality in a relationship of mutually consenting adults Locke does not surrender women's basic freedom or political capacities per se.[32]

For Locke, political life has chiefly to do with one's standing as a citizen who is a rights' bearer. This can be distinguished from the issue of what qualifies one to take part in public deliberations, that is, law making. Both men and women have equal standing as citizens. While argue that Locke did not include women in his account of law makers, this does not defeat their equal standing as citizens. Locke indeed see some men as more qualified to be law makers than other men. Membership as an equal citizen in the political system and qualifications for deliberating as a law maker, however, are two different values.

Critics of Locke argue that he ascribed differential rationality to women and the poor. Another distinction should be drawn between membership as an equal citizen in the political system and legislative competency. For Locke, women, the poor, and day labourers are equally rational in that their reason meets the threshold that distinguishes them from children, and thus entitles them to be free, but are perhaps less likely to possess the more sophisticated reasoning that law, making requires.[33] Further, in his *Thoughts on Education,* he designed a form of education for girls thus encouraging their rational development. Since rationality is directly linked to political authority, he has given even space to women's political development. Though these are not explicitly mentioned in any book, yet a collection of his several thoughts leads to this conclusion.[34]

Political Philosophy of Jean Jacques Rousseau: Exclusion of Women's Political Participation

Rousseau has not elaborated on the role of women in the political domain yet we can assess his contributions from the role of family where women occupy an integral space. He has emphasized on the role of the family and declared it to be important in two different aspects:

- In defining one's notion of self and understanding sex roles.
- Family serves to educate men to live in society in general and political society in particular.[35]

This analysis of the role of family by Rousseau over the history and its present-day incarnation pays special attention to the role of women. Therefore the role of women is crucial to the fate of transformational revolution that would in turn affect developments of private as well as political authenticities. The three model family analysis presented in his book, *La Nouvelle Heloise,* assumes that all members living in the family to be morally virtuous.

However in the context of political power being given to women, Rousseau opined that women who enter public life on the term of *amour proper* would do more violence to their nature than the men caught up in that mode of interaction. The mere presence of women in public life would undermine the masculine excellence and exacerbate *amour proper.* Thus in the realm of public sphere their participation is categorically excluded by him. Thus reading Rousseau helps in two manners:

- He remains useful to anti-feminism, so reading him is an exercise of "Knowing the enemy." However he understands many aspects of the structure of male dominance which form the critical perspective of feminist function as an effective criticism of that system, often virtually without revision.
- The larger message for feminist thinkers is that they cannot afford to do less than examine the whole of the social structure for any attempt to examine the relation between men and women in isolation from other questions as it may turn to be misleading.[36]

Political Philosophy of Machiavelli: Construction of a Secular Political Community

There are several feminist criticisms against Machiavelli on the grounds that he split the public and private sphere, thereby demarcating that power, force and violence are structures of political sphere whereas feminine domain is cowardly and unworthy. He tends to militarise both international and domestic politics, and thereby constructs a form of knowledge where men dominate both women and nature.[37]

In the light of these criticisms let us analyse the role of Machiavelli in recognising women's contribution to the political domain. It is important to note that he does not give general laws on nature where a male's sphere of politics is different from a female's domestic sphere.[38] He recognises that women have the *virtue* to rule, and in two of his plays he gives the role of Prince to females. Despite his scorn for the feminine term, he teaches Prince the art of "deception" which is essentially the feminine form of art.[39] Further, he does not set reason against passion in the domain of politics and achievement of power; hence the whole debate of excluding women as they lack reason does not come into picture in this case.[40]

Moreover, his demarcation is that of public good and private interest and not the Greek demarcation of household and politics; thus the difference between the two needs to be kept in mind.[41] On the question of "How a state is ruined because of women?," citing Aristotle's assumption of fall of tyrants by reason of violence or seduction, Machiavelli claims that this is the result of lack of self-restraint on the part of the man/tyrant, and is not to be interpreted otherwise.

On coming to the point of education and attainment of virtue, Machiavelli claims that not only is the military service a method to learn civic virtues but civic religion, education and inspiration from exemplary leaders are other useful modes. Hence both men and women can learn these discourses of civic nature and become citizens of the republic.[42] There are instances in the form of excerpts from Machiavelli's writings which show that he was well aware of history where examples of some women doing much better than men in the domain of politics abound. In the *Golden*

Ass he portrays his hero talking to a woman "as friends speak to another" about many things including politics. Further he could not have conceived women to be soft and cowardly as his interpretation of *Fortuna* was a strong and active force. He is also the champion of the modern idea of citizenship as he contributed to a secular, republican and pluralist ideal of political community.

Overall, according to the feminist account of Machiavellian morality, the moral agent is an active politician seeking to overthrow the patriarchal order. Acutely aware of continuous movement and change in the equilibrium of existent forces, she strives for a new balance of these forces, "basing herself on that particular force which [she] considers progressive, giving it the means to triumph."[43] This is true in the contemporary era where women need to empower themselves from within, and benefitting from their underlying potentials they need to emerge as champions for the cause of society and public welfare.

Political Philosophy of J.S. Mill: Equal Political Freedom to Both Men and Women

J.S. Mill's book, *The Subjugation of Women,* covers a wide variety of issues related to women that persisted in the twenty-first century focusing mainly on the "nature" of women.[44] Other essays of Mill such as *On Marriage and Divorce, Nature,* and *The Contagious Diseases Act* have provided additional material for gender analysis. As a political economist, he identifies the economic inequality, and particularly the fact that by law, husbands become the owners of their wives' property, as the central aspects of women's gendered social inequality.[45] When he served in parliament he co-sponsored The Married Women's Property Act to redress this issue. In his view, property is a necessary condition of women's equality because having control over economic resources is essential to women's ability to maintain their self-respect within marriage, and particularly to exit an abusive one.

Mill articulates that achieving equal freedom for men and women is more than just a matter of eradicating repressive and oppressive forms of power (internalised notions of women's incapacities and systematically imposed rules and customs that guarantee sex inequality). It requires equal powers and equal opportunities for women to share in practices of self-formation and self-government with respect to education, employment and careers, marriage and divorce, self-government in economic enterprise, political freedom and self-government in families.

Mill criticises the education system prevalent in his times where women were taught to minister the needs and desires of others rather than pursue their own dreams and purposes; thus they face special barriers to develop their speculative faculties and freedom of mind. Thus he advocated reforming the social and political institutions of his times to foster equally the free development of both men and women. He recognises the imbibed virtues of autonomy and self-determination as tools to achieve political empowerment.

Mill promotes equal political freedom for men and women that is an equal voice in shaping laws which govern them on similar grounds.[46] Along with equal voting rights Mill also defends the equal rights of capable women to seek and hold office; thus just as men demonstrate their fitness through their success in electoral competition, the same idea holds true for women as well. Thus, today we see that the key aspects of Mill's feminist agenda have been achieved through women's suffrage, increasing the presence of women as political leaders across the globe along with more equal marital relations and economic opportunities. Thus the lesson derived from Mill's philosophy is to recognise the complementarity of freedom and equality as well as freedom and power and implement the same to further carry forth the task of achieving greater political participation in the country.

Political Philosophy of Marx and Engels: Contemporary Socialist Feminist

Marx, Engels, Stalin and Lenin all wrote extensively on the "women question." Their arguments specify a specific economic structure as prerequisite for women's development, and this forms the basis of the contemporary socialist feminism.[47] Marx holds in *German Ideology* as well as *Capital* that the division of labour has an original, natural and sexual basis but that does not mean that there is anything fixed, inevitable, eternal or destined to women's role in the society. Modern feminists have criticised Marx's theory on the grounds of sexist in the economic category. Since he emphasizes on the role of economic conditions as the basis for evolution of family and the gendered society, it is perceived that his too much emphasis on productive activities neglect the role of women who are non-economic, non-productive and traditionally excluded from the domain of economic activities. However, Marx believed that if economic conditions were fundamentally transformed, capitalists overthrown and production primacy overcome, then male domination would also come to an end in the society.

Further he talks in terms of abolishing the institution of family as he views the monogamous system of marriage to be a tool of suppression of women by men. Engels supports the same views by claiming that monogamy as an institution was inaugurated long with slavery and private wealth which have proven to be fatal for the society.[48] Thus with the passage of the means of production into common property an individual unit ceases to be the economic unit of the society. Private housekeeping gets transformed into a social industry. Thus the domination of women within the institution of marriage would be done away with, clearing the path for further liberation and empowerment of women. On the question of women's liberation, it is further reiterated that legal equality accompanied by the right to vote and hold political office remains vital.[49] Thus the cause of women's liberation has to come from all political, social and economic circles.

Conclusion

The contemporary relevance of political philosophy behind women's political participation is of great importance. This is because any attempt to limit the role of women in the political participation of the state or undermining the full capacity of the women would surely amount to wasting half the talent of the state. A brief and most cursory perusal of the political philosophy of some of the leading political philosophers reveals that the participation of women in the political process has always remained a matter of debate. Moreover, the dominant opinion being on the positive side, i.e., women must be allowed to play a constructive and complete role in the process of decision making. The most vehement support and constructive argument has come from Plato's philosophy of communism of wives and property. He has considered the institution of family and private property as the two greatest competitors to the unity and progress of the state. Accordingly, he seems to have advocated that permanent institution of family is a place of talent waste. Hence, he urged for emancipation of women by allowing them to participate in the affairs of the state on equal footing with male as guardians of the state. The scheme of communism of wives may not be that relevant in the contemporary society, however, the underlying principle in the philosophy is more relevant than it was in the past, i.e., the talent of nearly half the population should not be allowed to go waste, as it is neither in the interest of the state nor even to the inhabitants of the state. Rousseau through his philosophy of General Will has accorded equal rights to both the genders in the process of law making, as the whole of General Will is the Assembly, and the sovereign, and the law-making power is exclusive to the General Will. John Stuart Mill has been another ardent supporter of women franchise and their participation in the political process of the state. Therefore, such political philosophy becomes vital as the debate on Women's Reservation Bill for 33 per cent reservation in legislatures can be viewed as a step forward to provide opportunities to women to enter in the domain of politics that has been viewed as an exclusive male bastion. By ensuring more representation of qualitative female rulers in the legislatures, the law-making process is acknowledging the role of women and ensuring that the demand of certain sections of the society can be articulated and dealt with by more sensitivity and dedication.

References

1. Gupta, V.P, Plato: *Who gave us the Republic,* New Delhi, Vijay Goel: English-Hindi Publisher, 2008, p. 99
2. *The Republic,* 451b-457b
3. *The Republic,* 455d
4. *The Republic,* 452
5. *The Republic,* 540c5-9
6. Gupta, V.P, Plato; *op.cit.,* p. 100.

7. *Republic,* 551
8. *Republic,* 454 d
9. *Republic,* 454
10. *Supra* at 6 at p. 101
11. For detailed analysis see- Alison Jagger, *Feminist Politics and Human Nature* (Totowa, N.J: Rowman and Allenheld, 1983)
12. For detailed analysis see- Tuana Nancy, *The Feminist Interpretations of Plato,* (Pennsylvania: The Pennsylvania State University Press, 1994).
13. For detailed analysis see - Aristotle, *Generation of Animals,* translated by A.L Peck, The Leob Classical library, (Cambridge Mass.: Harvard University Press, 1949).
14. Aristotle, *The Ethics of Aristotle,* translated by J.A.K Thomas, Baltimore, Md.: Penguin Books, 1953, (Book 8, Ch. 10, p. 247).
15. Ibid.
16. Aristotle, *Aristotle's Politics And Poetics,* Trans. By B. Jowett and T. Twining, New-York, Viking Press, Comapss Books, 1957, (Book 1, Ch. 12, p. 21).
17. Mukherjee Subrata, Ramaswamy Sushila, *A History of Political Thought: Plato to Marx* New-Delhi, Prentice Hall of India Pvt. Ltd., 2005, p. 115
18. *Supra* at 16. (Book 1, Ch. 13, p.22).
19. Ibid.
20. Ibid. (Book 3, Ch. 4, p.65).
21. Ibid. (Book 1, Ch. 13, p.23).
22. Donna Haraway, "Situated Knowledge: The Science Question in Feminism and The Privilege of Partial Perspective," *Feminist Studies,* vol.14, no.3, Fall 1988, p.592
23. For detailed analysis see - Mannings, *Speaking from the Heart: A Feminist Perspective on Ethics* Lanham Md.: Rowman and Littlefield, 1992.
24. For detailed analysis see-Freeland, Cynthia, *Feminist Interpretations of Aristotle,* University Park: Pennsylvania University Press, 1998.
25. *Politics,* Book VII, 10, 1330a, pp.1-17.
26. Toronto, *Moral Boundaries, A Political Argument for an Ethics of Care,* New York: Routledge, 1993.
27. For detailed analysis see Ann E. Cudd & Robin O. Andreasen, *A Philosophical Anthology,* Blackwell, 2005, Review by Peter B. Raabe, Ph.D. July 17, 2005 (vol. 9, no. 28).

28. For detailed analysis see *Feminist and Ancient Philosophy*, Julie K. Ward, *Feminist and Ancient Philosophy*, Routledge, London, 1996.
29. For detailed analysis see Judith Chelius Stark, *Feminist Interpretations of Augustine*, University Park, P.A, Pennsylvania State University Press, 2007.
30. Augustine, Letter 228, in *Saint Augustine*, translated by Wilfred Parisons, New York: Fathers of the Church, 1956, p.144.
31. "Individuality, Politics and Critique of Paternalism in John Locke," *Political Studies*. vol.16, February 1968, pp. 163-77.
32. For detailed analysis see Nancy J. Hirschmann & Kirstie M. McClure, *Feminist interpretations of John Locke*, University Park, Pennsylvania State University Press, 2007.
33. Rodrigues, Helena, "In Defense of Women: Equality in Locke's Political Theory." Paper presented at the annual meeting of the The Midwest Political Science Association, Palmer House Hilton, Chicago, Illinois, April 15, 2004.
34. Bettesworth A. & Hitch C., *Some familiar letters between Mr. Locke and several of his friends*, 3rd edn. (London, 1837), p.88.
35. In *Social Contract*, Rousseau calls family as the "first model of political societies," Du Contract Social, Bk.1, Ch, 2, OC:3-352, Translated by Lynda Lange.
36. For detailed analysis see Vaughan, C.E., *Political writings of Rousseau*, Cambridge, Cambridge University Press, 1915.
37. For detailed analysis see Mary O Brien, *The Root of Mandrake, in Reproducing the World: Essays in Feminist Theory*, Boulder, Colo.: West view Press, 1989.
38. For detailed analysis see Machiavelli Niccollo, *Discourses on Livy*. Trans. Harvey C. Mansfield and Nathan Travcov, Chicago: University of Chicago Press, 1996.
39. For detailed analysis see Jane S Jaquetter, "Power as Ideology," in *Women's Views of Political World of Men*, New York: Transnational Publishers, 1984.
40. For detailed analysis see Karen Green, *The Women of Reason: Feminism, Humanism and Political Thought*, New York: Continuum, 1995.
41. For detailed analysis see Honig Bonie, *Political Theory and Displacement of Politics*, Ithaca: Cornell University Press, 1993.
42. Saxonhouse, *Women in History of Political Thought. Leo Strauss, Thoughts on Machiavelli*, Chicago: University of Chicago Press, 2001, p.71.

43. Arelene W. Saxonhouse, *Women in the History of Political Thought: Ancient Greek to Machiavelli*, New York: Praeger, 1985, p.152.
44. For detailed analysis see John Stuart Mill, *The Subjection of Women, in Mill, On Liberty and Other Essays*, ed. John Gray, New York: Oxford University Press, 1991.
45. For detailed analysis see Okin, Susan Moller, *Women in Western Political Thought*, Princeton: Princeton University Press, 1979.
46. Mill worked with women's suffrage associations and introduced legislations to enfranchise women in 1866 and 1867 during his term in Parliament.
47. *International Socialism, Marx and Engels on Women's Liberation*, vol.44, 1970, pp. 21-29.
48. *Karl Marx and Frederich Engels*, Berlin, Weimar, Aufbau-Verlag, 1968, 3:174.
49. L.H. Morgan, *Ancient Society*, Chicago, Kerr, n.d, p.499 (end of Ch. 5 of part III).

4

From Emancipation to Empowerment: A Historical Perspective about Women's Political Participation

— *Om Prakash*

Introduction

Since antiquity, the participation of women in the political activities has been marginal. In the Rig Vedic period, where society was largely egalitarian and women had enough freedom, there is no evidence of their participation in the two political institutions named *Sabha* and *Samiti*. They used to participate in a cultural institution named *Vidatha,* which was a folk assembly having important function of redistribution. Thereafter women's condition deteriorated, and in the succeeding centuries they were confined to the house for the service of male folk although with exceptions.

According to Myron Weiner, "The concept of political participation refers to any voluntary action, successful or unsuccessful, organised or unorganised episodic or continuous, employing legitimate or illegitimate methods intended to influence the choice of public policies, the administration of public affairs, or the choice of political leaders at any level of Government, local or national."[1]

Unlike the oriental world, women are moving in the direction of near equal participation in few of the countries of the occident, such as Germany, Sweden, Norway, Denmark and Finland. In these countries women have modified the very nature of politics, making enduring and substantial gains in every field. However, in all other countries, including the supposedly advanced democracies of western Europe and North America, where women exercise more freedom and have acquired the economic independence, female presence in legislatures remains small and relatively insignificant.

Indian Renaissance and Women's Participation in Political Activities

The nineteenth century social reformation movement was a great liberating episode for existing social evils and abominable practices like caste, polytheism, idolatry, animism, purdha system, child marriage, sati system, etc., on the one hand, and Indian women on the other hand. The Abolition of Sati Act 1829, Widow Remarriage Act, 1856, Age of Consent Bill 1893, etc., were some of the great legislations concerning women and had a great role in ameliorating their conditions.[2] However, the grass-roots conditions remained grim. Eminent women reformers participated in this movement as well as in the religious reform movement of this period. Pandita Ramabai's crusade for upliftment of women in the field of education and for widow remarriage is a glorious chapter.[3] Sarala Devi started the Bharat Stree Mahamandal for the education of women.[4] Swarna Kumari Devi started the women's organisation Sakhi Samiti in 1886 for widows, and she was one of the two delegates elected from Bengal to represent the state at the 1890 Congress session, these are a few such examples. These activities accelerated women's participation in public spaces, which paved the way for their entry into the independence struggle.

Political Participation of Women during Indian Freedom Struggle

The first mass movement in which the political participation of women was overwhelming was the *Swadeshi* movement of Bengal during 1905-8. Several nationalist women donated their precious jewellry, money, etc., to the movement.[5] They took active part in the boycott of foreign goods and in revolutionary activities as well. The disciple of Swami Vivekananda, Sister Nivedita, became a member of the National Revolutionary Council, and organised women for nationalist activities. Kumudini Mitra launched the journal *Suprabat* which invoked women to join the political mainstream and movement against colonial oppression.

There were several others seen as a threat by the British, including Madame Cama, who was described by the government as a threat, and the leader of the revolutionary movement and British government had even plans for her assassination but she managed to escape. Bhikaiji Cama, a Parsi woman nationalist, persuaded the International Socialist Congress to support the Indian Independence Movement, and also began a monthly journal by the name *Vande Mataram*.[6] Annie Besant became the first woman president of the Indian National Congress, who later on organised Home Rule Movement in 1917 for the demand of dominion status to be given to India on the lines of white colonies.[7] At a time when the nationalist activities were almost negligible, the Home Rule Movement of Annie Besant was a great episode to push the country towards the mass movement era of Mahatma Gandhi. In December 1917, Annie Besant and a few other women met Mr. Montague to demand voting rights for Indian women. During the same period several all-India women's organisations came into being. In 1917, Annie Besant, Malathi Patvardhan, Ammu Swaminathan, Mrs. Dadabhoy and Mrs. Ambujamal founded the Women's Indian Association. The organisation strongly supported the Home Rule Movement. In 1926, the All India Women's Conference was formed and actively took the question of women's suffrage, labour issues, relief and nationalist work.[8]

The 1920s also witnessed prominent women activists like Rajkumari Amrit Kaur, Lady Piroj Bai Mehta, Mrs. N. Sengupta who were advocates of women's right.[9] Several other women were active on causes other than the Independence movement including Prabhavati Mirza, a powerful trade unionist, Kamini Roy, a social reformist and eminent writer, and founder of a social welfare women's organisation.[10] Basanti Devi took active part in anti-British activities and was arrested for picketing foreign goods shops, and in 1922 presided over the Bengal Provincial Congress Committee.

The role of Sarojini Naidu, Kamala Devi Chattopadhyay, Aruna Asaf Ali are well known in the freedom struggle. A great supporter of women's rights, Sarojini Naidu worked with the

Congress and the Muslim League. She was instrumental in the passage of a resolution to support women's franchise and became the first Indian woman to become the elected President of the Indian National Congress at it's Kanpur session in 1925.[11] Kamala Devi Chattopadhyay participated in the *Satyagraha* movement of 1930s.[12] Aruna Asaf Ali's first major political involvement was in the salt march at which she was arrested and prosecuted. She was also active in the Quit India movement, edited *Inquilab* magazine of the Congress, and established the National Federation of Indian Women.[13] She came to be known as the Grand Old Lady of the Independence Movement and heroine of the1942 movement. Her underground activities during the Quit India Movement put the British intelligence and police on their toes.[14] During Quit India Movement, Usha Mehta ran an underground radio, where regular broadcasting was being done to provide directions and guidelines to the people and revolutionaries.

The Civil Disobedience Movement of Mahatma Gandhi brought thousands of women in the Salt Satyagraha, which is "generally remembered as the first time 'masses of Indian women' got involved in the struggle for Independence."[15] Several women's organisations were formed to mobilise women to participate in nationalist activities including processions, pickets, and charkha spinning such as the Ladies Picketing Board, Desh Sevika Sangh, Nari Satyagraha Samiti and Mahila Rashtriya Sangh. Beyond any doubt, the active participation of women in the political struggles for independence consummated in a Constitution based on the principles of equality and guaranteeing equal rights to suffrage for women, in the year 1947 itself.

Mahatma Gandhi told Mridula Sarabhai, one of the valiant fighters for the cause of women and freedom in 1930s, "I have brought the Indian women out of the kitchen, it is up to you (the women activist) to see that they don't go back."[16] The role of women and their participation in all streams of Indian freedom struggle is an avowed fact. From Gandhian non-violent movement to socialist, communist and revolutionary movements, from peasant movement to trade union movements, women's dominant presence was everywhere.

Indian Women's participation in Contemporary Electoral Politics

Although small in numbers yet there were a number of women member present in the Constituent Assembly. In the first meeting of the Constituent Assembly held on December 9, 1946, "nine women members were present, adding colour to a score dominated by Gandhi caps, and Nehru jackets."[17] After independence, women were expected to come forward and actively engage themselves in the political activities but due to various societal, economic and patriarchal factors such expectations remained in the margin.

Role of Women as Voters

Figures from the state election department of the last few decade show that though the number of women voters has steadily increased from 1990, it was the 2003 assembly elections that witnessed an unprecedented turnout of women voters. In 1990, there were 736 women voters per 1,000 men, which increased to 755 in 1993, 786 in 1998, and 841 in 2003.[18] Women could be seen queuing up in long, separate lines which was a significant departure from the earlier elections.

A researcher working in central Bihar found that despite the call of poll boycott given by the Naxalites the people were largely unmoved for such calls, "the overall effect of poll boycott on voter turnout seems to be negligible. In villages where Maoist had been active for years, in fact election-day was seen as an enjoyable occasion. Women dressed in bright colours and reds, their hairs oiled and adorned with clips, made their way to the polling booth in small groups."[19]

Several rural women in North India, instead of giving her name in the electoral rolls, wished to register as A's mother and B's wife. The election commissioner, Sukumar Sen, was outraged by this practice and directed his officials to convert the rolls by inserting the name of the women, in place of mere description of the voters.[20] There is increase in the percentage of the eligible women voting in elections from 46.6 per cent in 1962 to 55.4 per cent in 1967 and 59.1 per cent in 1971.[21] The northeastern states have shown a comparatively high percentage of women voters' involvement in elections up to 75 per cent.

In Kerala, a state known for its socio-economic, demographic and developmental features, a good proportion of women willingly exercise their franchise in elections. The state, in fact, has the highest percentage of women voting.[22] The proportion of votes cast by women in the elections held in Kerala was around 50 per cent. This enthusiasm is however absent when it comes to political participation.

In the 2008 election for the Rajasthan assembly the women voters virtually outnumbered the male voters in a number of constituencies despite having adverse male-female ratio of 1,000 males against 909 females. According to Aruna Roy, the Magsaysay award winner, one of the most important reasons behind this development is the National Rural Employment Guarantee Programme and the high level of human development indicators in the constituencies where women's voter turnout was higher. In the urban centres like Jodhpur and Jaipur the percentage of women voters was comparatively lesser.[23]

Women's Role as Electoral Candidates at Various Level

Articles 14, 15, 16, 19, 325 and 326 of the Constitution of India and the Representation of Peoples Act guarantee political equality and equal right to participation in political activities and right to vote respectively. While the voting trends are more or less satisfactory, the right to equal political participation is still a distant dream. Indian women have a long way to go as far as their participation as electoral candidate in election is concerned.

The representation of women in the Lok Sabha has been stagnant. Although women constitute about half of the total electorate, their representation in the Lok Sabha has not been adequate.[24] Women contesting elections still constitute only a meagre percentage of one or two of the total number of contestants.[25] For instance, in the Lok Sabha, the representation of women varied between 3.4 per cent (in the Sixth Lok Sabha) and 8.1 per cent (in the eighth Lok Sabha). In the first Lok Sabha, there were only 22 women members who formed only 4.41 per cent of the total 499 members. The Sixth Lok Sabha admitted the lowest number of women parliamentarians with 19 out of the total 544, comprising merely 3.49 per cent. The highest number of women members was found in the Thirteenth Lok Sabha with 49 members in a house of 544. This did not form even 10 per cent of the total strength.

Table 1

Representation of Women in Parliament

Year	*Members in Lok Sabha*			*Members in Rajya Sabha*		
	No. of Seats	*No. of Women*	*%*	*No. of Seats*	*No. of Women*	*Percentage*
1952-57	499	22	4.4	219	16	7.3
1957-62	500	27	5.4	237	18	7.6
1962-67	503	34	6.7	238	18	7.6
1967-71	523	31	5.9	240	20	8.3
1971-76	521	22	4.2	243	17	7.0
1977-80	544	19	3.4	244	25	10.2
1980-84	544	28	5.1	244	24	9.8
1985-90	544	44	8.1	245	28	11.4
1990-91	529	28	5.3	245	24	9.7
1991-96	509	36	7.1	245	38	15.5
1996-97	537	34	6.3	245	20	8.2
1997-98	545	40	7.3	245	19	7.8
1998-99	545	44	8.1	245	19	7.8

Source: Election Commission of India, *Statistical Report on the General Election, 1952 to 1999.*

During the 2002 elections held in Kashmir there were comparatively better participation of women. Several women candidates held that they are contesting elections to highlight the problems which are being faced by the people, especially the women. During the General Elections 2004 in Andhra Pradesh, out of a total of 279 candidates fighting for the 42 Lok Sabha seats, only 21 were women. Maharashtra's track record in respect of women contestants is similar – only 29 of the 412 candidates contesting the 48 Lok Sabha seats were women. In Karnataka out of 172 candidates for the 28 Lok Sabha seats only 10 contestants were women.

In the 2004 General Election, for the Lok Sabha, the Indian National Congress fielded the maximum of 45 women candidates, while the Bharatiya Janata Party (BJP) was second at the count of 30 and BSP fielded 20 candidates. However as far as the winning ability factor is concerned only 12 out of the 45 Congress candidates could win the election while for BJP only one-third candidates could make to the hustings. The total number of women candidates actually increased to 355 in the 2004 election in comparison to merely 284 in the 1999 election.[26]

Table 1 shows the poor representation of women in parliament since independence. In Table 2 the condition of their participation as candidates in the assembly elections is also similar.

Table 2

Parliament and Assembly Elections: Women as Contestants

Year	*Males*	*%age*	*Females*	*%age*	*Total*
1952	1,831	97.71	43	2.29	1,874
1980	4,478	96.93	142	3.07	4,620
1984	5,149	96.91	164	3.09	5,313
1991	8,374	96.26	325	3.74	8,699
1996	13,353	95.71	599	4.29	13,952
1998	4,708	94.56	271	5.44	4,979

Source: Women in India - A Statistical Profile, 1997, Department of Women and Child Development, New Delhi and Election Commission of India, Statistical Report on the General Election, 1952 to 1999.

Gujarat may have been the state where the participation of women in the cooperative movement set an example for the rest of the country but when it comes to women contesting elections, the scene is no different from the other states. For the 26 Lok Sabha seats in the state, 151 of the 162 candidates were men. Of the 182 candidates fighting for the 14 Lok Sabha seats in Jharkhand, only 13 were women.

The 73rd and 74th Constitutional Amendments have brought about significant changes in the prevailing situation.[27] With these Constitutional Amendments, over three million women are now actively participating in shaping the policies and programmes of the country, though only at the local levels of governance. However, such affirmative action is lacking at the higher echelons of governance at the state and central levels.

Today India has more than 500 district panchayats, around 5,100 block/taluka panchayats and about 2,25, 000 village panchayats, 90 municipal corporations, 1,500 municipal councils, and 1,800 nagar panchayats. All these bodies would jointly elect over three million representatives and a considerable number of them would be women.[28] The trend owes impetus primarily to the provisions made in the Act that one-third of the seats in the local bodies such as panchayats, nagar sabhas, municipalities and corporations shall be reserved for women.[29] This one-third reservation means the possibility of one million women in the panchayats and municipalities of India. It is estimated that there are already 7,16,234 women in panchayats in all the states excluding Manipur, Bihar, and Jammu and Kashmir, and several states went ahead and elected even more than one-third women members required under the Acts. It is evident from the low proportion of women in the state legislative assembly and women representatives of Kerala in the Lok Sabha, Rajya Sabha and local bodies. In 1957, for instance, the number of women in the state assembly was only six out of the total 121 members. In 1991, the number was eight in the house of 141.

According to the Coordination Unit, 1994, "The number of women contestants in parliamentary elections has not increased significantly over the years. Political parties seem uniformly reluctant to field women candidates."[30] In 1998, women constituted only around 8 per cent of the Lok Sabha.[31] In 1991 women in the Lok Sabha won 36 seats out of 509 (7.1 per cent) and in the Rajya Sabha they had a slightly higher representation of 38 seats out of 245 (15.5 per cent) that they were elected or nominated to.[32]

It is important to observe that with reference to the portfolios generally assigned to women as ministers they are classified under the soft category, for example, information and broadcasting, social justice and empowerment, health and family welfare, tourism and culture, water resources and human resource development. It has been said, "the reality is that women's participation in decision making at all levels from the national to the local, is dismally low. The challenge that faces the government and society in setting right this inequality in sharing of power in a diverse and complex country like India is how to overcome the attitudinal, institutional, cultural and social restrictions that have grown over the centuries."[33]

Women's Participation in Arenas Outside Formal Politics

Women's historical participation in movements such as the Telengana Movement (1948-50), a militant share croppers movement, was noteworthy. Women leaders, who did take the lead in the guerilla warfare that followed, subsequently felt isolated due to non-recognition of their contribution. They had to wage a war within the movement for a fare share in leadership.[34] In 1954 the left wing of the All India Women's Conference formed a separate organisation named as the National Federation of Indian Women. Noted freedom fighter and great political activist, Aruna Asaf Ali, while delivering the presidential address of the 12th Congress of the National Federation of Indian Women at New Delhi in 1986, said, "We are meeting at a moment of time when those of us who belong to the older generation of the great sisterhood of womankind must tell the younger generation as to what they should do to become effective participants in making decisions which will shape every aspects of our national and international life, particularly concerning economic, social and political developments...we are now beginning to realise that our strength will depend on how rapidly we can organise ourselves for multi pronged action to fight for our rights."[35]

Since there were not many activities on the front of movements which gave the impression that there were no movement of women in the 1950s and 1960s.[36] In the decade of the 1970s, which was obviously the most turbulent decade, thousands of women joined the various streams of movements, like price rise, and later merged into the total revolution movement of Jaya Prakash Narayan.[37] On 15 August 1976 a Satyagraha movement was led by Manibhen Patel, daughter of Sardar Vallabhbhai Patel, in Ahmedabad against imposition of Emergency. They raised slogans like "Remove Emergency" and "Release Political Prisoners," and took the Gandhian route of civil disobedience against the salt law to Dandi.[38] Although these movements never addressed the central issue concerning women yet they had a great liberating effect as they infused the much needed self-confidence among the women who were so far reluctant to cross the four walls of their house.

Another important movement started was the Anti-liquor Movement in Maharashtra by the Bhil tribal women. The greatest drawback of liquor is linked with the wife-beating practice by the husbands. So this movement was directed against the liquor selling shops. The Uttaranchal region of the then Uttar Pradesh had earlier in 1960s witnessed the similar movements influenced by the noted Gandhian, Vinoba Bhave, and Sarla Behn. The decade of the 1990s also witnessed a powerful anti-liquor movement in Andhra Pradesh which compelled the government to restrict the sale of liquors and other prohibitory clauses were inserted regarding licensing and sale of liquor.

The Chipko Movement began as an environmental movement but as women began to participate in mass, it was celebrated as a mass-based women's movement. "In the Chipko movement it was the women who came to the forefront and transformed the struggle."[39] They protected the trees in their area from contractors with their own bodies even when the men were not around to help. The movement served as a precedent to other communities where women started resisting mining for environmental reasons.

What Perils Women's Political Participation?

There are a number of factors responsible for negligible political participation of women in India. Information plays a central role in electoral politics. Unequal access to information and other economic and non-economic resources is a barrier to women's political participation. Most information on governance is available in a language that is inaccessible to women. Because of the high rate of illiteracy and low levels of education among women they are deprived of information. Oral transactions invariably take place in the public sphere, which is inaccessible by women, as they are confined to their households. As their mobility is restricted they do not have the exposure to public life, thus limiting the scope of their interaction with others and the acquisition of information. So not having enough access to information impairs the recognition and enjoyment of the right of women to vote, contest elections, become members of political parties and other social networks.

It has been found in studies in Karnataka that often women are not taken seriously, not because of their lack of experience, but because of their lack of knowledge. The areas where information is lacking are: the Constitutional Amendments (their powers and duties), gram panchayat's jurisdiction, financial matters, benefits and disadvantages of taking loans, a broad understanding of the working of banks and other relevant institutions and governmental bodies, and so on.[40]

Limited access to economic resources, such as income, land, house and credit facilities impairs women's effective participation in electoral processes, viz., contesting elections, campaigning, building and sustaining their constituencies, and fulfilling their role as elected representatives. The efficacy of an elected representative, particularly in the panchayati raj institutions is dependent on their accessibility to government officials, as most programmes are routed through them. The resistance among the government officials due to gender insensitivity impedes the effective functioning of women elected representatives.

The family responsibilities and cultural values, traditions and practices of confining women to the household activities have excluded them from actively participating and fulfilling their role as elected representatives. The burden of multiples roles on women restricts the exercise and enjoyment of their rights in various political processes. The demands of the job and family in the absence of support mechanisms impede their effective discharge of responsibilities as elected representatives.

Generally, unmarried women are less represented in the gram panchayats. In a study done in four districts in West Bengal on 50 gram panchayats women members four of these women were widows and four were unmarried, while 42 (84 per cent) were married.[41] Given the fact that women wield less power within the family and in the institution of marriage, representation of "married women" need not necessarily indicate their real participation since in most cases the men are the actual decision makers. Though the marital status is not a bar for participation in politics, in practice acceptance of married women contesting elections is more accepted.

Some legislatures are also hindrances in the way of women contesting elections. For instance, to control the population growth, the states of Rajasthan, Haryana and Orissa have legislated that candidates standing for elections cannot have more than two children. The average age at which women gets married, 19, is lower than that of men, 21. By the time they stand for election they already have two or more children, and therefore are not qualified to contest election.[42]

Caste has posed to be a more difficult barrier than gender in electoral politics. In Rajasthan, two different caste groups had their women candidates running for a gram panchayat seat reserved for women. The *jats* (higher caste group) tried to persuade the *harijans* (lower caste group) to withdraw their candidate as it becomes an issue of prestige for them. The *harijans* were forced to withdraw their candidate and were given monetary compensation for doing so.[43] Despite reservation, caste dynamics in elections still pose barriers for participation. At the parliamentary level, caste is one of the reasons why the 84th Amendment never got passed in the Lok Sabha. At the lower levels where reservation has been put in place, caste politics takes other forms. The one major problem with reservations for lower castes, according to Kishwar, is that they have been "permanently ghettoised to reserved constituencies."[44]

In West Bengal 14, out of 50 gram panchayat women members (28 per cent) felt that women with a personal income were capable of being active members of the panchayat.[45] Women tend to have fewer resources at their disposal than men that could be used for election campaigns. Asha Ramesh and Bharati Ali interviewing

PRI members found that "while some women did not know how much was spent on their election as their husband or a male member of their family took care of it, there were some who did not want to disclose such information."[46]

According to the 2001 census, there is rampant illiteracy among women, it being around 46 per cent as against 24 per cent for men. Among the Scheduled Castes and scheduled tribes women's illiteracy is as high as 76 per cent and 81 per cent respectively. Illiteracy rates of women vary widely by region. For instance, in Kerala, which has achieved almost universal literacy, the illiteracy rate is just around 9.08 per cent as against 52.47 per cent in Bihar.[47]

Money and muscle power are used to threaten opponents and the voters; and impose their decisions on the electorate and to raise the kinds of funds required to get into and stay in power. Violating women's dignity is an integral part of politics instilling fear in women, thereby restraining their entry into politics. In addition, corruption is also insitutionalised systematically. Criminalisation and corruption are not part of women's value systems and therefore they are kept away from politics in general.

Inadequate organisational support directly affects the political participation of women. Elections in the country are fought on party lines. The poor representation of women in political parties does not give them the strength to negotiate gender issues and concerns that need to form a part of the party agenda. Fewer women in political parties impedes women from seeking positions in decision-making arenas which are crucial in changing the profile of political parties and also affect the number of women fielded for elections and being elected. Madhu Kishwar, in her discussion of women candidates from Shetkari Sanghathana in Maharashtra showed that they did not get elected despite a very enthusiastic election campaign where the organisation was able to play a supportive role. She claimed this outcome was because "money and muscle power play a crucial role in determining the outcome of panchayat and zilla parishad elections." [48] The civil society initiatives have not been strong enough to counter the local anti-social elements and power politics.

The research efforts of the Gender Studies Unit at the National Institute of Advanced Studies, Bangalore, on 'engendering governance' revealed that the priorities of male and female representatives differed. The women prioritised and addressed issues of long-term effects such as education, health, violence against women, basic amenities while men took up issues of immediate and visible relevance such as roads, community and commercial centres, tanks, bridges, etc.[49] The visual prioritisation tends to subsume the women's agenda and therefore undervalues the contribution made by women, which is in the larger interest of the community.

India ratified the Convention on the Elimination of All forms of Discrimination against Women (CEDAW) in the year 1993. The Preamble of CEDAW states, "Discrimination against women violates the principles of equality of rights and respect for human dignity; is an obstacle to the participation of women, on equal terms with men, in the political, social, economic and cultural life of their countries; hampers the growth of the prosperity of society and the family and makes more difficult the full development of the potentialities of women in the service of their countries and of humanity."[50]

In 1974, the government appointed a Commission on the Status of Women in India and its report, Towards Equality, changed the perspective of women from targets to agents of change in development. This report is the first and only comprehensive document on the status of women in India. It was in fact the first to recommend 30 per cent reservation of seats for women in decision-making positions, as women were either not being represented or were inadequately represented. In 1975 which was declared as the International Women's Year, the Lok Sabha passed a resolution to initiate comprehensive programmes for women. The Sixth Plan document was the first to have a chapter on 'Women and Development.' In 1984 a separate Ministry was created for women and children. The government's main emphasis remained on economic empowerment through its programs.[51]

Recommendations and Conclusion

The 85th Constitutional Amendment Bill pending in the parliament, providing reservation for women, is the most urgent need to move forward. This will provide space for women to ensure that their concerns and perspectives are incorporated while planning for action. Assurance for an enabling environment for women in the elected bodies is another necessity. Women must be taken seriously in their elected post by allotting important portfolios. There should be special mechanisms to induct women at all levels of decision-making to ensure, that they form a critical mass to contribute and influence administrative planning and policy measures. The Representation of Peoples Act needs to be amended making it mandatory for every political party to have one-third of its cadre to be women.

Non-Governmental Organisations are to create awareness amongst women through mass media about the electoral process and also the candidates contesting for election, thereby eliminating powerful men taking advantage of the ignorance of women and controlling their decisions in exercising their right to vote. Also it is required to disseminate information on the functions and responsibilities of the elected representatives. It is necessary to earmark special funding assistance to enable women to contest elections. Media should endeavour to put out stories of 'best practices', i.e., success stories of elected women who are performing their political duties. The Right to Information campaign Act can be very useful as far as empowerment of women is concerned.

References

1. Myron Weiner and John Osgood (eds), *Electoral Politics in Indian States: The Impact of Modernisation,* Manohar Publisher, Delhi, 1977, p. 273.
2. Raja Ram Mohan Roy had a great role in the abolition of the Sati, as he could convince the Governor General William Bentinck as to why this system was inhuman and it must be abolished. Although the British had initial fear due to religious intervention in the affairs yet later on agreed to take initiative. Similarly Ishwar Chandra Vidyasagar was instrumental in passing the Widows

Remarriage Act 1856. The efforts of B. M. Malabari is memorable in passing the Age of Consent Bill.

3. For details please refer, Nicol Mac Nicol and V. Mangalwadi, *What Liberates a Woman: The Story of Pandita Ramabai, a Builder of Modern India,* Good Books, 1996, Delhi.
4. Rajmohan Gandhi in his work mentioned that Sarla Devi was an influential women of the time, and for some time she had her influence on the life of Mahatma Gandhi. The possibility of having an affair between them has also been discussed by him, however such description is absent in the autobiography of Mahatma Gandhi and the personal accounts of Sarla Devi.
5. Bipan Chandra, *India's Struggle for Independence 1857-1947,* Penguin, 1988, pp. 128-29.
6. In the year 1905, which was also a year of movements in India due to Lord Curzon's decision to partition Bengal, Madam Cama along with her friends designed the India's tricolor flag with green, saffron and red stripes with the slogan Vande Mataram. This flag was raised by Madam Cama on August 22, 1907, for India's Independence at the International Socialist Conference in Stuttgart, Germany.
7. B. L. Grover, *A New Look at Modern Indian History,* S. Chand and Co., Delhi, pp. 440-42.
8. M.G. Agrawal, ed., *Freedom Fighters of India,* Isha Books,Vol. IV, Delhi, 2008, pp. 23-25.
9. Ibid.
10. For details please refer to Sukumar Sen, *Bangala Sahityer Itihas,* Vol III, Eastern Publishers, Calcutta, 1976.
11. She was the first Indian woman to become the Governor of the largest state of the union, Uttar Pradesh.
12. M. G. Agarwal, op.cit., p. 26.
13. *Fragments From the Past, Selected Speeches and Writing of Aruna Asaf Ali,* Patriot Publication, New Delhi, 1989, p. 45.
14. Ibid., pp. 15-17.
15. Kumar, op.cit., 1995, p. 78.
16. Bipan Chandra, *India After Independence,* Penguin, New Delhi, 2000, p. 451.
17. *The Hindustan Times,* December 10, 1946.
18. Election Commission of India, *Statistical Report on the General Election,*1952 to 1999.

19. Bela Bhatia, "The Naxalite Movement in Central Bihar, unpublished" Ph. D thesis, Faculty of Social and Political Studies, Cambridge University Press, 2000, pp. 114-20.
20. Ramchandra Guha, *India After Gandhi: History of World's Largest Democracy,* MacMillan, 2007, p. 134.
21. Radha Kumar, *The History of Doing: An Illustrated Account of Movements for Women's Rights and Feminism in India, 1860-1990,* New Delhi, 1993.
22. Susheela Kaushik, "Women and Political Participation," in Fredrich Ebert Stiftung, *Women in Politics: Forms and Processes,* 1992, p. 39.
23. Sunny Sebastian, "Female Voters Outperform Male Counterparts in Rajasthan," *The Hindu,* December, 7, 2008.
24. Ranjana Kumari, "Introduction," in Fredrich Ebert Stiftung, *Women in Politics: Forms and Processes,* New Delhi: Har Anand Publications, 1993, p. 5.
25. Susheela Kaushik, op.cit., p. 49.
26. "Dismal Presence of Women in Successive Lok Sabhas," *The Hindu,* March 14, 2009.
27. The Constitution (Seventy-third Amendment) Act 1992, covering the panchayati raj institutions and the Constitution (Seventy-fourth Amendment) Act covering the urban local bodies (Nagarapalika Act) were passed by the Indian parliament on 22 December 1992 and came into force in April 1993. As per these Acts, the panchayats, with a population of over two million, will have a three-tier system of village panchayats (at the lowest level), block panchayats (at the intermediate level) and district panchayats (on the top). In the urban areas, there will be three types of municipalities, namely, the municipal corporations, municipal councils and nagar panchayats depending on the size of the population.
28. George Mathew, *Restructuring the Polity: The Panchayati Raj,* New Delhi: Indian Renaissance Institute, 1987, pp. 4-5.
29. The Constitution (73rd Amendment) Act, 1993 has been in force from April 1993. The provisions relating to women include: (a) Not less than one-third of the seats will be reserved for women (including those for Scheduled Castes and Scheduled Tribes). These may be allotted by rotation to different constituencies of a panchayat. (b) Seats will be reserved for SCs and STs in proportion to the total population of the SCs and STs to the population of the

area. There would be reservation for women in the seats that have been allotted to SCs and STs. Not less than one third of the SC and ST seats may be reserved for women. (c) Not less than one-third of the total number of seats for the offices of the chairpersons at each level would be reserved for women. This would be rotated among different panchayats at each level.

30. Padma Ramchandran, "Women in Decision Making," In *What is Personal is Political Coordination Unit,* New Delhi, 1995.
31. National Centre for Advocacy Studies, 1998.
32. *Women in India - A Statistical Profile, Department of Women and Child Development, Government of India,* New Delhi, 1995, p. 71.
33. Padma Ramchandran op.cit.
34. P. Sundarayya, *Telengana People's Struggle and It's Lessons,* Foundation Books, New Delhi, pp. 246-51.
35. *Fragments From the Past, Selected Writing and Speeches of Aruna Asaf Ali,* Patriot Publishers, New Delhi, 1989, p. 353.
36. Bipan Chandra, op.cit., p. 453.
37. Ram Chandra Guha, *op.cit.,* pp. 502-505.
38. Satya Samachar, 20 Sepetember 1976, in *Emergency files of Hari Dev Sharma,* Nehru Memorial and Museum Library, New Delhi.
39. Ram Chandra Guha, *The Unquiet Woods: Ecological Change and Peasant Resistance in the Himalayas,* Oxford University Press, New Delhi, 2005, pp. 156-161.
40. Srilatha Batliwalla, B.K. Anitha, Anitha Gurumurthy, and S Wali, Chandana. *Status of Rural Women in Karnataka,* Women's Policy, Research and Advocacy Unit (WOPRA), NIAS, Bangalore, 1998.
41. Ruma Bannerjee, "Women in Panchayati Raj: A Study in West Bengal" *Development Dialogues,* Calcutta, 1995.
42. Bidyut Mohanty, "Panchayati Raj, 73rd Constitutional Amendment and Women," *Economic and Political Weekly,* Vol. XXX, Number 52, 1995, p. 3346.
43. Bidyut Mohanty, "Panchayati Raj, Seventy-Third Constitutional Amendment and Women: Some Emerging Trends," Institute of Social Sciences, New Delhi.
44. Madhu Kishwar, "Women and Politics: Beyond Quotas" *Economic and Political Weekly,* XXXI, Number 43, 1996, p. 2871.
45. Ruma Bannerjee, op.cit.

46. Asha Ramesh, and Bharati Ali, "Towards Political Empowerment –Profiling Elected Women Members in Karnataka and Gujarat. A Report," 1998.

47. Census of India, 2001.

48. Kishwar, op.cit.

49. *Interim Narrative Report 2002-2003,* Gender Studies Unit, National Institute of Advanced Studies, Bangalore.

50. *Convention on the Elimination of All forms of Discrimination against Women,* United Nations Organisation, 1979.

51. Shakuntala Narasimhan, "An Overview of Past State Initiatives," *Empowering Women: An Alternative Strategy from Rural India,* Sage Publications, New Delhi, 1999.

5

Political Participation of Women in Ancient India: With Special Reference to Kalhan's *Rajtarangini*

— ***Manorama Upadhyaya & Jagruti Upadhyaya***

यं कामये तं तमग्रं क णोमि तं ब्रह्माणं तम ी तं सुमेद्या ।[१]

Whomever I want, I make him Rudra, Brahma, Rishis and the learned. – This mantra of *Rig Veda* about the feminine power establishes women as an all powerful entity. The idea of Shakti, the Goddess as the slayer of Demon Mahisha, presents before us a lofty ideal of a strong feminine. Yet, women and their definition as being persons 'out of history' have been truly the most oppressive aspect of women's condition under patriarchy. Women remained at best, punctuation marks or footnotes in a narrative essentially concerned with the achievements and ideas of men.[2] Distorted presentations of women who have actually wielded power have been made. The use of pejorative terms such as 'Kitchen Cabinet' or 'Petticat government' is fairly common. Their casual use indicates the prejudice against women who have never been regarded as having legitimate access to power.

India produced some outstanding Muslim queens who inherited their parents' title and governed kingdoms efficiently and wisely. They issued *Farmans* and *Sanads* and struck coins in their names (a prerogative only enjoyed by the king). The right of females to enjoy sovereign power was familiar to those of the Persians[3] and this system was introduced in India by the Turks. The names of Sultana Razia, Mallika-e-Jahan Lad Malika, Maham Anga, Noor Jahan are significant examples of political power wielded by women in medieval India. But, as the Muslim period in India was accepted as the initiator of evils in society (especially towards women), their role in politics has been neglected with a jaundiced eye.

Though Indian women showed themselves at their best in the Indian National movement and when practically all male leadership were locked up in jail, "women became dictators of war councils, set up to direct the day-to-day activities,"[4] their role being marginalised. Throughout the historical times, women have been discriminated against and disadvantaged economically, legally and sexually. Even in the modern societies and democratic governments of the West, women's participation in politics was negligible. The power of franchise was granted to them as late as 1918 in England after they had proven their mantle in the world scenario during the trying times of World War I. The Bill of Rights spoke of equal political rights, yet women in America and France could not get their political rights and participation until the 1930s.

Participation of women in politics is not a modern issue of contemplation. In the patriarchal ancient Indian society women were not considered fit enough to participate in running the administration. Male hegemony even today is so strong; it raises several questions, whether the real power wielding authority lies with women or not. The 'ghunghat' politics of modern day panchayati raj system raises questions as regarding the credibility of the decisions taken by women.

In ancient India, we have conflicting ideas amongst the *Smritikaras*, regarding the sovereign status of women. Political thinkers are not unanimous as to whether it is desirable to permit women to become rulers of the state. One school saw no objection in allowing them to ascend the throne. There is a proposal in the *Ramayana* to offer the crown to Sita, when Rama was banished to the forest[5].

आत्मा हि दारा : सर्वे ïां दारसंग्रहवर्तिनाम् ।
आत्मेयमिति रामस्य पालयि यति मेदिनीम् ।।

It says all women represent the better half of their husbands. As Sita is the soulmate of Rama, let her rule the country on his behalf. However, it could not materialise owing to Sita's determination to accompany her husband in banishment. The *Mahabharata* presents before us a combination of contradictions. At one place it catagorically states that a state ruled by a woman, or a gambler, or a child falls prey to many difficulties.[6]

यत्र स्त्री यत्र कितवो बालो यत्रानु ाासिता ।
मज्जन्ति तेव ाा राजन् नद्याम मप्लवा इव ।।

However, at another place Bhishma advices Yuddhishthira to sanction the coronation of the daughters of those kings, who had died in the war and left no male issues. He says:

कुमारों नास्ति ये ाां च[7] कन्यास्तत्राभि ेचयः ।।

It also speaks of "Stri Rajya" in the Shanti Parva.[8]

The examples of queens reigning independently in their own right are few. Women in the ancient Indian political scenario appear to act more as political advisors (sometimes more wiser than their male counterparts), yet few have ascended the throne, as a daughter was never considered the natural successor to the throne of her father. We find mostly examples of dowager queens acting as regents for their minor sons, yet the fact remains that they ruled wisely, that their administration never lacked development and welfare of their people. Their role in politics became more important as they bore the onus of governance on their responsible shoulders; and carried forward the load of their state in turbulent times.

There are quite a few fine examples, however, of women as reigning monarchs in Kalhan's *Rajatarangini* and inscriptional evidences testify to several queens and princesses having taken an active part in the administration. The paper attempts to trace such examples with special reference to *Rajatarangini*. The paper examines political participation of women in ancient India, as counsellors, regents, power wielders and factual rulers.

Women as Counsellors

Women in the *Mahabharata* are strong-willed personalities, wise counsellors, efficient leaders and managers. As Amartya Sen has aptly remarked, "There can be little doubt that men have tended to rule the roost, but despite that, the participation of women in both political leadership and intellect has not been negligible. The sharpest questions have come from women interlocutors. They do not always conform to the tender and peace-loving image that is often assigned to them. When Yuddhisthira is reluctant to engage in a bloody battle with the usurpers of his throne, with appropriate anger the most eloquent instigator is his wife Draupadi.[9]

Draupadi is one feminine character in the *Mahabharata*, typical of the age. She is the most forceful and consistent personality of the epic. Though in theory, the slave and property of her husbands, in actual practice, Draupadi often dominated her husbands and their council. She is even mentioned in the epic as Pandita (learned). It is profoundly instructive to study how Kunti educates her sons in the proper use of power. Her maturity and ability to observe life closely and use the learning from experience, for arriving at swift decision to benefit simultaneously both society and her children, sets her apart from all other persons in the epic. Damayanti takes the responsibility for running the administration when Nala is negligent about the affairs of his state. The Sanjay—Vidura dialogue, the Swetaketu Survarchala discussion, the Janaka Sulabha *samvad* are best examples of the wise council and the role played by women in politics. These dialogues discuss in detail the theories of politics, role of kingship, inter-state relations, etc.

Both Atharvaveda and Kautilya[14] also speak of women counsellors. Mahishi the chief queen has been termed as one of the Ratnins in the Ratnavimshi ceremony, i.e., the king designate had to hold counsel with the chief queen and sought her approved for ascending the throne, as the *Atharvaveda* says for the Ratnins:

एते वै रा ट्रस्य प्रदातारः ।

Women as Regents and Power Wielders

Women in ancient India not only helped their husbands with their wise counsel in moments of crisis they did not hesitate even to take up arms to protect the life and honour of their country. Since the ancient times dowager queens have successfully ruled their respective kingdoms. Though queens usually did not assume the reign of government when their husbands were alive, they did not hesitate to assume full control of the administration as regents when their husbands died or sons were minor or taken prisoners. During the captivity of the king Udayana of Kausambi, his mother had taken full charge of the administration and had discharged her duties in a manner that excited the admiration of even the experienced ministers. Curtius records that when the ruler of Massaga had died fighting Alexander, the queen directed the attack against the foreign invaders. In second century B.C. queen Nayanika was at the head of the administration of the extensive Satavahana empire of Deccan during the minority of her son. The Nanag hat cave inscription speaks of appointment of Nayanika as the regent of her minor son Vedsri.[17] In the fourth century A.D. Prabhavati Gupta, the daughter of Chandra Gupta II, ruled successfully as a regent for many years when her son Divakarsena Pravarsena II was a minor. We find two inscriptions of Prabhavati Gupta - one from Poona and another from Riddhpur (Amarvati). The Poon Copper Plate inscription was issued in her 13th regional year. The copper-plate found from Bhandara in Maharasthra speaks of Prabhavati Gupta to have ruled from A.D. 390 to 410. It is to be noted from the Charter, land grants could only be issued by either the sovereign or the person holding sovereign authority.

There are such few examples in the Rajput period also. Minaldevi, mother of great Siddhraj Jai singh of Gujarat, ruled over her kingdom in the end of eleventh century. Similarly, administration of Mewar was taken up by Kumardevi in 1193, when her husband Samarasi died on the battlefied alongwith Prithviraja III. During the time of Harsha, his sister Rajshree, after the death of her husband, Maukhari, Grihavarman of Kannauj, occupied a seat of honour by the side of her brother and also participated in state deliberations.[18]

Women as Factual Rulers: With Special Reference to *Rajatarangini*

Inscriptions testify to several queens and princesses taking an active part in administration. It is notable that Queens in south India had more of their say in policy matters and they wielded actual authority than in northern India. They issued charters in their names, issued land grants and governed portions of kingdoms. It was probably because of the system of matriarchy prevalent amongst the Dravidians. Megasthenes speaks of the queen rulers in Pandya country in third century B.C. in Malabar and the territory around.

The Chalukya queens of Badami are known to have been highly religious and charitable. They accompanied their kings in the battlefield; they were well educated and gifted in many arts; and they were even vested with the responsibility of administration and governance.[19] Vijaybhattarika, queen of Chalukya Chandraditya, ruled the kingdom efficiently after her husband's death. The Nerur and Kochere inscriptions speak of her reign.[20] She ruled over a portion of Bombay and Deccan by the middle of seventh century. We have got a charter issued by her in the fifth year of her reign. In A.D. 786 we find Silamahadevi, the crowned queen of the Rastrakuta king Dhruv, making a land grant on her own authority. She also issued royal orders in her name.[21] Obviously she felt that being the crowned queen, she had an inherent right to issue routine administrative orders, without any reference to her husband, or the latter may have expressly invested her with certain important power of making land grants. Revakanammadi, a daughter of Rastrakuta Amoghovarsha I and wife of Erraganga, was the governor of the district of Edetore in A.D. 837 Malila devi, a queen of Chalukya Somesvara, was governing the extensive province of Banawasi in A.D. 1053 Ketaladevi, another queen of the same king, was the governor of Agrahara of Ponavad. Akkadevi, an elder sister of Jayasimsha III, was ruling over the district of Kinsukad in A.D. 1022 Kumkumadevi, a sister of Vijayaditya, was ruling over a portion of Dharwar district in Karnataka in A.D. 1077. Laxmidevi, the chief queen of Vikramaditya VI, was in charge of the administration of 18 religious endowments.[22]

Hindu princesses, even when entitled to the throne in their own right, did not usually become the legal heads of their state. Their consorts usually became *de jure* as well as the *de facto* heads of the government. Thus, when Gauri, a Ratta princess who was an heir to fiefdom in Karnataka, married a prince of Banahatta family, in the tenth century, her husband became the ruler over the principality.[23]

In northern India, notable examples of women sovereigns are found only in the *Rajatarangini* of Kalhana. The region of Kashmir was liberal in its attitude towards the ruling capabilities of their womenfolk. Queen Didda is the most famous example of women sovereigns, who ruled Kashmir for 22 years in tenth century. We have an inference in *Rajatarangini* going back to the time of Lord Krishna that when King Domodar of Kashmir was killed by Lord Krishna, he crowned his pregnant Queen Yashomati as a sovereign.[24]

अन्तर्वत्नी तस्य पत्नी यदा यदुकुलोद्वह :
राज्ये य ोवतीं नाम द्विजै : क णोऽम्य ेचयत् ।।

King Jalauksirfe Queen Ishandevi had not only control over Kashmir, but had influence over other regions also. She established 'Matrachakra' all over.[25] Similarly, it is stated elsewhere that Tajeen, the son of Pratapaditya, ruled the throne jointly with his wise queen Vakpushta.[26] The *Rajatarangini* speaks of "Stri Rajya" or women sovereigns in the region of Pragjyotishpura (Assam) and their women army who had successfully repulsed the attack of Lalitaditya of Kashmir.[27]

After the death of king Shakarvarman (7th century), his queen Sugandha[28] accepted the prayers of her people and ministers and ascended the throne. She is considered to be one of the most successful monarchs after Didda. We find the influence of Doma queen in the tenth century Kashmir politics. She had formed her people (similar to that of Noor Jahan's), and she and her relatives ran the administrative affairs of their own accord. The role of Suryamati in relieving her kingdom from bankruptcy and the re-establishment of administration in the eleventh century Kashmir is also notable.[29] We have references also of women commander-in-chief[30] in *Rajatarngini.*

In Orissa when king Lalitabharmandeva and his son died towards the end of the ninth century A.D., the widowed queen mother was requested by the feudatories to accept the sovereignty. In compliance to their request, we are told, she ascended the lion throne like Katyayani and ruled till the birth of a grandson. In one *Jataka,* we find a king of Banaras renouncing the world and his queen assuming the reins of administration at the request of the subjects.[31] We have coins of Chandragupta-Kumardevi type, which suggests they ruled the Gupta kingdom jointly. Uma Chakravarti does not agree with the view. She says that the role of Kumaradevi in Gupta administration is highly hypothetical.[32] The Lichchavi kingdom was inherited by her son Samudra Gupta under the *putrika* tradition, but she factually ruled the kingdom, this contention cannot be agreed upon.

Ordinary women took considerable part in the administration of the country. There were democratic assemblies in the Vedic Age. The marriage hymn expresses the hope that the bride would be able to speak with composure and success in these public assemblies down to her old age of'kuh Roa fonFk ekonkfl.[33] It is thus probable that some ladies used to take an effective part in the public discussions of democratic assemblies of the age. In the later Vedic period and the periods later, the state of affairs changed, a text expressly informs us that women do no longer go to public assemblies.

तस्मात्पमांस: सभां यान्ति न स्त्रिय:[३४]

Thus, it can be seen clearly, that women in ancient India did not have wide political powers. We have a few examples of women sovereigns; they existed merely as counsellors and the power behind the scene.

References

1. Rigveda : X 125, 145
2. S. Jay Klemberg, ed. "Retrieving women's History: Changing Perspectives of the role of women in Politics and Society," Oxford: Berg UNESCO Press, 1998, p.323
3. Rekha Mishra, "Women in Myghal India," Delhi: Munshiran Manoharlal Publications, 1967, p.7

4. Kamala Devi Chatopadhyaya, "Woman of India," As quoted in P. Thomas, *Indian women through the Ages*, p.331.
5. *Ramayana*, Ayodhya; 37/24
6. *Mahabharata*: Udyogaparva, Ch 38/43.
7. *Mahabharata*: Vanaparva, Ch. 51/25.
8. *Mahabharata*: Shantiparva, Ch. 4/6-7.
9. Amrtya Sen, *The Argumentative Indian*, Penguin Pub, 2005, pp. 7-8
10. P. Thomas, *Indian Women through the Ages*, Bombay & Calcutta: Asia Publishing House, 1964, pp.131-132.
11. *Mahabharata*: Udyogparva, Ch. 16
12. *Mahabharata*: Shantiparva, Ch. 2/20
13. Ibid., Ch. 18
14. Kautilya's *Arthashastra*, Ch.2.
15. *Pratigya* – Yaugandharayana, Act I.
16. J.W. Mc Crindle, *The Invasion of India by Alexander the Great as Described by Curtius Arrian, Diodorus, Pluaorsh and Justin*, West Minster, 1986.
17. प्राचीन भारतीय अभिलेख संग्रह vol. I मक श्री राम गोयल pp.424-27 राजस्थान हिन्दी ग्रन्थ अकादमी, जयपुर
18. Chatterjee, G.S., *Harshavardhana*, p.87, A.L. Basham, *Wonder that was India*, p.91.
19. Seminar paper presented by M.S. Nagaraja Rao on the Chalukyan queens of Badami–Banglore 1978, p.166 as quoted in *Women in Early Indian Societies*, p.287.
20. For a detailed study see: दक्षिण भारत का इतिहास, याम मनोहर मिश्र वि व प्रका ान नई दिल्ली 1995
21. *Epigraphica Indica* XXII, p 98
22. A.S. Altekar, *The Position of Women in Hindu Civilisation*, New Delhi: Motilal Banarasidas, 2005, p.190
23. Ibid., p. 186
24. Kalhana's *Rajatarangini*: Ch. I/70
25. Ibid., Ch. 1/122.
26. Ibid., Ch. 2/11.
27. Ibid., Ch. 4/173.
28. Ibid., Ch. 5/243.

29. Ibid., Ch. 7/180-209.
30. Ibid., Ch. 8/1069.
31. A.S. Altekar, *The Position of Women in Hindu Civilisation,* New Delhi: Motilal Banarasidas, 2005, p.185
32. Kumkum Roy, ed., *Women in Early Indian Societies,* Delhi: Monohar Books, p.147
33. *Rigveda* X, 85/26
34. *Manusmriti,* 10/7.4

6

Role of Women in Politics: Constitutional Provisions

— Shubhadha Pednekar & Baserat Fatima

In twenty-first century, women are participating in politics all over the world. They are emerging as the builder of democracy. They are the voters and the partners of the leaders, and accordingly act in politics indirectly, but during the past few years they have started participating in politics as policy makers and particularly in India, the rights ensured by the Constitution and various national policies have helped them in doing so.

The history of women's rights starts with the political thinker J.S. Mill. In his essay *The Subjection of Women,* he says, "We simply don't know what women are capable of because we have never let them try...one cannot make an authoritative statement without evidence." He attacks the argument that women are naturally less good at some things than men, and should therefore be discouraged or forbidden from doing them. Until conditions of equality exist, no one can possibly assess the natural differences between women and men. Women are brought up to as if they are weak emotional and docile – a traditional prejudice. Mill felt that emancipation and education of women would have positive benefits for men also. By emancipation of women they would be better able to connect on an intellectual level and thereby improve relationships.

International Aspect

Women's rights are accepted on an International level. The Convention on the Political Rights of Women, 1953, desires to implement the principle of equality of rights for men and women. The Convention recognised that everyone has the right to take part in the governance of the country directly or indirectly, through freely choosing representatives, and has the right to equal access to public services in this country, and desiring to equalise the status of men and women in the enjoyment and exercise of political rights.

Women shall be entitled to vote in all elections on equal terms with men, without any discrimination. They will also be eligible for election to all publicly elected bodies, established by law of the land, on equal terms with men without any discrimination. They will also be entitled to hold public office and to exercise all public functions established by national law on equal terms with men without discrimination.

THE ICCPR 1966

The International Covenant on Civil and Political Rights, (ICCPR) stated: "The State Parties to the present Covenant, recognising that, in accordance with the Universal Declaration of Human Rights, the ideal of free human beings enjoying civil and political freedom can only be achieved, if conditions are created whereby everyone may enjoy his civil and political rights as well as economic, social and cultural rights."

Realising that the individual, having duties to other individuals and to the community to which he belongs, is under a responsibility to strive for the promotion and observance of the rights recognised in the present Covenant.

Art. 3 of Part II mentions that the State parties to the present covenant undertake to ensure the equal right of men and women to the enjoyment of all civil and political rights set forth in the present Covenant.

CONVENTION ON ELIMINATION OF DISCRIMINATION AGAINST WOMEN, 1979

The state parties to the International Covenants of Human Rights have the obligation to ensure the equal rights of men and women to enjoy all economic, social, cultural, civil and political rights. The state parties were convinced that the establishment of the New

International Economic Order based on equity and justice will contribute significantly towards the promotion of equality between men and women. Particularly related to political participation of women certain obligations are put on the state parties. The State Parties undertook to take all appropriate measures to eliminate discrimination against women in the political and public life of the country and, in particular, to ensure to women on equal terms with men, the right:

a) to vote in all elections and public referenda and to be eligible for election to all publicly elected bodies.
b) to participate in the formulation of government policies and implementation thereof, and to hold public office and perform all public functions at all levels of the government.
c) to participate in non-governmental organisations and associations concerned with the public and political life of the country.

The Mexico Plan of Action (1975), the Nairobi Forward Looking Strategies (1985), the Beijing Declaration as well as the Platform for Action (1995) and the Outcome Document adopted by United Nations General Assembly (UNGA) Session as Gender Equality and Development and Peace for the twenty-first century, titled, "Further actions and initiatives to implement the Beijing Declaration and the Platform for Action" have been endorsed by India for appropriate follow-up.

Constitutional Provisions

Fundamental Rights

Art. 14 of the Constitution of India reads as follows:

The state shall not deny to any person equality before the law and equal protection of the laws.

But at the some time, a legislature is entitle to make reasonable classification for purposes of legislation and if the law in question is based on national classification it is not regarded as discriminatory.

Art. 15 (1) specifically bars the state from discriminating against any citizen of India on grounds only of religion, race, caste, sex, place of birth or any of them.

Art. 15 (3) the state is not prevented from mauling any special provision for women and children.

Here, under Art. 15, the word discrimination involves an element of unfavorable bias.

Art 19 guarantees to the citizens of India six freedoms –of speech and expression, peaceful assembly, association, free movement, residence and practising any profession and carrying on any business. These freedoms are necessary to promote the basic rights of the citizens, as well as certain democratic values. But these freedoms are not absolute, but can be controlled, curtailed and regulated to some extent by the laws of the parliament or the state legislatures. They can impose 'reasonable restrictions' on these freedoms.

Art. 21 is the heart of fundamental rights. It states that everyone has the right to life and personal liberty. In various cases, the Supreme Court has come to impose positive obligation upon the state to take steps for ensuring to the individual a better enjoyment of his life and dignity.

Directive Principles of State Policy

Art.39 requires the state to direct its policy towards securing: that all citizens, irrespective of sex, equally have the right to an adequate means of livelihood that there is equal work for both men and women.

Art. 42 requires the state to make provision for securing just and humane conditions of work and maternity relief.

Art. 44 requires the state to strive to secure for the citizens of India a uniform civil code throughout India.

Much progress has not been made towards achieving the ideal of uniform civil code yet the Supreme Court has interpreted the provision in favour of women in different cases.

Art. 51-A lays down fundamental duties: to renounce practices derogatory to the dignity of women.

Reservation of seats in panchayats and municipalities has been provided in Articles 243 D and 243 T of the Constitution. Not less than one-third (including the number of seats reserved for women belonging to the scheduled castes and scheduled tribes) of the total number of seats to be filled by the direct election in every panchayat shall be reserved for women, and such seats may be allotted by rotation in different constituencies in a panchayat:

- Not less than one-third of the total number of offices of chairpersons in the panchayats shall be reserved for women.
- A similar provision is there related to the municipalities also.
- Not less than one-third seats in municipalities shall be reserved for women.
- The offices of the chairpersons in the municipalities shall be reserved for women. And the state legislature may make any provision for such a reservation for women.

It means, these two amendments have totally changed the picture of panchayats and municipalities. The male dominance which was and is in rural politics is prevented by these provisions. The women in rural areas have started participating in politics. Earlier, the relative or wife of a politician entered into the field because of the reservation policy, but slowly the influence of power changed the character of the local bodies. Experience shows that in villages earlier it was not possible for a woman to sit and discuss with men about a family matter, now women are discussing political matters in meetings. As always, it is not easy to change the mindset of the village community to accept the dominance of a woman sarpanch, but today, they have started appreciating the presence and decisions of the women. It may take a few more years, for the women to change their own mindset and also of the community, but still it is a step forward 'towards equality.'

It means that the process in panchayat Raj institutions has opened exciting possibilities for women's participation in the political field. These provisions ensure a real and effective participation of women. For educating the rural women in politics, the urban leadership should come forward. The Singamma Foundation of Karnataka is attempting to build the Indian women's movement to bridge the between urban leadership and the vast number of rural women by creating networks for advocacy at the national, regional and local levels.

Women make up half of the population as now it is well accepted that they must have right to vote, also they must have the right to participate in the political policies because ultimately these policies are going to affect them. Women have to be allowed to participate in the decision-making process to protect their own interests as well as the interests of the society at large.

The National Commission for Women (NCW) was established in 1990. For its establishment, earlier the report was asked by a committee. The Report was submitted as *Towards Equality.* Unfinished Agenda – Status of Women in India 2001. The report submitted the status of women in India and the need for establishing a Commission for Women. THe National Commission for Women Act was passed by the Parliament in 1990 and accordingly the Commission started functioning. In the Act, the functions of the Commission are mentioned in which particular mention of S. 10 (a) (f) (i) (m) are quite relevant which are as under:

S.10 (1)(a) to evaluate and examine all matters relating to the safeguards provided for women under the Constitution and other laws:

f) look into complaints and take *suo moto* notice of matters relating to:
   i) deprivation of women's rights;
   ii) non-implementation of laws enacted to provide protection to women, and also to achieve the objective of equality and development;
   iii) non-compliance of policy decisions, guidelines or instructions aimed at mitigating hardships, ensuring welfare and providing relief to women, and to take up the issues arising out of such matters with appropriate authorities;

i) participate and advise on the planning process of socio-economic development of women;

m) make periodical reports to the government on any matter pertaining to women and, in particular various difficulties under which women toil.

Accordingly, in the programme agenda of 2005-06 the National Commission for Women has undertaken.

- National and local level campaigns for reservation of women.
- Interaction with women in governance in all spheres including legislative, social services, local self-government and public sector undertakings.

In accordance with this agenda in 2005-2006, the IC Centre for Governance, New Delhi, in coordination with the Vadilal Gandhi Foundation arranged a National Level Essay Competition on the topic, "Women at Grassroots Level' in which 'Symbiosis Law School' , Pune, received first prize.

National Policy for the Empowerment of Women, 2001

The policy stated particularly that our Constitution empowers the state to adopt measures of positive discrimination in favour of women. Within the framework of a democratic polity, our laws, development policies, plans and programmes have aimed at women's development in different spheres. The empowerment of women has been recognised as the central issue in determining the status of women. The goals and objectives of the National Policy are as follows:

- the enjoyment of human rights and fundamental freedom by women on an equal basis with men.
- equal access to participation and decision making of women.
- strengthening of the legal systems aimed at elimination of all forms of discrimination against women.
- changing of the social attitudes and community practices by active participation and involvement of both men and women.

It has been stated that equality can be achieved through power sharing and decision making in the political process. Participation should be ensured at all levels. All measures will be taken to guarantee to women equal access to and full participation in decision-making bodies at the legislative, executive, judicial and statutory bodies. Women-friendly personnel policies will be drawn up to encourage women to participate in the development process. The legislative structure will be reviewed and effective implementation would be promoted.

Today, if we analyse the consequences of political participation of women, it has negative as well as positive results because of the provisions made by the state and policies implemented; it is the duty of everyone not to discriminate against women. The presence and participation of women are welcome and appreciated. It is true that literacy in political matters will be achieved by a person only after a certain period of time but when a woman gets elected, she may not be able and well-versed with the situational matters; she may be dependent on her male counterpart but definitely in five years or maybe in lesser time than that she will stand empowered to work independently. The experience is that women candidates who were elected for the first time for a reserved seat later may have been elected independently without reservation.

In the Pune Municipal Corporation, the seat of the chairperson is reserved for a woman mayor. For all these years, only a woman candidate is holding the chair of the mayor and men are deprived of the highest position in the municipality. This example shows how the participation of women has increased in the last 15 years. Political participation is necessary for women because whenever one talks about empowerment of women the empowerment must be social, economic and political. Social empowerment is a long-term process. It includes the change and development in the personality of the women as well as their acceptance by the society. A society takes a long time to change its attitude and approach. In a country like India, where a multi-ethnic, multi-linguistic, multi-religious, multi-cultural society exists, this process will be a slow process yet to be achieved.

Economic empowerment is not only important for women but for everyone who relates with them. It gives status to the woman to stand proudly before the society, as well as elevates the status of the family and community to which she belongs. But economic empowerment is related to many factors, such as educational qualifications, and so it is based on the personal achievement.

Political empowerment is important in all the necessary ways because it will lead to social and economic empowerment. Now, as the participation of women in panchayats is increased it leads to their social and economic empowerment. It has brought considerable changes in the personality of a rural woman. She is aspiring to everything which she can achieve through the ways and means which have been made available to her.

As long back in 1866, Mrs. Gaskell, in her novel *Wives and Daughters* stated that masculine resistance to the development of feminine identity is because possessing a strong identity means possessing power as well. If such power is possessed by women then it will be easy for them to develop feminine identities. Nevertheless, now that we have entered the new millennium it is clear that state policies and programmes will play a prominent role in the development of the society as a whole.

The number of women elected to panchayats in Bihar in 2001 show the emerging role of women that they are scheduled to play in panchayats. Women in villages have shown deeper concern in employment and development in their villages. Women, who have been participating in politics, have at the same time more interests in the social and economic development of the village, than in the party politics. Women have better feelings of togetherness and community life than men, and that is why they are getting more and more support.

The Bihar government recently announced 50 per cent reservation in village panchayats. It has been observed that the women working at the panchayat level may have the least interest in party politics. The village panchayats with the participation of women work as a family unit and as separate independent units of development, as was expected by the Gandhian panchayats. But still, with all the national policies drafted in favour of participation of women in politics the tendency of women is towards low participation because of the male-oriented authority structure, lack of social protection to women and anti-feminine public attitude. One of the major causes is lack of proper education. Female illiteracy is due to poverty, social customs, lack of motivation and apathy on the part of the girls because the education level of women has a positive effect on their decision-making power. For the upliftment of women, changes in the value system are required. Women should be made aware of their political and legal rights. The basic attitudes of men and women need to change.

According to Swami Vivekananda, "A nation would not march forward, if the women are left behind." Today, the issue of women's political participation is on the forefront in established democracies all over the world, and also in developing countries that are moving towards democracy. Women are registering their votes and at the same time emerging in the politics as being successful candidates to earn the votes. Conditions for promoting political participation may not be all comfortable but the women's groups are finding that they can become a force for democratic change. The representatives of The Asia Foundation have reported how women's political participation is occurring in Nepal, Mongolia and Sri Lanka. As a neighbouring state, one should have a better idea about their position in the respective countries.

Political Participation in Nepal

In 1990, when Nepal restored parliamentary democracy, a Constitutional Mandate was passed to ensure the participation of women in national elections, and 5 per cent of all candidates who sought seats in the House of Representatives were reserved for women. Prior to the 1977 local elections, the government passed an act that requires 20 per cent of the elected seats in village development committees to be set aside for women so that at least one woman gets elected to each of the nine wards that comprise the village development committee. But the major impediment in the proper participation of women in politics is illiteracy. Most of them do not have the basic education, nor do they have support from their families they cannot afford to shun their livelihood to spend time in politics, and hence the Asia Foundation Programmes support women's political participation. The Foundation is increasing women's awareness and advocacy skills. It helps women to put their issues on the public agenda, influence policies and facilitates their participation in the political process.

Political Participation in Mongolia

In 1992, Mongolia promulgated a new Constitution which guaranteed equal rights for men and women. A number of women's organisations comprised politically conscious and active women. Women these vote in equal numbers with that of men, but in formal politics women have a limited role. Only eight of

76 seats in the parliament are occupied by women. The same apathy is at the local level. On the other hand women participate actively in civil life at the local and national levels. They do it through NGO's, and the issues which are important for women are focused but in political and economic environment these issues are neglected. As the role of a woman as an active citizen is important for the country's development, NGO's paid attention towards creating awareness in areas of legal literacy, women's political and civic participation and voter's education. The successful example of is to increase the number of women in parliamentary elections.

In the legislative process, NGO's initiatives are: first, women for social progress work with the parliament secretariat on a new election management law, which is an effort towards strict gender interest; the second initiative is Women's Lawyers' Association and the Centre against Violence that drafted Mongolia's first domestic violence laws. The women who are active in public affairs have a very sophisticated view of their involvement in political process. The women view their participation in political and civic life not as an end in itself, but as a means to influence the country's laws and regulations.

Political Participation in Sri Lanka

In comparison to Mongolia and Nepal, in Sri Lanka the democratic institutions and processes have been in place for a number of years and women's suffrage is there since 1931. However, the ability to vote has not resulted in a great deal of participation on the part of women. Presently, there are 12 women who are members of parliament, 90 per cent of whom are in place by virtue of a kinship to a father, brother or husband. It is important to recognise that simply getting into the political process is not enough. It is noteworthy that women's group were very important in the run up to the 1994-95 election in Sri Lanka when the focus was on peace and conflict. Further, women from other areas, for example, from outside Colombo, are starting to mobilise more. It is interesting to see the emergence of solidarity among the wives and family members of soldiers, including those who are missing in action and others who are pushing the government and LTTE. In fact, they have become a very local group calling for a different approach to setting the conflict.

The Agromart Foundation working with the Asian Foundation deals with women's participation issues, having passed through an interesting transition to represent this view and awareness among women's groups. The Agromart Foundation is performing with the Asia Foundations Support. First, the publication of the only women's magazine in Sri Lanka with a focus on women's rights, women's political participation and issues related to garbage collection as government responsibility and other topics. Second, Agromart is involved in advocacy training, i.e., creating awareness amongst the women of their rights.

Some Cases and Incidences Revealing Women's Commitment to Society

Sunita Devi and her husband Shreekanth were activists of the CPI (ML) People's war. On March 3, 2000 Shreekanth was killed in a police encounter in Jehanabad. But instead of weeping over the fact that she had lost her husband she was overwhelmingly grieved because a committed revolutionary had been killed, and she resolved to bring her only son to be a revolutionary.

Kanthi Devi, the leader of Nari Mukti Sangharsh Samiti, feels that people's war is a symbol of sheer human will power. She said, once I entered the agrarian struggle, I realised the need to understand the various aspects of women's life and struggle.

In the present scenario, the first and most important issue is the reservation for women in parliament and state legislatures. Looking at the experiences in village panchayats and empowerment of the women at the grassroots level, the need for reservation in legislatures is realised. The urban sector will help the women to come forward and enjoin the political fraternity, but the bill is yet to be passed.

A somewhat different issue can be discussed here and that is about the number of women judges in Indian courts. The participation of women in village panchayats is achieved and legislatures are being discussed but the participation of women in judiciary also should be discussed and accordingly some initiatives be made to enhance their participation. The encouragement for the women to enter the field of judiciary is the need of the hour. Judiciary is an important pillar of democracy and governance, such as legislature and executive, and more and more participation of women in the judicial process will definitely change the face of justice in India.

Conclusion and Suggestions

As in Mongolia, NGOs are playing an important role towards enhancing the participation of women in politics; it will also work in India. NGO leaders should help to increase the number of women in the elections. The women who are otherwise active in public affairs must have a strong motive for their involvement in the political process. The women's NGO movement should continue to play a key role in advancing India's democratic development. The onus for political participation also lies with the corporate sector. The corporate who are coming forward with social and environmental issues should also think about proper planning towards participation of women employees in politics. The service sector which is otherwise having an apathy towards politics if starts engaging their human resources in politics, it will give an appropriate framework to politics.

At the same time the private sector will contribute to women-related issues, particularly towards the economic and political development of women. In the British regime, it was the contribution of intellectuals and academicians who brought renaissance in the Indian society. Today, it is time for the intellectuals to participate in politics so that the entire political scenario changes for the better and people are able to live in a civilised society.

Works Cited

1. Mishra, O.P., *Law Relating to Women and Child.* Allahabad: Central Law Agency, 2003.
2. Batra, Manjula, *Women & Law.* Faridabad: Allahabad Law Agency, 2001.
3. Rao, Mamta, *Law relating to Women & Law.* Lucknow: Eastern Book Company, 2005.

4. Shakuntla, *New Dimensions of Women Empowerment*. Ed. Ajit Kumar Sinha. New Delhi: Deep and Deep Publications Pvt. Ltd. 2008.
5. Sinha, K.K. *New Dimensions of Women Empowerment*. Ed. Ajit Kumar Sinha. New Delhi: Deep and Deep Publications Pvt. Ltd.
6. Srivastava, G.. *Women's Higher Education in the 19th Century*. New Delhi: Concept Publishing Company.
7. Roy, K., *Women's Oppression and Protective Law*. Delhi: Rajat Publications, 1999.
8. Pillai, J.K., *Women and Empowerment*. New Delhi: Gyan Publishing House, 1995.
9. Roy, A., *Human Rights of Women*. New Delhi: Rajat Publication, 2003.
10. Neshla, *Women in Haryana*. KUK Publishing House, 1991.
11. Sinha, K.K., *Panchayat Dilemma, People, Power and Poverty, Serials*. Delhi, 2006.
12. S. Uma Devi, *Role of Women in Economic Development*, IEJ Conf., 1998. (She discusses a radical approach as a fight against patriarchal family structure. It is more a question of development of the household than the urban question of development of the market).
13. Jain, M.P., *Indian Constitutional Law*. New Delhi: Wadhwa and Company, 2007.

The Asian Foundation. Strengthening Democracy Through Women's Political Participation. www.du.ac.in/course/material/ug/ba/hrge/08.pdf (Accessed January 21, 2009).

State Initiatives. http://www.india-seminar.com/2001/505.htm (Accessed January 22, 2009).

National Policy for the Empowerment of Women (2001). www.wcd.nic.in/empwomen.htm (Accessed January 21, 2009). Feminist Literacy Criticism. http://en.wikipedia.org/wiki/ The Subjection of Women (Accessed August 5, 2008).

7

Constitutional 73rd Amendment: Instrument of Political Empowerment of Women[1]

—Mushtaq Ahmad

Introduction

The role of women in panchayati raj Institutions (PRIs) is attracting a lot of serious attention in the present context. The constitution 73rd Amendment has been welcomed as the step focusing the nation's attention on the political structures and the processes of democratising rural India and their significance for the vulnerable sections of the rural society.

Attitudes have changed a lot today. Women now are not going to remain contended just looking after women's affairs as elected members of panchayats, whether it be village, block or the district level. If given the chance, they will play a constructive role in all the developmental activities and step into what was hitherto considered man's domain. The very idea that women in such large numbers will have a say in local self-government is a new concept and will not be easily accepted. Difficulties are bound to be there initially. Statutory empowerment will become a reality and relevant only when they are given adequate, planned and systematic training about their responsibilities, duties and rights which devolve on them as elected representatives.

Panchayati raj institutions serve as training grounds for the growth of leadership, democratic decentralisation of administration and involvement of people particularly women in accelerating the socio-economic development. In this paper an attempt has been made to discuss the steps taken by the Government of India for political empowerment of women through the Constitution 73rd Amendment and to highlight the constraints which come in the way of such empowerment.

Experience reveals that women have lived in two parallel worlds ever since the first community habitation. They have occupied positions of eminence and authority, and even gone into battle.

They have been objects of repression, uncalled-for violence and the petty tyrannies of the male breadwinner. 'Political empowerment of women'— an enigma to be desired, mankind has ever been willing to give women everything but equal status. This brazen conspiracy of the menfolk against the women has been perpetrated since all times. Even the human rights have been given to them but grudgingly. And the irony is that the 'man' is hardly ever conscious of the injustice done by him. But today, a stage has arrived when she is almost an equal partner in the voyage of life. The fact is that the match of mankind is irreversibly towards an era of equality, and the women is on the threshold of a life hitherto un-charted.[2] This is because of dynamic constitutional and legal provisions and other measures adopted by the government from time to time to transform Indian society to make it gender just. Their visibility in public life is increasing, still they face gender discrimination.

In this paper an attempt has been made to discuss the steps taken by the Government of India for political empowerment of women through the Constitution 73rd Amendment, and to highlight the constraints which come in the way of such empowerment.

United Nation's Response

Women constitute half of the world's population. But they are the largest excluded category in almost all respects. They have only 0.1 per cent of the global income. They own 0.01 per cent of the means of production. Nearly 70 per cent of the women live below the poverty line. Two-thirds of them are illiterate. They constitute almost invariably a small minority of those holding elected office. In 1980, they made up of just over 10 per cent of the world's parliamentarians. The figure rose to 14.8 per cent in 1988 and it came down to 12.7 per cent in 1997, and the situation is by and large the same till date.

The question of women's participation in politics began to assume special importance only since 1975 when the United Nations declared the decade as the " Women Development Decade," and adopted some resolutions for empowerment of women. The Nairobi Conference (3rd International Conference on Women) held in 1985 called on the participating countries "to take steps for ensuring women's participation in politics through reservation of 35 per cent seats in all elections."

In the 4th U.N. (World) Conference on Women held at Beijing in 1995, it was asserted by the participating countries that "women's empowerment and their participation on the basis of equality in all spheres of society are fundamental for the achievement of equality, development and peace."[3]

The Indian Scenario

After Independence, even in India, several efforts have been made to increase women's political participation. The participation of women PRIs was for the first time brought into focus in 1957 by the Balvant Rai Mehta Committee, which had recommended nomination/cooption of two women members in panchayat (at block level). The principle of nomination, however, did not produce the desired results.[4] Thus, the running theme in the debates from 1957 to 1989 was how to encourage the participation of women in political process. Thus, the next and more significant effort was 33 per cent reservation of seats for women in panchayat and municipalities through the 73rd and 74th Constitutional Amendments.

"You cannot draw the masses into politics without drawing the women into politics as well."[5] India is perhaps the first country to recognise this social fact underlined by Lenin in 1921 on International Working Women's Day. And to have concrete measures to draw women into politics at the grassroots level by giving them 33 per cent reservation in what may be called the 3rd –tier of governance-the Panchayati Raj.[6]

'Democratic Decentralisation' or panchayati raj as it is popularly known in India, aims at making the democracy real by bringing millions of people into the functioning of their representative government at the grassroots level. The main responsibility of panchayati raj institutions (PRIs) is to accelerate the pace of development and involve all people, both male and female in this process so that the felt needs of the people and their development aspirations are fulfilled. Involvement and participation of women in PRIs is essential for efficient, equitable and sustainable people-centred development. Democracy, governance and gender are therefore interrelated. Democracy is a form of political system, governance is an institution to implement its principles, and gender is a part of governance, to be ensured by equal participation of men and women.

In the context of the meagre representation of women in the Parliament and state legislatures *vis-à-vis* their population, the Constitution(73rd Amendment) Act, 1992 shall be considered a significant landmark in the process of political empowerment of women. The 73rd Amendment which became a Part IX of the Indian Constitution and thereby providing constitutional status to PRIs, has brought a silent revolution in the country by facilitating the entry of 33 per cent women into public life. Giving one- third reservation to women in PRIs basically aims at ensuring women's participation in political and development process for socio-economic justice at the grassroots level.

Constitutional Protection of Political Empowerment

Article 243-D inserted in the Constitution by 73rd Amendment deals with reservation of seats and political offices for women in PRIs. The main features of Article 243-D are:[7]

- Onethird of the total number of seats to be filled by direct election in every Panchayat shall be reserved for women and such seats may be allotted by rotation to different constituencies in panchayats (Art.243-D(i));
- One-third of the total number of seats reserved for women under Cl.(i) shall be reserved for women belonging to SCs & STs (Art.243-d(2));
- One-third of the total number of offices of chairpersons in the Panchayat at each level shall be reserved for women (Art.243-D (4)).

Articles 330 and 332 of the Constitution provides for reservation of seats in the Lok Sabha and state assemblies in favour of SCs and STs. The Constitution also provides that these twin types of reservation shall cease at the end of 50 years from the commencement of the Constitution, i.e.; in January 2006. However, the reservations introduced for women in the panchayats shall continue (Art.243-D (5)). This is a very significant provision as the reservation for women in PRIs has been made a permanent feature.

As a women welfare measure, the year 2001 in India was observed as the 'Year of Women Empowerment.' This veritably presupposes the nation's urge to hoist the status of women in society. The 73rd Amendment may be regarded as a watershed in the history of state initiatives in regard to political empowerment of women. It had indicated a noticeable shift in the approach of the Indian state towards women. Earlier women were generally viewed as objects of development only, but this amendment made women the subjects of development and an indispensable part of the decision-making process. As a result of the reservation of seats formal participation of women in politics at the grassroots level has gone up considerably.

The Present Position

Democratic decentralisation would be rendered meaningless unless gender equity is ensured. The pace of development in any society would be slow if women who constitute about 50 per cent of the population are not facilitated to participate in the development process. India with a female population of over 450 million possesses a vast reservoir of women power which exceeds a combined total population of South-East Asian countries.[8]

The available data in respect of the first post-73rd Amendment Panchayat elections reveal that, of the total number of 2.92 million elected representatives of panchayat, at various levels, about 10 lakh (1 million) were women, and a large majority of them were first-timers.[9]

The historic Amendment has greatly contributed to the political empowerment of women (including SCs and STs) and has thrown open political opportunities in the Panchayati raj institutions (PRIs) to these disadvantaged sections. Despite various constraints it can safely be said that the upsurge of women power in PRIs is noticeable as panchayats in India are gradually becoming gender sensitive. Women have started asserting themselves leading to a new kind of situation in the society. Reservation of seats has given them an unprecedented opportunity and has created conditions for a sort of social revolution without much hue and cry.[10]

Constraints

Unlike other political systems, based on egalitarian values, democracy has more scope for promoting 'gender equality.' But democratic structure being influenced, reflected and determined by historical culture, social, economic and political conditions of society, has some constraints in achieving equality in all walks of life. More than a decade has gone by since the passage of the 73rd Amendment Bill, and drastic and dramatic changes were expected by increasing women's representation. The dream of feminisation of politics has been achieved in quantitative terms (only at local level), yet to be achieved in qualitative terms.

Most of the women members do not know that they have been selected to represent womenfolk and work on behalf of them. So there is a need for creating feminist consciousness among them.

It further includes:

- Identifying women in trouble
- Identifying the requirement of women of the village and try to fulfil their needs tnrough panchayats.
- Raising women's issues in the panchayat meetings
- Monitoring development works.

The male members of the panchayat, viz., bureaucracy, field level officials and functionaries, have proved to be gender insensitive. The basic problems among women are illiteracy, ignorance, social and religious barriers and family obligations which prevent them from participating effectively in PRIs. The male members of the panchayat as well as their husbands keep them away from meetings, take signatures at their residence and treat them as dummy participants.

Of late, there is a paradigm shift in the development process by incorporating the 'gender concerns' as an important element of development strategy. Duly recognising the importance and involvement of women in the participatory model of development, India has taken up the theme of women's empowerment as one of the main agenda items to tackle rural poverty and socio-economic issues.[11]

Despite various constraints, one of the significant achievements of the provisions of the 73rd Amendment Act concerning reservation of seats and political offices in favour of women is that it has improved their awareness and perceptional levels, and had created an urge in them to assert for their rightful share in the decision-making exercise at the local level. They have begun to realise that political empowerment in the ultimate analysis holds the key for their social and economic betterment. Therefore, there is no need to be cynical about the prospects of the constitutional safeguards provided to the women.

CONCLUSION

If you feel sceptical about this process because of the adverse reports regarding the pitfalls of empowering women who are not ready to take their place alongside men due to inexperience and illiteracy, just visit eastern India where at least one rustic male has got a card printed describing himself as the *Sarpanch Pati*. A more eloquent comment on the kind of change that we are seeing would be hard to find. It may not be appropriate to expect miracles overnight in the historical and cultural context of the Indian social system. A brief spell of 14 or 15 years is too small in the history of a nation to judge the rationale of political empowerment of the women. The disabilities suffered by this deprived section of the rural society are bound to disappear in the long run. The women have now to take up the cudgels and take full advantage of the opportunities, and to participate in rural affairs through the medium of the new panchayat raj system. By nature they are suited to take the cudgels to perform this task but they have to come out with a firm determination. If they do not, their case would go by default forever and they cannot claim that they are being discriminated.

Enacting a law is not enough for ensuring the desired socio-economic transformation but an essential prerequisite for such a change. The traditional and conservative attitude of the rural community, illiteracy and ignorance, social forces, economic structure and the existing political milieu place obstructions in their effective participation. The women need to be properly educated and trained to fulfil their obligations as people's representatives, and actively help to overcome obstacles they encounter. The genuine women empowerment thus obviously is not a concomitant of their numerical or quantitative presence but depends on their qualitative participation, which, in turn, flows from the gender orientation, a frame of mind, an attitude, a perspective.

Works Cited

1. This Article has earlier been published in the Schoolasticus: A Research Journal of National Law University, Jodhpur.
2. Bhan, C & Raj. "Women's Empowerment for Gender Equality-A Functional Analysis", *Kurukshetra,* Vol. 49, No. 11, August, 2001.
3. Datta, P. "Women in Panchayats," *Kurukshetra,* Vol. 50, No. 4, December, 2001.
4. Report of Study Team on *Community Projects & National Extension Services,* Vol I, Govt. of India, New Delhi, 1957.
5. Lenin, International Working Women's Day, 1921.
6. Hemalath, H.M., 2003, "A Hand that Cradles can also Handle the Panchayat", *Kurukshetra,* Vol. 51, No. 5, March.
7. Article 243(D) of Constitution (73rd Amendment) Act 1992.
8. Anon, *Eight Five Year Plan 1992-97,* Vol II, Govt. of India Planning Commission, New Delhi.
9. Subramanyam, K.S, "Empowerment of Women and Marginalised Groups in Panchayats", *Kurukshetra,* Vol. 50, No. 7, March, 2002.
10. Patnaik, B.K., 2001. "Gender Economic Empowerment and Rural Poverty Alleviation," *Kurukshetra,* Vol. 50, No. 2, December, 2001.
11. Rani, L.D., *WomenEnterpreneurs,* A.H.P., Publishing Corporation, New Delhi.

8

Political Participation of Women: Issues and Challenges

— *Nirupama Prakash*

Politics is the process by which groups of people make decisions. It consists of social relations involving authority or power, and refers to the regulation of a political unit, and to the tactics used to formulate and apply policy. (http://en.wikipedia.org/wiki/Politics.) Though these units consist of both men and women, men have always dominated the field.

According to the International Institute for Democracy and Electoral Assistance, throughout the world women face obstacles towards their participation in politics. These barriers exist in prevailing social and economic systems, as well as in existing political structures. In 2007, the rate of female representation at the national level stood at merely 18 per cent globally. Although this figure has increased in recent years, minimal progress has been made, meaning that the ideal of parity between men and women in national legislatures still remains distant. (http://www.idea.int/gender/)

A century ago, almost no women held elected office. In fact, they were legally barred from voting in national elections until ratification of the 19th Amendment to the US Constitution in 1920. A few women, however, were candidates for political office even before they could vote. Now most of the women are educated and work in different fields yet their participation in the field of politics does not commensurate with their numbers in the society. Though thousands of women serve as mayors of cities and towns across the world yet still they are left on the periphery of political process.

Enhancing the active participation of women in politics and the representation of women in positions of power and decisionmaking is a key factor in mainstreaming gender issues in the political agenda of nations. Politics of gender has to be looked into.

In the Western world, only after countless demonstrations, hunger strikes and active lobbying did women get the right to vote. New Zealand was the first country to provide the right to vote to its women in the year 1893. There were two historical factors which played a decisive role in women's securing the right to vote: their increasing participation in "male" jobs during the industrial revolution; and their substantial contribution in world wars. In other parts of the world, women earned their access to the modern political process through active participation in the struggle against colonialism, for national liberation and in the formation of new states. In India, for example, women received the right to vote following independence as a natural extension of their active participation in the freedom struggle. Wars, revolutions and independence movements brought waves of women into the polling booth.

Beginning in the nineteenth century, women in several countries led prolonged struggles to obtain the right to vote. In Europe and North America in particular, opposition to women's suffrage was based mainly on the assumption that women and politics did not belong together, that politics was a "non-feminine" activity. By 1987, women had the right to vote in at least 115 countries. In most countries, they won the right to vote and the right to contest elections at the same time. Although they have voted in increasing numbers in countries with democratic elections, their numbers in elective or appointive offices remain unacceptably low Rao B D, 2000.

In the global perspective, although women are half the earth's population, they hold minimum per cent of seats in the world's 181 parliaments. Women around the world share a common condition; they are not full and equal participants in public policy choices that affect their lives. The top decisionmaking positions remain a largely male-dominated sphere where women have little influence. Women's exclusion from power in the public arena is in sharp contrast to their ability to make crucial decisions relating to the survival of their families. Not only do millions of women manage scarce resources related to household consumption and health matters, but they also organise, supervise, teach, heal, solve problems and make peace, providing our societies with the cohesion required for development.

Since the first world conference on women in Mexico City two decades ago, many women have entered the public arena. Even though more women serve as heads of states or governments, ministers, member of parliament, mayors and members of local councils than ever before, their numbers are usually too small to affect significantly the power structure that shapes society.

The candidates fielded by the various political parties are still dominantly male—women account for only 5 to 10 per cent of all candidates across parties and regions. In most parties, the women members are by and large thin on the ground if not invisible in the actual decision-making bodies, and rarely influence the more significant party policies.

Most often they are relegated to the "women's wing" of the party, and made to concentrate on what are seen as specifically "women's issues," such as dowry and rape cases, and occasionally on more general concerns like price rise which are seen to affect especially "housewives." Though there is proliferation of women leaders in national politics yet it is evident that they are still not actively engaged in the mainstream politics (Rao, 2000).

The Indian Context

There is a strong correlation between the status of women and their role in political participation. The Indian civilisation has produced great women ranging from *Brahma vadinis* (lady Rishi) to stateswomen, from ideal wife to warrior queen. It dates back to thousands of years. Hindu mythology shows that the status of Hindu women during the Vedic period was honourable and respectable. In the same age women had sufficient freedom to attend fairs, festivals and assemblies. During the post-Vedic period, they started losing their status in society, which they had attained in the Vedic age. They lost their independence. They became a subject of protection. Manu, the progenitor of Hindu race, stated that a woman should be kept day and night in subordination by the males of the family—the woman has to be protected by her father in childhood, by her husband in young age and by the sons in old age. He did not treat women on par with man. He believed that there is a vital structural difference between man and woman, each suited for different types of work. He regarded women as more emotional and less rational by nature than men. Man was responsible for hard work, earning the bread and women for household duties. The rigid institution of caste reinforced these notions.

During the Mughal rule, the socio-economic status of Hindu woman was further lowered. Social evils like the purdah system came into force. Child marriage was prevalent. Lack of education, early marriage, non-existence of employment opportunities, absence of absolute property rights were the main causes of inequality of sex in the socio-economic field. Economic dependence made a Hindu woman socially backward. Incidents of female infanticide and custom of sati could be witnessed. Women were thus deprived in many ways.

During the British rule in India, legislation was used to bring about significant modifications in the structure of society. Various reforms were initiated with respect to the status of women. The advent of British rule in India in the nineteenth century saw the rise of a new elite group influenced by Western liberalism. A variety of socio-religious reforms were undertaken by this group on issues related to women. By the end of the century a nationalistic movement had emerged. This continued for the next 50 years carrying a common interest of all the political leaders, i.e., achieving freedom from British rule. This struggle for freedom, broadly speaking, marked the beginning of a political awaking among women in India (Evrette, 1979).

The first Indian National Congress was founded in 1889 and 10 women attended its first meeting. Subsequently women started attending annual meetings regularly. Gandhiji's emergence as a political leader worked as an instrument in bringing thousands of women out of their homes to join the freedom struggle. Under his leadership women in large numbers joined the satyagraha movement and many went to prisons willingly. The non-cooperation movement started in 1921 and gave a forward kick to the participation of women in politics. Gandhi's civil disobedience movement and *Dandi yatra* (march) campaign brought a large number of women into public life. This helped the traditional housebound women to emerge as a powerful instrument of political action. They demanded equal right of representation for the fair sex in Indian provincial legislature which at first was denied by the British government but finally came through in 1935.

With India attaining freedom in 1947, our Constitution guaranteed equality before law and equal protection of law, prohibiting discrimination on the ground of sex. It also empowered the state to make special provisions for women and children, to provide for securing just and humane conditions of work and for maternity relief (Yogendra, N *et al*, 2005).

Now in independent India women are holding important political and administrative positions, like governors, chief ministers, and ministers in cabinet and state governments, presiding officers of legislative bodies, judges of high courts and secretaries to the Government of India. But still their representation in the parliament remains at a very low level; it never got beyond 10 per cent at any point of time. The Government of India made efforts to improve the socio-economic status of women through its five year plans. The Ninth Five Year Plan commits to "Empower Women through creating an enabling environment where women can freely exercise their rights both within and outside their homes, as equal partners along with men."

In 1999 the historic 85th Constitutional Amendment Bill was introduced seeking to reserve 33 per cent of the seats for women in legislative bodies; 33 per cent of seats in all local bodies have been reserved for women by the 73rd and 74th Amendments passed in 1993, and this has brought over a million women into panchayats and urban local bodies (Panda 2001). In many states women panchayats have been acclaimed and commended.

During 1987-92 Karnataka had 14,000 women in its development councils. In 1991 in Orissa, 22,000 women were elected to panchayats. In Kerala 30 per cent of seats were reserved for women whereas women won 35 per cent and the corresponding figure in 1994 in Madhya Pradesh was 43 per cent. Just in two to three years there was a manifold increase in the per centage of elected women to local government bodies (Sen S, 2000). However, still our Parliament is a man's world.

Women represent half the population of a country and have the right to half the seats and parliamentary decisions that affect their lives; then why is the reservation 33 per cent? If the aim of this Bill is to promote gender equality, 33 per cent quota does not pass the test of equality. Some have argued that parties should simply ensure that 33 per cent of their candidates for elections are women. Opposing the bill many have argued that reservations of 33 per cent will only bring urban elite women to power. Everybody agrees on the principle of equal participation for women, but none will lift an honest finger to ensure equal representation. Preventing women from creating their own leadership, and obstructing them from policy-making decisions is simply a continuation of the gender subjugation. Only women in positions of power can inspire more women to take up these paths (Gupta V. 2005).

A study conducted by Dr. Susheela Kaushik in Haryana and Rajasthan has revealed that while awareness and confidence on political participation and role have increased and are more widespread among the women of all classes and castes, it would be quite sometime before they can break through the barriers of patriarchy (familial, societal and state), and emerge as equal players in politics. Women need more time; more of support structure and services; more sensitisation of programmes especially for men and officials on women's rights and empowerment, affirmative actions on the part of political parties and NGOs, and longer period of uninterrupted reservation for women, particularly of schedule castes, OBCs and tribes (Kaushik, 2001).

Though the provisions relating to reservations in panchayats were passed without much debate and opposition, yet immediately after the first round of election there was a great deal of scepticism (Sharma R, 2001). For instance, if women panchayat presidents do not yield to powerful landowners or contractor lobbies, they face no-confidence motions and eventual removal from office. In some cases, women panchayat members also have to face violence, intimidation and harassment for questioning male dominance and asserting their rights as elected representatives. Although there is greater social acceptance of women in panchayats, women sarpanches, in conservative areas, face daily obstacles in their work. In some areas, male officials do not hold elected women members/presidents in high esteem. Women are also doubly disadvantaged – forced to carry the burden of household chores as well as official duties. Even if women are selected in large number, the power equation never changes. Women leaders in panchayats are being used as proxies.

But according to Indian writer and activist Devaki Jain, "The positive discrimination of PRI has initiated a momentum of change. Women's entry into local government in such large numbers, often more than the required 33.3 per cent, and their success in campaigning, including the defeat of male candidates, has shattered the myth that women are not interested in politics, and have no time to go to meetings or to undertake all the other work that is required in political party processes. PRI reminds us of a central truth: power is not something people give away. It has to be negotiated, and sometimes wrested from the powerful." By asserting control over resources and officials and by challenging men, women are discovering a personal and collective power that was previously unimaginable. Women leaders in the panchayati raj institutions are transforming local governance by sensitising the state to issues of poverty, inequality and gender injustice. Through the PRI, they are tackling issues that had previously gone virtually unacknowledged, including water, alcohol abuse, education, health and domestic violence. (Mathew, 2004).

Strategies for Enhancing Participation of Women in Politics (UNIFEM Study)

The participation of women in politics and decisionmaking is influenced by the actions of political parties and the extent to which parties are committed to the promotion of women's involvement in politics. Quotas and reservations are a first step in increasing women's participation in the political world (UNIFEM, 2005). The following are the few strategic measures:

1. Create or Strengthen National Machineries and Other Governmental Bodies

In keeping with the commitments to the Beijing Platform for Action, national machineries and mechanisms have been set up in South Asian countries.

In Bangladesh, the Ministry of Women's and Children's Affairs facilitates the mainstreaming of gender equality in all areas. Bhutan has a National Commission for Women and Children to coordinate and monitor gender-related issues. India started its institutional interventions for women about six decades ago. The Department of Women and Child Development (DWCD) is located within the Ministry of Human Resources Development of the Government of India, and several other agencies have been set up to work with women. The National Commission for Women (NCW) was established in 1992 through an Act of Parliament "to examine legal safeguards provided by the Constitution, recommend measures for their effective implementation and improvement, take *suo moto* notice of abuses of women's rights and correct these conditions in collaboration with the appropriate authorities," among others. State level commissions for women have been set up in most states. Crimes against women cells have also been set up in most states to mediate between the police and survivors of violence. Legal-aid cells and all-women police stations have been initiated in some states. The National Crimes Records Bureau has been instituted for monitoring registered cases of violence against women, and recently district level bureaus have also been set up for the purpose.

The Ministry of Gender, Family Development and Social Security in the Maldives implements its activities through the Gender Equality Council. The setting up of the Ministry of Women and Social Welfare in 1995 was deemed a path-breaking initiative for Nepal as there had been no women in the cabinet in the first half of the 1990s. The National Commission for Women, formed on Women's Day 2002, is entrusted with promoting the welfare of women.

The Government of Pakistan has developed institutional arrangements at the federal and provincial levels. A National Commission on the Status of Women was set up in 2000. A

National Policy for Development and Empowerment of Women has been in place since 2002, which aims at gender equality and social, political and economic empowerment of women.

Sri Lanka's Ministry of Women's Empowerment and Social Welfare acts through the National Commission on Women (NCW) by monitoring the implementation of the Women's Charter of 1993, the national document that provides for the eradication of sex-based discrimination, enhanced gender equality and standards in the areas of political rights, education, health, and also violence against women.

CEDAW observed that in every country in South Asia, the "national machinery is weak in implementation" without distinction as to whether the national machinery has a ministry level status or not. The challenge of promoting gender equality and advancing women's status does not end with the creation of an implementing office. Almost all countries highlighted the lack of resources for institutional machineries looking into women's programmes in the region. National machineries for the advancement of women are also bogged down by the same stereotypes and prejudices that women face in society. The Third Beijing Biennial Regional Ministerial Meeting aptly observed the "marginalisation of the Women's issue." The change of mindset about women and about gender relations is necessary for the successful realisation of governmental commitments.

2. Integrate Gender Perspectives in Legislation, Public Policies, Programmes and Projects

With a view to implementing international commitments made through the Beijing Platform for Action (BPFA), CEDAW, and other instruments, as also continuing efforts at perspective building can be seen across South Asia. The recent trend at gender budgeting exercise in most countries in South Asia intends to highlight the existing biases and suggest ways of promoting equality. Gender budgeting is not a separate budget for women, but an analysis of the government budget to see what its gender-differentiated impacts are, and to enable better translation of policy commitments into resource commitments. A gender sensitive budget is one that improves the gender balance in outcomes and more effective targeting of expenditures. It is one of the most recent and effective tools for gender mainstreaming. Governments may allocate budgets for a certain purpose but given gender differentials in society, the impact on men and women, boys and girls is not the same. The challenge is to provide budgets and programmes that are able to counter pre-existing social biases.

3. Generate and Disseminate Sex-disaggregated Data and Information for Planning and Evaluation

A conscious effort is needed to generate nuanced information on the situation of women and men from the household level and upwards to ensure realistic inputs to planning and policy making. Sex-disaggregated data is crucial to counter the long-standing issue of women's invisibility.

4. Increase Women's Participation and Leadership (Capacity Building, Gender Training and Awareness Raising)

As women are relatively new to politics at the local level, capacity building and training in political processes are extremely important across South Asia. In Bangladesh gender training is being conducted in the National Institute for Local Government for ward commissioners, government officials, etc., The programme schedule includes women's empowerment, gender and development, women's rights, etc. Programmes are also conducted by NGOs on awareness raising and sensitisation for political empowerment of citizens. In India, both government and non-governmental organisations conduct capacity building programmes for elected women members. In Kerala, systematic gender training programmes for women in panchayats have been conducted and technical training on gender budgeting imparted.

Initiatives Undertaken by UGC Centre for Women Studies, BITS, Pilani

The UGC Centre for Women Studies organised Two Days Orientation Workshop on 'Convention on the Elimination of All Forms of Discrimination against Women (CEDAW) for University and College Teachers' during January 12-13, 2008 at BITS, Pilani.

The Convention on the Elimination of All Forms of Discrimination against Women (CEDAW) constitutes the international Bill of Rights for Women. Among the International human rights treaties, the Convention takes an important place in bringing the female half of humanity into the focus of human rights concerns. The Convention is a unique instrument, as it is formulated on the principles of equal rights between women and men in the private and public spheres. The Convention is an instrument to protect and promote equal access and enjoyment of the rights for women through law and policy reforms.

Women can enjoy the rights only if they are aware and have knowledge of their rights under national and international conventions. Raising awareness about women's rights can go a long way in realising their interventionist role. In this background, the objectives of the Orientation Workshop on CEDAW were as follows:

- To provide knowledge and develop skills in the application of principles of the Convention on the Elimination of All Forms of Discrimination against Women.
- Raise awareness of teachers of the advantage of basing the struggle for women's human rights on the feminist principles and international human rights norms, with special reference to CEDAW.
- Create a clarity on key concepts and principles pertaining to women's rights advocated by the Convention: equality, discrimination and state obligation under treaty law.
- Create familiarity with the obligations that the state has undertaken through ratification of international human rights treaties and by being a party to the recommendation and plans of actions of the UN World Conferences.
- To create awareness on the reporting mechanism and its benefits for women.
- To raise awareness on the Optional Protocol to the CEDAW Convention.
- To create awareness on the legality of the declaration and reservation on CEDAW.

- To identify areas of priority and strategies for action in relation to CEDAW and the Optional Protocol.

Prof. Pam Rajput, Executive Director, Women Resource and Advocacy Centre, Chandigarh, and Member, UGC Expert Committee on Gender, and Ms. Kamal Singh, Gender Expert and Former Head, Governance and Social Justice, British Council, New Delhi, were the resource persons for the Workshop. There were 47 delegates from nearby academic institutions and BITS, Pilani, who attended the Workshop. This activity helped in making women aware of their rights.

The UGC Centre for Women Studies, BITS, Pilani conducted a programme on 'Creating Awareness and Inculcating Decision Making Skills among the Rural Poor/ SC/ ST Women on Financial Inclusion Scheme and Bhama Shah Financial Yojana for Women Development' in Jherli Gram Panchayat near Pilani on August 30, 2008. Access to financial services such as banking and insurance has been found to be an effective tool against disasters/ events that creates an impact on poor communities. Though each member of society should have easy access to the financial services, the drive is focused towards women because of the following reasons:

- Despite several schemes and directed efforts by the Governmental and non-governmental organisations, women are still excluded from the formal channels of banking and finance due to lack of awareness.
- Women do not have the decision-making power for appropriate utilisation of funds.
- Access to financial services to women will provide them greater control over household decisions and resources.

The objectives of the programme were to:

- Create awareness about available government schemes on financial services and their benefits among women comprising mainly landless labourers and marginal farmers. The programme aimed to bridge the gap between rural households and formal financial sector by providing them requisite information.
- Train women on decision-making capabilities and appropriate utilisation of available funds provided by the government under the Bhama Shah Yojana.

The Bhama Shah Financial Strengthening Yoajna for Women Development launched by the Government of Rajasthan which provides an incentive of Rs.1,500 to a woman for opening a bank account which only she can operate through a smart card. Preliminary interactions at villages near Pilani revealed that most women are not aware of this scheme, and even if they are, most of them do not have any decision-making power as mostly their husbands take the money from the woman in the family, and the money is not always used in a productive way. This money, if used pragmatically, can not only free the poor from the clutches of money lenders but also help in overcoming difficult times, such as buying medicines when needed, or may be used for any other household purpose. Therefore there was an immediate need to educate women regarding the scheme and its proper utilisation wherein women would be the decision-makers.

This activity created awareness about the available banking and financial services and their benefits for rural women and also helped in inculcating decision-making power amongst rural women for utilisation of funds.

Works Cited

Everett, J. M., *Women and Social Change in India,* Heritage Publisher, New Delhi, 1979, pp.40-43.

Gupta, V., Reporter, *India Together,* Civil Society Information Exchange, September, 2005.

Kaushik, S., *Sustainable Politics, Women in Panchayati Raj: Second Round of Elections,* Centre for Development Studies and Action, New Delhi, 2001.

Mathew, G., *Times of India,* April 29, 2004,

Panda, S., "Reservation for Women in Union and State Legislatures: A Perspective," *Indian Journal of Public Administration,* Vol. XLVII., No 4, October-December, 2001, pp 686.

Progress of South Asian Women 2005, UNIFEM and Institute of Social Studies, New Delhi.

Rao, D. B. *et.al., Status and Advancement of Women,* A.P.H Publishing Corporation, New Delhi, 2000

Sen, S., "Towards a Feminist Politics? The Indian Women's Movement in Historical Perspective," *Policy Research Report on Gender and Development,* Working Paper Series No. 9, April 2000, p. 48.

Sharma, R., "Women's Reservation Bill: A Crisis of Identity," *Indian Journal of Public Administration,* Vol. XLVIII, No 1, January-March, 2001, pp. 56-64.

Tripathy, R.C., *History of Ancient India,* Motilal Banarsidas, Delhi, 1967 pp.32-49.

Yogendra N, Sahu, S.N. and Lakshmi, "Political Empowerment of Women," *Indian Journal of Public Administration,* Vol. LI, No. 1, January-March, 2005, pp.36, 40-41.

9

Representation of Women in Indian Parliament: Dichotomy of Gender Equality and Gender Bias

— *Asha Bhandari, Iswarya Balakrishnan & Sindhu V. Reddy*

The litmus test of any civilisation is the position of a woman in society, and it is for this very reason that she has always remained an object of intellectual controversy in the history of mankind. Power relations in all the social, political, economic and cultural spheres act as a deterrent to women's performance at home or in the public. This is heart-rending as it reflects the status of the women of our nation in general and particularly in the field of politics.

The representation of women is still poor in all areas of decisionmaking, and the principle of equality enshrined in Article 14 of Indian Constitution has not yet been attained in the arena of political participation and representation. It is extremely despicable that even after 62 years of independence and 14 general elections women still remain under-represented in India.

Democracy is a widely accepted term which has been much debated, has figured in the Constitution of many countries across the globe. Democracy and politics are two sides of the same coin, and politics has the distinction of being male dominated. As a result of this, one debate which arises is the challenges that a woman has to face for being a part of the parliament, the struggle she has to undergo to enter it and what she faces after she enters it. Gender equality cannot be attained if our deep-rooted bias against women prevails.

The causality of gender bias and the power gap between women and men is difficult to explain. For a plethora of reasons, women still remain under-represented, viz., their family background, economic shortcomings, cultural and religious background, gender identity, level of education, age, job and time budget. Ironically, these factors are in fact a result of female under-representation, creating a vicious cycle. Causes may vary from one nation to another but some of the major reasons include religion, nation, ethnicity and economical situations. The very need for an emphasis on a higher political representation of women is so that it may lead to the break down of stereotypes about women and emphasize on equality of both genders. This requires higher participation of women in the decisionmaking process: at the grassroots and national level.

The paper is an effort to look into the women's representation in Indian parliament as a dichotomy of gender equality and gender bias. The existing position of women within the party structure is analysed with a special emphasis on the 15th *Lok Sabha* (House of the People) elections, barriers faced by women in political participation and, finally, on understanding the potential of positive contribution of political parties and the need for party reform regulations in order to bring equality. The paper is divided into three parts where Part I discusses the key terms: gender bias, gender equality, Women Participation, representation in politics and need for gender equality in politics. Part II is the portrayal of women representation in Indian parliament, their share in political parties, which in turn presents a real picture of existence of gender bias in the political representation. Part III focuses on the obstacles faced by women at the entry level in politics and also the problems of those women who are in political positions, and the need for political parties to understand the potential positive contributions of women.

Part 1

'Gender bias' can be loosely defined as the unjust and unequal treatment or the obvious favouritism of one gender over the other, as a result of which one class of people have not improved their level of living. In India, this kind of a bias exists right from the time of the birth or planning of a child, and can be at workplaces and in political arena. This type of an unequal treatment has its impact, directly or indirectly, on the lives of every citizen in the country at some point in time. Gender equality may be said to be a social order in which all the genders are given the same opportunities, face the same challenges and the contributions of both the genders given the same importance. So, essentially, men and women are equally important in society, and there lies no discrimination on the basis of gender, caste, sex, race, etc. Both the genders have equal responsibilities.

Need for Gender Equality in Politics

Article 2 of the Universal Human Rights Declaration of 1948 (HRD) states:

> Everyone is entitled to all the rights and freedoms set forth in this Declaration, without distinction of any kind, such as race, colour, sex, language, religion, political or other opinion, national or social origin, property, birth or other status.

Equal dignity, rights, power, and possibilities for all human beings have been stressed on in many international declarations, conventions and treaties including the Constitution of India, which calls for equality and especially gender equality. Political rights and political participation form an aspect of women's empowerment, help in increasing gender equality, and enhance the quality of life of women. Political participation will mean taking part as well as providing participation in politics. One of the measures of political participation is by means of political representation. Representation would mean that only citizens who are legally authorised should be elected to the parliament and form the government, reflecting our values of equality and equal representation. This representation of citizens in the legislature is a reflection of the society as a whole, and therefore it is imperative that all groups should be represented equally. Female political participation is determined by the percentage of female members of the parliament and the positions they hold in the government or the parliament, and also the ministries held by them.

Table 1
Women's Presence in the Lok Sabha, 1952-2004

Year	*Seats*	*Women MP's*	*% of Women MP's*
1952	499	22	4.4
1957	500	27	5.4
1962	503	34	6.8
1967	523	31	5.9
1971	521	22	4.2
1977	544	19	3.3
1980	544	28	5.2
1984	544	44	8.1
1989	517	27	5.2
1991	544	39	7.2
1996	543	39	7.2
1998	543	43	7.9
Average till 1998	527	31	5.9
1999	545	49	8.65
2004	5		
2004	539	(May 2004)	8.16

Source: Election Commission of India

A number of reports suggest that policy results will improve with the participation of women in politics. Many scientists explain that women are often more trustworthy and public-spirited than men. Therefore, a higher female participation would promote a more peaceful government.[1] Also, three recent studies found a positive correlation between women's increased participation in public life and a reduction in the level of corruption.[2] A national Constitutional Amendment in India, which vested the women with the right to be elected to the village councils rather than being appointed, resulted in nine villages voting for all women's states. It also led to an increase in women's mobility and decisionmaking, closure of liquor dens, resulting in less wife-beating and in more girls attending schools.[3] This shows the impact female political leadership has on advancing the gender equality agenda by setting an example as well as pushing through actual laws that benefit women.[4] It also establishes that the complex task of social modernisation could be achieved by enhancing political participation.

PART 2

Empirical data suggests that the parliament, the apex decision-making body in India, itself has not been able to remove the disparities in the attainment of the goal of gender equality. It appears to a utopian ideal to expect the same from it, considering the abysmal representation that has been persistent in the House of the People since the first general elections. Even the Council of States, where nomination is done to attain equal representation of the society, has not been able to attain this target as female members still remain sparse. To elucidate the above, the authors have used the available data indicating the inadequate representation of women in the parliament and lack of power given to them, where representation is given.

Table 2

Female Contestants and Winners in Parliament Elections in India

Year of General Elections	*Female Contestants*	*Per Cent of Female Winners*
6th	70	27.1
7th	142	19.7
8th	164	25.6
9th	198	13.6
10th	325	11.4
11th	599	6.7
12th	274	15.7
13th	284	17.2
14th	147	29.93

Source: Election Commission of India, CSO, 2004.

From the above figures we understand that though there was a steady increase in the number of females contesting from the 6th up to the 11th general elections, with a remarkable leap in participation especially in the 11th general elections, still in the very next elections the participation was down by more than half. This shows a trend of inconsistency in participation in national level politics by women, even sans the introduction of any reservation.

Table 3

Performance of Women Candidates in 1998 and 2004

	1998				*2004*			
	No. of Seats	*No. of Cont.*	*Women Elected*	*Fds*	*No. Seats*	*No. of Cont.*	*Women Elected*	*Fds*
Andhra Pradesh	42	18	2	12	42	21	3	12
Arunanchal Pradesh	2	0	0	0	2	0	0	0
Assam	14	3	1	0	14	6	0	5
Bihar 54	22	4	13	40	14	3	9	
Goa 2	1	0	1	2	1	0	1	
Gujarat	26	7	4	3	26	11	1	6
Haryana	10	6	1	4	10	8	1	5
Himachal Pardesh	4	1	0	0	4	2	1	1
J & K6	2	0	2	6	4	1	3	
Karnataka	28	10	0	7	28	10	2	6
Kerala	20	10	1	6	20	15	2	10
Madhya Pradesh	40	28	4	21	29	30	2	23
Maharashtra	48	20	2	15	48	29	5	21
Manipur	2	1	1	0	2	1	0	1
Meghalaya	2	2	0	2	2	0	0	0
Mizoram	1	0	0	0	1	0	0	0
Nagaland	1	0	0	0	1	0	0	0
Orissa	21	10	2	6	21	9	2	4
Punjab	13	9	1	7	13	10	2	4
Rajasthan	25	20	3	14	25	17	2	12
Sikkim	1	0	0	0	1	0	0	0
Tamil Nadu	39	13	1	11	39	23	4	17

(Contd...)

(Contd...)

Tripura	2	1	0	1	2	0	0	0
Uttar Pradesh	85	56	9	40	80	61	7	37
W. Bengal	42	21	5	9	42	34	4	24
Andaman & Nic. Islands	1	0	0	0	1	1	0	1
Chandigarh	1	2	0	2	1	1	0	1
Dadra & Nagar Haveli	1	0	0	0	1	1	0	1
Daman & Diu	1	1	0	1	1	0	0	0
National Capital Terr. of Delhi	7	10	2	7	7	15	0	12
Lakshadweep	1	0	0	0	1	0	0	0
Pondicherry	1	0	0	0	1	1	0	0
Chattisgarh	–	–	–	–	11	12	1	10
Jharkand	–	–	–	–	14	13	1	9
Uttaranchal	–	–	–	–	5	5	0	4
Total	543	274	43	184	543	355	45	239

Source: Election Commission of India, General Elections, 1998 & 2004 (12th and 14th Lok Sabhas respectively)

The above table helps us to conclude that the representation of women, when considered state-wise, has still remained largely the same when a comparison is drawn between their participation in parliament in 1998 as against 2004. Even though the number of women being elected and contesting has witnessed a marginal increase from 43 to 45 and from 274 to 355, respectively between 1998 and 2004, still there is a huge decline in the number of contestants itself in 2004 to 239 when compared to 274 in 1998.

In the Rajya Sabha, the representation of women seems to remain constant at about 8 per cent of the total seats. The only exception was seen in the 1991-1996 elections wherein their representation was at 15.5 per cent and their representation from then has been one of decline stagnating at around 8 per cent, indicating a continued marginalisation of women in these institutions.[5]

Table 4

Performance of Women in National Parties vis- a-vis Others

1998 (Candidates per cent)

Party	*Cont.*	*Won*	*Fd*	*Won*	*Fd*	*Valid Votes*
BJP	32	15	9	46.88	8.13	7,123,516
BSP	10	1	8	10.00	80.00	467,623
CPI	6	2	3	33.33	50.00	858,173
CPM	8	3	1	37.50	12.50	2,523,655
INC	38	10	12	26.32	31.58	7,420,392
JD	10		10		100.0	279,592
SAP	3		2		66.67	248,150
National Parties	107	31	45	28.97	42.06	18,921,101
State Parties	26	6	11	23.08	42.31	4,218,679
Registered Parties	64	5	53	7.81	82.81	4,125,359
Independents	77	1	75	1.30	97.40	784,252
Total	274	43	184	15.69	67.15	28,049,391

Source: Election Commission of India, General Elections, 1998 & 2004 (12th and 14th Lok Sabhas respectively).

Table 5

2004 (Candidates per cent)

Party	*Cont.*	*Won*	*Fd*	*Won*	*Fd*	*Valid Votes*
BJP	30	10	3	33.33	10.00	6940,884
BSP	20	1	16	5.00	80.00	1081,843
CPI	2		1		50.00	292,866
CPM	8	5	1	62.50	12.50	2,730,678
INC	45	12	12	26.67	11.11	11,922,098
JD	5	2	12	40.00	60.00	787,051
SAP						
National Parties	110	30	29	27.27	26.36	23,755,420
State Parties	66	14	30	21.21	50.00	10,241,047
Registered Parties	62	1	14			928,616
Independents	117		117		100.00	744,908
Total	355	45	239	12.68	67.32	35,669,991

Source : Election Commission of India, General Elections, 1998 & 2004 (12th and 14th Lok Sabhas respectively)

Women Candidates and the 15th Lok Sabha Election

Even the grand 15th Lok Sabha elections saw women as the silent victims. They were not duly represented and although the Women's Reservation Bill, which is pending in parliament, required to be pushed forward by the new government, the elections merely witnessed tokenism by political parties in fielding women candidates to contest.

The presence of a number of powerful women like Mayawati and Sonia Gandhi may deceptively give a picture of women empowerment in the country but this is sadly not what the *status quo* is. It is highly noticeable that the number of women in the cabinet has been declining. The 15th Lok Sabha elections saw our Prime Minister's ministry have only nine women members in comparison to his previous ministry comprising 10 women members. Most comfort however was brought by the fact that Mr. Singh decided to have four women cabinet ministers, including the elevation of Kumari Selja from the level of Minister of State with independent charge as compared to the presence of merely two women members in the cabinet in his previous regime.

On the other hand, political parties are still insensitive and apathetic to women, and this was evident in these elections. The Congress pitched 40 women candidates out of the 443 candidates declared by it, which is even less than 10 per cent. Opposition BJP did no better by fielding only 43 women candidates out of the total 427 seats being contested by the party. The self-claimed flag-bearer of the cause of women reservation, the Left parties, have the worst record of not even giving 5 per cent ticket to women candidates. While the CPM has only fielded four candidates out of the 80 declared seats, the CPI has also given only three candidates out of the 45 seats it is contesting. Third Front leaders and Fourth Front have equally the worst record in this regard. While the Samajwadi Party fielded mere 6 candidates out of its 75 candidate in UP, Lalu Yadav-led RJD has also given merely two seats to women in its quota of 28 seats in Bihar.[6] The chances of a woman winning an election have apparently been undermined by these parties.

Representation of Women within the Political Parties

The scene has been quite bleak for women's representation and active participation in political parties as well. The contribution of the parties can be gauged through the number of women candidates that are fielded by them during elections.[7] This figure over the years has been very discouraging.

Although women played a prominent role in obtaining independence for the nation, their participation in politics was very negligible immediately after the independence. The candidates fielded by the various political parties are still dominantly male.[8] The statistics clearly indicate that during the 1952 elections the percentage of women contestants were as low as 2.29 per cent. In the later years the number of women contesting elections increased at a very low pace. The two elections where there has been a noticeable increase in the number of women contestants are those held in 1998. This occurred at the time when the Committee for the Status of Women, 1974, made their recommendations, and the 73rd and 74th Constitutional Amendments were introduced.[9]

Participation in Decision-making Role

Another observation with regard to the status of women within the party system is with respect to the nature of the position that they hold. Women are often assigned roles that are along their roles in the domestic sector. This only reaffirms their lack of faith in women to handle positions of power, and is nothing but stereotype, in fact. This happens in spite of the existence of female wings in many of the political parties.

Women in the decision-making bodies of the major political parties vary from a mere 5.1 per cent in the CPI (M) to 12.5 per cent in the BJP. This shows that all parties do not place women in leadership positions, and therefore women's access to decision-making bodies remains abysmal. They are given trivial and traditional roles like serving food and refreshments, cleaning and maintenance. Men continue to rule in formal leadership roles (56 per cent) compared to women (26 per cent). This applies even in organising events (65 per cent v. 44 per cent). Also, another noticeable fact is that there are more women MPs in the Lok Sabha but less in the cabinet in the 15th Lok Sabha. The new ministerial team of Prime Minister Manmohan Singh has nine women out of a total of 78 ministers as against 10 women in his previous ministry.[10]

Although the Women's Bill has seen 14 years since it was first introduced proposing 33 per cent reservation for women in the state legislatures and the parliament, it has only been a source of debate with no plausible outcome as such.[11] Women have not yet been able to participate in politics due to the absence of equality and especially due to gender bias. This is quite evident from the fact that the women's bill has not yet been passed, and the basic arguments by those against it delve on women not being able to handle political posts. Women constitute 3.4 million voters out of an electorate of 710 million in 2009, and yet comprise only 9 per cent of the total strength of the lower house of the parliament.[12]

All the above data clearly point to the dire need of qualitative representation of women in the decision-making process of the country. But in the furtherance of the same and attainment of the gender equality, it is important to identify and analyse the challenges faced by them in their march into the political field in India.

PART 3

Factors Impending Women's Advance in the Political March

Looking beyond the numbers is important. Somehow, none of these recognise the basic fact that women contribute equally to this society with men, that they demand and deserve a share in decision making with regard to policies and planning, and that their struggle for equality is today an integral part of the struggle of the Indian people to ensure the strength and stability of the Indian democracy.[13] It is also imperative to understand that the cycle of politics is only complete with choosing a candidate with shared concern but holding officers accountable for those concerns. The political challenges that women connected with the parliament happen to face can be broadly divided into the following broad categories.

Gender-based politics

The entire system of politics is setup as per the male norms and values. It is based on the norms of competition rather than cooperation and mutual respect, and this environment is alien to women due to their inherent nature and experience.[14] This drives women to reject or not opt for this type of male-centric politics. Hence their participation is very low.

Need for "contacts"

It is well known that Sonia Gandhi entered politcs only after the death of Rajiv Gandhi; Mayawathi needed the patronage of Kanshi Ram; and Jayalalitha of M. G Ramachandran. Most of the successful women politicians have entered the political arena only through the shadow of a male politician. Also the support and approval of the family members, especially the husband, is very vital to a woman's participation in politics. Therefore, these factors are always a consideration for a woman while considering her career in politics. This seems to be unfair as the male population does not usually have such factors to worry about.

Impact of Mass Media

The fact that women are largely alienated from the political decision-making process is also ignored by the media.[15] Women are stereotyped and are portrayed to fit only domestic roles, and are hence incompatible with the image of political leadership. Such a portrayal of women by the media taints their opportunities for a good political career, the chances of their winning and also discourages them from any interest in politics, whatsoever. A general observation is also that the media only concentrates on the physical attributes, like their hairstyle, scowls, the type of saree and so on, of the contesting woman at the times of campaign coverage, speeches and in instances of publicity stunts. An instance of this would be a journalist recollecting his adolescent encounter with Mrs. Indira Gandhi, and describing a scowl which cannot be missed and hence fit to be captured by a camera. He said, "I understand why big and powerful men were scared witless by this little woman in a crisply ironed saree."[16] The media has hence been biased, and their views are a classic example of hyperbole when it comes to judging women politicians. They use many other scales to assess them rather than looking at their leadership skills. Character-assassination and general mud-slinging are common practices, and women are the targets. Thus, the perception by media, of these women, needs a dramatic change. It is important that a distorted picture of these women is not presented by the media, one of the four pillars of a democracy, to the people. An objective view is hence called for. The political *gurus,* mentors, relatives, friends and colleagues of the women who have ruled the parliament have been very unsparing in their comments about such women leaders, which shows an attitude of general underestimation on their part of these women. In this context, we should recall the portrayal of Mrs. Indira Gandhi as *Gungee Gudiya*[17] by Ram Manohar Lohiya or as Little Princess by Morarji Desai.

Multiple roles and socio-economic obstacles

> It is very difficult for a woman to make up her mind to enter politics. Once she makes up her own mind, then she has to prepare her husband, and her children, and her family. Once she has overcome all these obstacles and applies for the ticket, then the male aspirants against whom she is applying make up all sorts of stories about her. And after all this, when her name goes to the party bosses, they do not select her name because they fear losing that seat.—*Sushma Swaraj*[18]

As sociologist Shoma Munshi puts it: "Men use money and success as power; women in turn use sex to gain power. How else would she negotiate in the very system which restricts her?"[19] It is clearly obvious without explanation that the socio-economic status of a woman has a direct relation with her political participation. Though hinted at above, we wish to elaborate on the dual burden on the women politicians in the form of domestic tasks and their professional role. In most countries women are carrying a disproportionate share of domestic work. The needs of the family precede their participation in political life. Striking a balance between home and their job as a politician becomes hard as their work might involve travelling, working late hours, etc. Even the timing of the parliamentary programme and sitting times are not suitable to them as it doesn't consider the dual burden that they carry. Also, they are overworked as they are involved in various committee works and networks apart from working for their own party.

Ideological and psychological impediments

> Once we're in parliament, we should not give the impression that we are very special, gifted women, especially created by God to serve as special preachers. No, we should tell other women that you are just like us, and you can also reach parliament, with some struggle, with some education, with some talent. *Sushma Swaraj*[20]

Women lack the necessary confidence to help them scale heights in politics. They do not believe in themselves which is one of the sole causes for their under-representation in formal political institutions, including parliaments, governments and political parties. All this can be easily achieved by them with the requisite amount of self-confidence. They should do away with the perception that women can do nothing big. It is up to them to fight for their rights. They can make a huge difference in the working of our political system but they rarely come to the front. An instance of a good political leader, in our opinion, is Ms. Menaka Gandhi who has put in her heart and soul in the portfolios allotted to her, each time. Indian women's lower educational level, inferior social status and lack of autonomy are reflected in their lower participation in politics. Increasing criminalisation, corruption and compromises required to sustain one's political career also deter them from entering mainstream politics.

Absence of party support

Financial flux is one of the problems faced by them as they are not funded even at the time of campaigning,[21] which in turn happens to be one of the most important criteria to win elections. The selection procedure of nomination, within the party, is also biased towards men which is a cause of concern. Women are not given the due importance and are not heard when they voice their views, in the right light. The candidates fielded by the various political parties are still dominantly male as pointed out above: women account for only 5 to 10 per cent of all candidates across parties and regions. In most parties, women are relegated to work on merely women's issues and are not given substantial work. The only party which has given importance to women in the inner party structures is the All India Anna Dravida Munnetra Kazhagam (AIADMK) which has made conscious moves to bring women into decision-making posts. Most women politicians have found it difficult to rise within party hierarchies, and have managed to achieve clear leadership only when they have effectively broken out and set up parties on their own. Jayalalitha and Mamata Banerjee are clear examples of this. Allocation of only soft portfolios is another issue. The quest for greater political representation of women is still relevant.[22] Very few women reach the level of cabinet ministers and most of them remain deputy ministers or ministers or ministers of state. It is seen that the few women who have been able to reach the top posts have been given only portfolios in the social service sectors of Health, Education, Social Welfare, Women and Child Development, etc.[23]

Lack of unity

Women's organisations and women parliamentarians have spent a great deal of energy during the last decade fighting for 33 per cent of seats for women in parliament and state legislatures. But it is quite noticeable that while concerned with political issues, women parliamentarians or organisations have barely stood up for their colleagues. Due to their inability to support the other's cause or defend them, it serves as an advantage to the party bosses to snub women and show them their "place." Women hardly lobby for each other or form interest groups, and unfortunately, at least in India, women politicians do their best to pull each other down rather than lend support to each other.

Suggestions

Party reform regulations: Need of the hour

In India most endeavours towards enhancing political participation of women have translated merely by increasing the number of women leader in the decision making process. This traditional approach seemed to be flawed as is evident from the fact that even after 60 years of independence we have been unable to nurture a sizeable number of women in order to bring out a substantial change. There is a need to explore other avenues of political participation. The potential contribution of political parties towards the cause of achieving gender parity cannot be stressed upon enough. The only way to break the stereotype is by raising women to higher positions within the political parties.

Restructuring of the internal party structure is important and are the need of the hour. Measures ought to be taken either voluntarily by parties or should be enforced through legislations. All parties must compulsorily put up a specified percentage of women candidates in the elections. Women should also be given decision-making roles instead of the usual stereotypical roles. Training could be provided in areas such as organisation of the campaign, building of the electoral image, oratory skills, communication and media campaign, financing work with volunteers and NGOs, parliamentary procedures, techniques and practices, process of preparation and adoption of the law.

For elected women representatives as well, training centres should be set up to enable them to discharge the responsibilities of a public office. Parties could also utilise the experience of seasoned politicians, senior party members and political advocates to coach potential women candidates. Since lack of financial resources acts as a major impediment. Special funds could be set up by the parties to offer cash contributions or interest-free loans to women candidates or to reimburse their campaign expenses.

The women's wing in a political party should be compulsory and ought to be involved in policy decisions, and should not just be decorative instruments. Prior scheduling of meetings and other such steps to allow women to manage their time and maintain a balance between their domestic life and demands of public office

To conclude, it is hoped that the potential contribution of political parties to ensure effective participation of women at the decision-making level is capitalised upon in the light of the fact that merely giving women a reservation will not be effective unless the political atmosphere is conducive to their growth. This will be the sole factor that will help in removing the dichotomy of gender equality and gender bias in the Indian legislatures.

References

1. Thorsten Nilges, "Gender Inequality in Politics", *Human Rights: A Gender Perspective*, October 10, 2007, Retrieved from <www.koed.hu/mozaik15/thorsten.pdf >
2. Lecture delivered by Winnie Byanyima, *Women and Leadership: The Missed Millennium Development Goal,* Ministry of Community Development, Culture and Gender Affairs & UNDP, Trinidad & Tobago, October 11, 2007, Retrieved from <www.undp.org.tt/Speeches/Women-and-Leadership.pdf>
3. Ibid.
4. Ibid.
5. Shanta Mohan & Ors, *Baseline report on Women and Political Participation in India,* p. 14, Retrieved from <http://www.iwraw-ap.org/aboutus/pdf/FPwomen_and_pol_pax.pdf.>
6. Press Release, "Women candidates' 'winning percentag' better than their male counterparts in 15 th LS elections," Retrieved from <www.csrindia.org>
7. Yogesh Vajpeyi, "After 60 years, wait has not got shorter for women," *The Business Line,* March 27, 2009, Retrieved from <http://www.thehindubusinessline.com/2009/03/27/stories/2009032750170401.htm>
8. Ibid.
9. Ibid.
10. "More women MPs in Lok Sabha, but less in Cabinet ", *The Business Standard,* May 27, 2009, Retrieved from < http://www.business-standard.com/india/news/more-women-mps-in-lok-sabhaless-in-cabinet/63000/on>
11. Kalpana Sharma, *"A law with flaws,"* June 14, 2009, Retrieved from <http://www.indiatogether.org/2009/jun/ksh-wbill.htm>
12. Manjula Pooja Shroff, "Women's Bill: A measure of equality"?, *DNA,* October 31, 2009, Retrieved from <http://www.dnaindia.com/india/column_women-s-bill-a-measure-of-equality_1305258>
13. Malini Bhattacharya, "Women Power," *Frontline,* Vol. 25, Issue 11, May 24- June 6, 2008.
14. Sarah Childs & Mona Lena Krook, "Critical Theory and Women's Political Representation," *Political Studies,* 2008, Vol 56, pp. 725-736.
15. Shvedova, N., "A Woman's Place: How the Media Works Against Women in Russia," *Surviving Together,* Vol. 12, No. 2, 1994.

16. C. S. Anuradha, "Women Political Leadership and Perception," *Case Study of South Asia,* Retrieved from <www.pondiuni.edu.in/journals/ssas/13_anuradha.pdf>
17. Meaning Dumb Doll.
18. Retrieved from <http://www.upi.com/Features/Voice_Young_Voters/2009/06/11/Feminising-politics/12446778316654/>
19. Sheela Reddy, *Madam Pompadour's Chessboard* ,< http://www.outlookindia.com/article.aspx?263690>
20. Nadezdha Shvedova, "Obstacles Women's Participation in Parliament", Retrieved from <http:/ www.online womeninpolitics.org/beijing12/obstacles_wpp.pdf.>
21. Shvedova, op.cit.
22. Malathi Subramanian, "Political participartion and representation of women in Indian Politics," Retrieved from <http://www.du.ac.in/course/material/ug/ba/hrge/08.pdf>
23. "Human Development is South Asia : 2000", Retrieved from <http:// / www. Mhhdc.org/reports/HDRSA% 202000.pdf>

10

Political Participation of Women in Panchayati Raj Institutions: Understanding the Quantity-Quality Nexus

— *Asha Bhandari*

Recent decades have witnessed an international trend towards democratic decentralisation in order to strengthen local governance. A significant contribution of this decentralisation is that it provides constitutional status to women in local governments to enhance their political participation. A clear example is the 73rd Constitutional Amendment Act of India (1993)[1], which transferred power to people through decentralised panchayati raj institutions (PRI - local government institutions), with one-third reservation of seats for women.

Various state governments have shown more commitment towards women political empowerment and increase reservation for women from one-third to 50 per cent.[2] While this paved the way for women to exercise their political rights in local governance, and is gradually giving a new thrust to more woman-friendly grassroots governance, it has not been able to guarantee a non-discrimination or conducive environment for women to participate qualitatively in the decisionmaking process. India today has more female politicians than the rest of the world together. But the presence of women is not necessarily synonymous with their participation. There is a need to examine as to whether the massive rise in the numerical strength of women has bought any substantive change in the status of women.

This paper makes an endeavour to discuss the interplay of the quantity and quality of women's role in politics. I wish to explore the hypothesis that whether a quantitative and numerical rise in the representation of women in the political field would also make a qualitative change in the life and status of women and thus result in the political empowerment of women in the real sense of the term. The test of the hypothesis is based on the secondary data collected from various studies related to participation of women at the grassroots level.

Political Participation: Conceptual Framework

The definition of political participation includes a large arena comprising a wide range of activities, such as in trade unions, cooperatives, collectives, informal and formal political action[3]. However, the scope of definition of political participation for the present purpose is limited to addressing women's participation only in electoral politics (formal politics) consisting of women's constituencies at various levels from the grassroots to the state legislatures and parliament at the centre.

Political participation for the paper has been defined to mean participation of women in terms of their numbers-quantity (i.e. the presence or absence of a critical mass), the quality of their participation and their involvement in effective decisionmaking in political institutions, and the electoral processes as candidates and elected representatives both.

PRI: A Quantitative Rise of Women's Representation at the Grassroots Level

Political participation of Indian women, though in a miniature form, started with the freedom movement. It did not translate into continued participation in public life in the post-independence era. The framers of the Constitution perhaps believed that law would lead to social change. Hence, the Constitution of India is based on the principles of equality, and guarantees equality before law and equal protection to all its citizens, guarantees fundamental rights and freedoms, also prohibits discrimination on the basis of religion, race, caste, sex, and place of birth.

Articles 325 and 326 of the Constitution of India guarantee political equality—equal right to participate in political activities and right to vote respectively.

The passage of the Constitutional 73rd Amendment Act 1992 marks a new era in federal democratic set-up of the country and provides Constitutional status to the panchayati raj institutions (PRI). The 73-rd Amendment, introduced in 1993, proposed that 30 per cent of government seats be set aside for their as a means of further guaranteeing women's representation in panchayati raj institutions. Similarly the 74th Amendment introduced the similar reservation for women in municipal council and municipal corporation in towns and urban areas. However such affirmative action are lacking at the state and central levels.

Table 1

Women Representation in PRI in India

Panchayat Level	*Total No. of PRI*	*Elected Repre-sentatives*	*Women Represent-atives*	*Women (%)*
District panchayat	534	15138	5,785	38.2
Intermediate panchayat	6,085	155960	58,347	37.4
Village panchayat	233,669	2,608,808	977,298	37.4

Source: The State of the Panchayat, A Mid-term Review and Appraisal, Ministry of Panchayati Raj, Government of India, November, 2006.

The panchayati raj[4] as a system of self-governance was introduced for the first time in 1959 following the Balwant Rai Mehta Committee report (1958) that recommended a three-tier structure[5] of local self-government consisting of gram panchayats at the village level, taluka panchayat samitis at the sub-district level, and zilla parishads at the district level. The system of governance in India has undergone considerable changes over the last 15 years with the implementation of quotas for women in local parliaments, the PRIs. India has adopted a bold affirmative action in providing for one-third reservation for women in all institutions of local self-governance. This was the starting point for the revolution in the field of decentralisation and recognisation of the principle of gender equity through empowerment of women. The provisions for women in the 73rd Constitutional Amendment are:

- To provide a three-tier system of PRI for all states having a population of over 20 lakh.
- Tc hold panchayat elections every five years.
- To provide reservations of seats for women, SC and ST—not less than 33 per cent.

At present there are more than 27 lakh representatives elected to three levels of panchyat. Of these nearly 977,298 are women elected to gram panchayats, 58,347 women to panchayat samitis and 5,785 women to *zila parishads*. Out of a total number of representatives 19 per cent belong to SC and 12 per cent to ST. As per the statistics available more than 10 lakh women had entered the *panchayats* in 24 states, and this has been one of the greatest experiments in democracy ever undertaken anywhere in the world or at any time of history.

The state-wise break up of elected women in panchayats is given in Table 2.

Table 2

State-wise Women Panchayat Members in PRI's

	Gram Panchayat		*Panchayat Samiti*		*Zila parishad*	
States	*No.*	*%*	*No.*	*%*	*No.*	*%*
Madhya Pradesh	131,671	33.9	2,393	33.4	304	34.4
Maharashtra	77,548	43.7	1,407	49.0	658	46.2
Manipur	625	36.6	NA	-	21	34.4
Orissa	336,023	35.8	2,188	35.1	296	34.7
Punjab	30,875	35.0	922	33.4	103	32.7
Rajasthan	40,044	35.2	2,108	38.4	391	37.6
Sikkim	366	40.4	NA	-	32	32.0
Tamil Nadu	36,824	33.7	2,319	35.3	227	34.6
Tripura	1,852	34.6	106	35.4	28	34.1
Uttar Pradesh	273,229	38.8	24,673	37.6	1,122	41.6
Uttaranchal	20,482	37.9	1,133	35.9	119	33.1
West Bengal	18,150	36.6	2,953	34.9	246	34.2
Union Territories						
A & N Islands	261	34.3	25	37.3	10	33.3

(Contd...)

(Contd...)

Chandigarh	53	32.7	6	40.0	3	30.0
D & N Haveli	45	39.3	NA	–	4	36.4
Daman & Diu	30	39.0	NA		7	35.0
Lakshadweep	30	38.0	NA		8	36.4
Pondicherry	330	36.1	40	37.0	–	–
Total	977,298	37.5	58,347	37.4	5,786	38.2

Source: The State of the Panchayats, A Mid-Term Review and Appraisal, Ministry of Panchayati Raj, Govt. of India, November, 2006.

Table 3

Women's Participation in PRI's Before 1965 and After 2005 (Comparison)

States Political Participation	*Overall Percentage of Women in Gram Panchayats before 1985*	*in Gram Panchayat after 2005*
Gujarat	Only 2 women	33.3%
Haryana	Only 1 woman	36.1
Karnataka	Only 1-2 women	43.0
Madhya Pradesh	2 women	33.9
Kerala	1 woman	37.3
Punjab	2 women	35.6
Rajasthan	2 women	35.2
West Bengal	2 women	36.4
Uttar Pradesh	0	38.8

Source: Panchayti Raj Development Report 1995, Institute of Social Sciences, New Delhi. The state of Panchayats, A Mid-Term Review Ministryof Panchayti Raj, Govt. of India, 2006.

The representation of women in these institutions has shown an increasing trend in many states. This shows the numerical rise of women in the political field. Before 1985 whereas only two women in each of the states of Gujarat, MP, Punjab, Rajasthan and West Bengal participated in panchayats their representation after 2005 has increased to 33.5 per cent, 33.9 per cent 35.6 per cent and 36.4 per cent respectively.

The above analysis shows that representation of women in this institution has shown an increasing trend in quantitative terms. These achievements, however does not mean that rural women have no problems and are treated equally. Although there are many changes yet still certain socio-economic and political barriers are present which obstruct women towards performing their task and in participating actively in public life.

Understanding the Challenges: Obstacles and Factors Mediating in Women's Qualitative Participation in Politics

Broad-based political participation of women has been severely limited due to the inbuilt structure of the Indian traditional society and the perception of the male dominance in politics. There are a number of factors that constrain women's participation in public life and decisionmaking including: economic dependency, illiteracy and limited access to education, discriminatory cultural and social attitudes and negative stereotypes perpetuated in the family and in public life, etc. I would like to substantiate the above argument on the basis of various studied conducted at the grassroots level.

Women Candidate-Surrogates for Male Family Members

Women's participation in politics has been limited to the family connections rather than conviction and commitments. Consequently they have been left at the periphery of political life. The most crucial obstacle in the journey of political participation is the nomination of the candidature itself. Most of the women fill the candidature because of the pressure of their male members or due to the pressure of political parties. Many are surrogates for husbands and fathers who could not contest because of the reservation. Some were put in place by the wealthy and powerful, for their malleability—a kind of puppet to serve the vested interest while appearing to be an elected representative.[6] One of the studies conducted in the village of Orissa found that most of the women enter into politics because of the mandatory provisions of reservations and thus forced by their male family members. They enter into politics not because of their choice but due to force. This concept has been defined as "figurehead elected women representatives who are supposed to do the bidding of male members of the family rather than take their own decisions."[7] A study conducted in three districts of Punjab (Hoshiyarpur, Patiyala and Gurdashpur)[8] reveal that women candidates are consulted only after the decisions have been taken by their male partners. Voters especially men, prefer cultural feminist to radical feminist candidates, to represent them as they will not threaten their status quo or question the institutional set-up. These are internal contradictions present in politics that hamper quality participation of women in politics.

Masculine Model of Political Participation

The political field is generally considered as a male domain. Reservations introduced from 'the top' which bring women into a predominantly male political system, cannot break traditional patterns of socio-economic and gendered power, nor bring awareness to women and marginalised sections overnight.[9] The assumption is that when women are different from men in levels of literacy, workforce participation, and university education—and thus not equal to men in the social spheres—they are less likely to be seen as men's equals in the political sphere.[10]

Elections in India, as in all other modern democracies, have become very complicated, violent, dirty and expensive, inviting thereby very many legitimate and not so legitimate ways of funding and managing them. Women cannot obviously fit into this matrix of election. The participation cost in formal politics is too high for them. Violence has also come to dominate the PRI's election in many states, thus making participation of women more difficult. Some such incidents are: Ms Leelavathy from Villipuram, Tamil Nadu, who was working towards getting permanent water supply to Villipuram as part of her election campaign was murdered in broad daylight by armed men because it was contrary to the interests of the mafia henchmen who sold drinking water to the people.[11]

Another classic case is that of a village in Madurai district of Tamil Nadu, a southern state in India. In Melavalavu, the dominant castes of the area murdered the panchayat president and the vice-president who both belonged to a lower caste, merely because they dared to fight the panchayat elections.There have been reports from four districts of Madhya Pradesh – Raigarh, Chattarpur, Raisen and East Nimar – of a lady sarpanch being stripped naked, another lady sarpanch being gang raped, an upa-sarpanch (deputy president) being tortured and a dalit panchayat member being beaten up.[12]

Most incidents of violence have resulted from caste war[13] in Rajasthan where two different caste groups had their women candidate running for the *gram panchyat* seat reserved for women. The Jats tried to persuade the Harijans to withdraw their candidate. As it became their prestige issue she was forced and give money to compensate for the same. Examples of harassment, sexual or mental, writing of vulgar letters, character assassination of active women members are very common. Muslim women have to face 'fatwa' or physical attacks. In such situation participation of women becomes impossible.

A Rise of New Class of Sarpanch Pati or Pradhan Pati

Despite all the advancements made in the previous years the way women are defined by their culturally attributed role as mothers, wives, daughters only, still constitutes one of the largest obstacles for women to enter politics nationally and locally. Although reservation has provided some chance to the womenfolk for participating at the grassroots level but the real function is done by their male partners.[14] The subordinated position of the ordinary women in families, their routine and normal duties like looking after the family, bringing up children, performing both the paid and unpaid work, do not allow them much ooprtunities to participate freely in public political activities.

The linkage between 'personal' and 'public' is missing and women do not feel automatically impelled. Political exercise needs tremendous mobilisation. Their daily work, household chores, patriarchal family norms, possibility of violence further discourage them. Participating in public space is totally out of question.[15] Sometimes it also happens that a number of villages come under one gram panchyat, in such cases representation and participation of women become difficult as women have much less mobility than men[16].Sometimes the men in the village refuse to talk to a 'woman pradhan' and her husband is forced to come to all meetings. Such pervasive resistance of women pradhans all over, lad to the birth of a parallel power base called 'Pradhan-Pati'

Prof B.S. Baviskarin in his study on *Impact of Women's Participation in Local Governance in Rural India*[17] SAP Network 2003: summary of workshop in "Women's Empowerment in the Context of Local Government in India states that "if a woman does not come out of her house or remove her veil and signs on the dotted line (or gives her thumb impression) as directed by her husband acting as *Pradhan Pati,* it is a case of zero empowerment. Hence due to such norm it becomes extremely difficult for women to enter the PRIs, and even when they enter they are mostly confined to household responsibilities letting the male members of her family (mostly husband) run the office for her. Male influence is of such high order that this peculiar power structure of elected women performing their duties under the stewardship of their husbands has thrown up a new tribe of power brokers called sarpanch patis.[18]As a result, a new class of sarpanch patis has emerged who manage the affairs of the panchayat on behalf of their wives. As a consequence women are not getting the actual chance to participate in the decisionmaking process.

Lack of Awareness About Women's Political Role

Though women are elected to the panchayats yet evidence indicates that most are not aware of the roles associated with becoming an elected official. One pilot study on GP members in Kerala found that women political leaders were still not clear about the exact roles they were expected to play in this system. Swain and Mahapatra[19] claim that 49 per cent of women leaders said they were not aware of the role of PRIs, 12.5 per cent thought their role was to attend GP meetings, while only 17.5 per cent thought their role was to solve people's problems. Only 20 per cent were aware that the GP could sponsor people's development projects through a governmental programme. Furthermore, this showed that women GP members were not aware of where the resources lie for them to be able to meet the needs of their constituencies.

In Karnataka and Gujarat, Asha Ramesh and Bharati Ali[20] analysed the performance of GP women members. They found that while most women attended GP meetings, not many supervised work and a few handled work outside the village. This is also because of other factors such as lack of mobility. Furthermore, the range of responsibilities that of GP members need to undertake, from planning to monitor and finally to implementation, are rarely spelled out as part of their duties. In a study conducted by Stephen and Rajasekaran, the women members of the Rajoor panchayat were not aware of their roles and responsibilities. Though women were seven as against five male members, they were unable to influence the decisions made in the Gram Panchayat.

All proceedings of the GP meetings were controlled by the local political leader of the Congress party, despite women being in the majority. Dr. Sangita Dhal in her study on *Grassroots Democratic Processes and Women: A Case Study of Panchayati Raj in Orissa* states that most had little knowledge of politics including issues such as the Panchayat Raj Act, the operation of political parties in the village and the reservation of seats for women in PRIs. Elected men were much more aware.[21]

No Direct Participation in PRI Meetings

From a study done in Punjab, it was found that very few of the members, male or female, attended meetings. However of those who did, fewer women members (3.33 per cent) attended all the meetings compared to their male counterparts (5.83 per cent). Women who did not have escorts did not attend any meetings at all (4.11 per cent). Overall, the study revealed that a large number of co-opted members than those elected remained uninterested in the GP meetings. The same is identified by the study conducted by Sukhdev Singh and Verminder Kaur in Punjab (2007) which states that often the traditional role of women deny them the chance to attend the meeting. A little above one-third of them were invited for all the meetings and almost 20 per cent were never invited to participate in the decisionmaking process. A majority of the women have not even participated in the meeting.[22]

Unable to Raise the Issues in Policy Making

Lack of space for participation in political bodies has also not resulted in the neglect of their issues and experiences in policy making. Women who are in positions of power are seen not to be advancing womens' issues. This may be as a result of wanting to be associated with men who are considered to be the 'norm', or, while women try to learn from the men their thinking, experiences and interests influence them. The ability to take up the issue pertaining to gender sensitive discourse is also limited. Issues such as violence against women, female foeticide and infanticide, women's health, livelihoods, etc., are rarely taken up.

In a study of tribal women in PR in MP, Abha Chuahan[23] revealed that nearly 63 per cent did not raise any issue in the panchayat of their own accord, and the few who did mainly confined their concerns to health, child welfare, and drinking water.

In Gania block in Orissa, although a young and energetic female sarpanch wanted to tackle the issue of alcoholism in the area, she could do nothing about it as the elite class males of the village who would be instrumental in deciding her re-election were the liquor consumers. Antagonising them would make her lose her political support.[24] A tribal woman sarpanch was stripped naked while unfurling the national flag on August 15, 1998 (Independence day) in a district in Rajasthan. In another case a tribal woman sarpanch in Madhya Pradesh was stripped naked in a gram sabha meeting because she was not consulting the leader of the dominant caste.

Moreover, political parties also play a significant role in directing the affairs of the panchayat. Winning an election requires political party backing. Due to this the elected candidates (men/women) remain loyal to the party. Since political parties are most controlled by the males, women find it extremely difficult to make their voices heard or have to become mere 'rubber stamps' to the dictates of the party. George and Krishnan give the instance that the first ever tribal woman block panchayat president in Attappady block in Palakkad district of Kerala could hardly do any work due to the boundaries laid by the political party, which she represented.

The dominating attitude of the male official obstructs the smooth functioning of women officials. Women are forced to maintain silence as the men have numerical majority in most of the gram panchayats. This amounts to disregard and rejection of most of the resolutions tabled by the women members. If they try to oppose tactics of the male members, they are pressurised to keep their mouth shut. In this situation the argument that more women would lead to women participation is really questionable.

Illiteracy and Lack of Knowledge of Institutional Mechanism

The lack of knowledge and awareness of elections and electoral processes among women is a major barrier towards participating in elections. Also, the low level of literacy among the majority of the women prevents them from accessing information about the various political candidates, parties, party manifestos and the debates that precede elections which are critical for making an informed choice of the most appropriate candidate. Most of the information is in print media, and hence a serious handicap for a large majority of women, who are illiterates. For the elected women representatives who are relatively new in the political field, the lack of knowledge of the roles and responsibilities associated with political institutions impedes their effective participation in decision-making processes of governance including that of financial management. Hira Devi, SC candidate and Panchayat Pradhan of Soloi Gram Panchayat, Gongri village, Himachal Pradesh, was very confident of her abilities, and was involved in initiating a number of village development projects. However, being educated only till class five, she claimed that education was the main obstacle that came her way as she failed to understand clearly various schemes and policies of the government.[25]

Women's' Individual and Personal Capacity

In personal life, women are subject to discriminating laws and continue to be denied the right to seek remedy for family violence. This goes without saying, it affects their general well being so much so that they seldom show enthusiasm in taking the benefit of the Constitutional guarantee of equality and equal opportunities given to them in public life. The other consequence of this is that the political sphere remains under the dominance of a few women linked to power through family, business, finance or social position leaving out many of those who are genuinely politically committed. Therefore, the role these women tend to play is characteristically defined by the motivation for preservation and protection of their family, party, financial or class interests. Another important factor here is that since their power base is not sown in popular support, they suffer from a sense of insecurity, which works as a hindrance to their ability to face serious challenges posed by the discriminations, inequalities, lack of access to resources on the basis of class, creed, religion, ethnic identity and gender which are stark realities.

Conclusion and Suggestions

An affirmative action through the 73rd Amendment Act created a massive rise in the numerical strength of women in panchayati raj institutions. But there are both individual and institutional factors in the mechanism that has put women in a disadvantaged position, affecting their chances to get involved in political decision making in the real sense of the term.

Individual factors address the extent to which individual characteristics favour political participation. In general, women are less interested in politics; they have not learned to develop political capacities, because public sector activities are usually seen as male. As a consequence women lack confidence in their own political capabilities. Their lower level of education, professional experience, income and time available have put them in a disadvantageous position as compared to men.

Institutional factors are related to the organisation of society, its norms and values. To become active as a politician, women are hampered by their care-taking tasks and their responsibility for the household. Limited access to leadership, managerial skills and training, lack of female role models and mentors, disproportional expectations, and violence against women are the few structural barriers present in the society.

Women's participation also depends on the gender equality policies within a country. The existence of women's organisations to promote the political participation of women and to give support to elected women is very important as well. Institutional factors related to the political system are registration procedures, voting procedures and civic education. Women politicians are further hampered by the working conditions and by an organisational culture, which is not adapted to women's circumstances.

Reservation has succeeded in bringing the womenfolk in rural India into the political mainstream The statistics collected by the Centre for Women's Development Studies 1999 show that 95 per cent of women claimed they would never come to acquire positions in panchayats, if there were no provision of reserving seats for them. However, it needs to be emphasized that although changes are happening, they are occurring gradually. It may also be observed that villages that are socio-economically more advanced are ones where women have more exposure to information and education. Therefore, there need to take various proactive measures if political empowerment is to be translated into real empowerment and not mere lip service. As Hust in his book *Political Representation and Empowerment: Women in the Institutions of Local Government in Orissa after the 73rd Amendment to the Indian Constitution* argues that reservation for women in political bodies can only be an enabling condition for the larger project of women's empowerment. For actualising real political empowerment of women, numerical strength cannot be disassociated from the larger structural elements of social relations. Women's participation in public life and decisionmaking depends on several factors, including:

- An awareness of her rights and ways to claim them.
- Access to information about laws, policies and the institutions and structures which govern their lives and the effective implementation of this kind of legal framework.

- Confidence, self-esteem and the skills to challenge and confront existing power structures.
- A strong networking of women's organisations at the national and regional level and positive role models.
- A strong and sincere commitment from the side of governmental institutions and political parties, declaring women's development as an important policy and setting up special departments and/or programmes.

The above factors indicate that there is a need to develop an enabling environment, meaning a political, legal, economic and cultural climate that allows women to engage in decision-making processes in a sustainable and effective way. Pamela Singla in her study on *Participation in Panchayati Raj –A Case Study of Gurgaon District in Haryana* states that "the majority of the women leaders have exhibited their determination to occupy the public space, however there are hurdles in the process of empowering women. In order to overcome the hurdles the elected women representatives require the assistance of the state and various agencies to provide them proper orientation, information, counseling and training." Poornima & Vinod Vyasulu also argue that women in Panchayati raj in India who have been supported and nurtured by NGOs and those who have been involved in larger peoples' movements have gained a more assertive stance which gives them an edge over other women in the local government.

The following ways may help in developing the favourable environment at the grassroots level:

- *Capacity Building*—To organise training courses for women interested in politics, dealing with the necessary skills and knowledge for campaigning, presentation, negotiation, and handling with the media, as well as gender-awareness and self-esteem and offer possibilities to practices these capacities in the form of work placements.
- *Role of NGOs*—Supporting NGOs who organise support for women candidates and provide moral, psychological and / or financial support to women candidates.

- *Database*—Setting up a database with names and profiles of women candidates for decision-making posts in (local) government, political parties, organisations and committees. A collection of data on how women politicians have managed to make a difference through their legislature will be very helpful for other women politicians.
- *Access to information*—Give women practical information about the current situation vis-à-vis the condition, position, and the political participation of women throughout the world, and about any research being carried out in this regard. Set up information systems (use of the Internet).
- *Gender training*—To organise joint training sessions, in which both men and women can discuss the importance of gender issues and of parity and non-discriminatory working relationships in government. Male politicians can become more aware of women's and gender issues. Women are encouraged to address their areas of interest and to network with male colleagues.
- *Moral support*—The lack of a support base can lead to women politicians becoming despondent and even withdrawing from politics, thus reinstating the status quo. There is a need to provide women with support from interests groups within the political process, as a type of political mentor system, or create another system of mentoring for inexperienced women politicians.

Political participation of women is essential to ensure that women's concern and issues are integrated into mainstream decision-making process. This would be a major step in facilitating them to exercise and enjoy their rights granted in the Constitution, toward achieving substantive equality for them. It is necessary to go beyond the present boundaries and create dynamic partnership within the government, and between the government and civil society to translate the dreams of women empowerment in reality.

To conclude, I would like to use the words of Amartya Sen who has rightly expressed:

"The expansion of women's capabilities (both quantitative and qualitative) not only enhances women's own freedom and well-being, but also has many other effects of all."

References

1. The demand for greater representation of women in political institutions in India was not taken up in a systematic way until the setting up of the Committee on the Status of Women in India (CSWI) which published its report in 1976. Before this the focus of the growing women's movement had been on improving women's socio-economic position. The CSWI report suggested that women's representation in political institutions, especially at the grassroots level, needed to be increased through a policy of reservation of seats for women. In 1988, the National Perspective Plan for Women suggested that a 30 per cent quota for women be introduced at all levels of elective bodies. Women's groups insisted that reservation be restricted to the panchayat (village council) level to encourage grassroots participation in politics. The consensus around this demand resulted in the adoption of the 73rd and 74th Amendments to the Indian Constitution in 1993. The 73rd Amendment, introduced in 1993, proposed that 30 per cent of government seats be set aside for women, as a means of further guaranteeing their representation in panchayati raj institutions. Similarly the 74th Amendment introduced similar reservation for women in municipal council and municipal corporation in towns and urban areas.
2. There is a proposal which seeks to amend Article 243 (d) of the Constitution providing one third reservation for women in panchayat by enhancing it to 50 per cent. Bihar,Chhattisgarh, Uttarakhand, Himachal Pradesh and Madhya Pradesh are among the few states which have already implemented 50 per cent reservation for women in PRI, while Rajasthan has announced that it would implement the proposal in the next PRI election in 2010. Kerala too has announced 50 per cent reservation in PRI.
3. Baseline Report, prepared by Women and Political Participation in India, National Institute of Advanced Studies-Gender Studies Unit (NIAS), Women's Voice, National Alliance of Women (NAWO) and Initiatives-Women in Development (IWID) coordinated by International Women's Rights Action Watch Asia Pacific (IWRAW Asia Pacific) Kuala Lumpur, Malaysia.

4. Article 243 of the Indian Constitution says, 'Panchayat' means an institution of self-government. Article 243G entrusts the State legislatures to "endow the panchayats with such powers and authority as may be necessary to enable them to function as institutions of self-government."

5. In the rural areas a three-tier structure has been adopted. They are:

    (a) Grama panchayat consisting of a village or group of villages having a population of not less than 5,000 and not more than 7,000, or the geographical distance of an area within a radius of 5 km from the centre.

    (b) Taluk panchayat for every taluka.

    (c) Zilla panchayat for every district.

    In the urban areas there are the municipal bodies called the nagara palike i.e., nagara panchayats. There are also the municipal councils for smaller urban areas and municipal corporations for larger urban areas, based on the size of population.

6. Poornima and Vinod Vyasulu, Women in Panchayati Raj: Grassroots Democracy in India, Experience from Malgudi, Background Paper No.4, Meeting on Women and Political Participation:21st Century Challenges, United Nations Development Programme, 24-26 March 1999, New Delhi

7. SAP Network 2003: summary of workshop in "Women's Empowerment in the Context of Local Government in India," New Delhi on October 20-21, 2003.

    http://action.web.ca/home/sap/india_resources.shtml?x=48752&AA_EX_Session=88d7f8d350980bba1d32cf3d6f0fcf35 visited on December 12,2010.

8. Sukhedev Singh and Virmender Kaur, Gender bias in identity formation: A study of role of women in panchayti raj institution in Punjab, studies available at www.isical.ac.in

9. www.ids.ac.uk/bridge/dgb9.html -

10. Matland, Richard E., 1998: "Women's Representation in National Legislatures: Developed and Developing Countries." *Legislative Studies Quarterly*. vol. 23, no. 1, pp. 109–125.

    Taken from Upasna Mahanta, Leaving the 'proxy woman or politician' dichotomy: A qualitative study of the possibilities and obstacles for elected women's participation in Indian local governance B.A. Thesis in Political Science Minor Field Study Spring 2008, Department of Political Science, University of Gothenburg

11. See Mythily Sivaraman, 'Blow to Goodness', *The Hindu,* May 18, 1997.
12. Mathew, George, Panchayati Raj Institutions and Human Rights in India, *International Council in Human Rights Policy,* 2002, available at – http://www.ichpr.org/paper_files/116_w_04.doc
13. Panchayayti Raj, *Update,* Institute of Social Science, vol.8, April 2001.
14. Singh Sukhedev and Virmender Kaur, op.cit.
15. Hust Evelin, "Political Representation and Empowerment: Women in the Institutions of Local government in Orissa after the 73rd Amendment to the Indian Constitution," *Heidelberg Papers in South Asian and Comparative Politics,* Working Paper No.6, August 2002, available at - http://www.sai.uni-heidelberg.de/SAPOL/HPSACP.htm
16. Poornima and Vinod Vyasulu, op.cit.
27. SAP Network 2003: summary of workshop in "Women's Empowerment in the Context of Local Government in India," New Delhi on October 20-21, 2003.

    http://action.web.ca/home/sapindia_resources.shtml?x=48752&AA_EX_Session=88d7f8d35 0980bba1d32cf3d6f0fcf35
18. Raghunath, 2000 reference taken from Poornima and Vinod Vyasulu, Women in Panchayati Raj: Grassroots Democracy in India, Experience from Malgudi, Background Paper No.4,Meeting on Women and Political Participation:21st Century Challenges, United Nations Development Programme,24-26 March 1999, New Delhi.
19. "Leaving the proxy woman or politician dichotomy: A qualitative study of the possibilities and obstacles for elected women's participation in Indian local governance," B.A. Thesis in Political Science Minor Field Study, Spring 2008, Department of Political Science, University of Gothenburg
20. Ramesh, Asha & Ali, Bharti, 2001: 1/3: *Reservation Towards Political Empowerment,* Karnataka
21. SAP Network 2003, op.cit.
22. Sukhdev Singh and Virmender Kaur, op.cit.

23. Chauhan, Abha, "Women's Participation in Panchayats in Scheduled Areas With Special Reference to Madhya Pradesh," *A Decade of Women's Empowerment Through Local Government in India,* Institute of Social Sciences/South Asia Partnership Canada/ International Development Research Centre, October 20-21, 2003, available at - http://action.web.ca/home/sap/attach/SAP%20W &E%20 workshop%20Abha.doc
24. Hust Evelin, op.cit.
25. *Panchayati Raj,* Update, op.cit.

11

Affirmative Action and Reservations for Women in Legislatures

— Amar Pal Singh

Introduction

Democracy is a political method by which every citizen has the opportunity of participating through discussions in an attempt to reach voluntary agreement as to what shall be done for the good of the community as a whole.[1] It resolves itself in practice into a continuous search for agreement through discussions and compromise and action on the basis of which maximum measure of agreements is obtainable. The real test of democracy is the creation of equality of opportunity for the hitherto deprived sections of society. It requires both a favourable social atmosphere and an individual attitude.

The issue of women's reservation during last two decades, more or less, has been a bone of contention amongst various political parties; the problem with this has been that all actors involved in the debate are not acting in the true traditions of democracy, as talked about above. While proponents of Women's Reservation Bill (WRB) would treat the Draft of WRB (81st Constitutional Amendment Bill), as sacrosanct and non-negotiable, the people opposed to it would do everything to subvert the process of providing a modicum of democratic protection to half of the population of the country by giving what is due to them. And the result is that every political party for the last more than a decade has been assuring its support to the Bill which disarms women activists. And then a farce rather than a tragedy is played out by so-called radical politicians, jumping into the well of the House, tearing copies of the Bill and making impossible for proceedings to continue—the House gets adjourned, the Bill is thrown into the dustbin till it is revived in subsequent years with the same result.

It has got to be understood by people on either side of the fence that unless the democratic methods are employed in the process of presenting this or that opinion the current process would take us nowhere. This paper is an attempt to highlight this farce and not the tragedy of Women's Reservation Bill that has continuously been enacted by all the actors involved and then try to arrive at some kind of working strategy for resolving the entirety of the issue of women's reservation, empowerment etc.

We know that women constitute half of the population of the country, and the United Nation's data avers that they contribute two thirds of the working hours and even then earn just one tenth of the total income, and own just one-tenth of the total properties in the country. They make up 70 per cent of world's absolute poor, and two-thirds of them are illiterates. One-half of the population of women in Asia and Africa are malnourished and they are also subjected to lot of domestic violence. Evidently the democratic norms would require some kind of protective discrimination in their favour which in any case is the norm all across the democratic world. Therefore when the demand of women's reservation is made, they are not asking anything more than what is due to them.

Understanding the Affirmative Action Programme

The Affirmative Action Programme, as it is understood in the United States of America, where this term is said to have originated, basically refers to the policies aimed at addressing the problems of historically and socially deprived sections of society in order to promote their access to education or employment. The motivation for affirmative action is a desire to redress the effects of the past and current discrimination that is regarded as unfair, and serves to encourage public institutions, such as universities, hospitals and governmental and non-governmental organisations, including the police forces, to be more representative of the population. Professor James E. Jones, Jr. defines affirmative action as "public or private actions or programs, which provide or seek to provide opportunities or other benefits to persons on the basis of, among other things, their membership in a specified group or groups." According to Professor David Benjamin Oppenheimer the practice of affirmative action comprise of five methods: quotas, preferences, self-studies, outreach and counselling, and anti-discrimination.[2] As an extension of his categorisation-based definition, affirmative action can and often is divided into "hard" and "soft" affirmative action, with the former consisting of quotas and preferences, and the latter encompassing various outreach, self-evaluations, marketing, and labour market development.[3]

It may be noted that the idea of affirmative action programme has germinated from the principles of Distributive Justice. It is worth noting that philosophers of various hues may have differences of opinions as to the conception of justice and equality, they would all suggest some kind of distributive justice mechanism to shape the society in the mould of their philosophy. In fact, the idea of distributive justice is not something new. Aristotle himself talked about distributive justice. According to him justice is of two types: complete justice and particular justice. He further subdivides particular justice into Distributive justice and Corrective Justice. Distributive Justice consists in proper allocation of reward to each person according to his worth and dessert. It thus looks beyond equality in a purely formal sense. Its central concern is to redress the bias of contingencies in the direction of equality. In a democratic world it is taken for granted that policies for the redress of severe social and economic disadvantages are in themselves desirable. Such policies of distributive justice aim at different sectors of society and at the widest possible base. Either we call such policies as protective discrimination, benign discrimination or preferential policies; they are the means for achieving the ideals of distributive justice. Justifications for affirmative action lies in the needs either to remove the grossly unjust inequalities in the system or to raise particular sections of the society to the level of human existence and assure them their due dignity. Women's reservation is a way of seeking women's emancipation by way of state intervention, i.e., affecting social reform by the instrumentality of the political system, which is the practice adopted all across the democratic world.

It is in accordance with the widely accepted democratic norms that the Indian Constitution adopts justice and equality as the basic organising principles of India's socio-political system. The equality has come to be embraced as a cardinal value against the background of elaborate, valued and clearly perceived inequalities.[4] What is laid down in terms of equality is a twin concept, i.e., equality before law and equal protection of laws, while the former ensures equal status to everybody, from a prince to a pauper; the later concept, is aimed at achieving substantial equality by classifying the advantaged and disadvantaged and provide the disadvantaged ones with affirmative action programmes. The result has been an array of programmes that are termed here as policy of affirmative action or protective or compensatory discrimination. In fact the measures for ensuring equal protection of laws involve the element of protection as well as that of compensation or reparation to offset the systematic and cumulative deprivations suffered by lower castes in the past. These protective discrimination policies are authorised by constitutional provisions that permit departures from norms of equality, such as merit, even-handedness and indifference to ascriptive characteristics.[5]

Affirmative Action Programme in India

The array of affirmative action programmes in India can roughly be divided into three broad categories. First are reservations which allot or facilitate access to valued positions or resources; such as reservations in legislatures, including the reservations for scheduled castes and scheduled tribes in the Lok Sabha,[6] reservations in government services and reservations in educational institutions. The second type of protective measures are employed though less frequently in land allotment, housing and other scarce resources, like scholarships, grants, loans, health care, etc., third type of protective measures is specific kinds of action plans for removal of untouchability, prohibition of forced labour, etc. In the classification of Prof David Benjamin Oppenhiemer the first type of affirmative action would be 'hard' affirmative action, and the second and third types of affirmative action would be a typical case of soft affirmative action.

For the purpose of providing protection in terms of political representation, Article 330 of the Indian Constitution provides that seats in proportions to the population of scheduled castes and scheduled tribes in particular states are reserved in the Lok Sabha. The states which are predominantly tribal are excluded from the operation of Article 330. Earlier section 2 of the 23rd Amendment of the Constitution 1969, excluded the operation of Article 330 to the tribal areas of Nagaland, but the exclusion has now been extended in respect of the states of Meghalaya, Mizoram and Arunachal Pradesh by the 31st Amendment Act as these states are predominantly tribal in nature.[7] Similarly under Article 332, seats are reserved in the legislative assemblies of the states in favour of scheduled castes and scheduled tribes in proportion of their population in that particular state. Once again the states of Meghalaya, Nagaland, Mizoram and Arunachal Pradesh are excluded from the operation of Article 332, simply because of the predominant tribal population in those states. Articles 331 and 333 do the same in favour of members of the Anglo-Indian community.

Reservation in government services as a measure of Affirmative Action has been incorporated under Article 16(4) of the Indian Constitution. This particular provision falls under the head of "Right to Equality." In order to give effect to the general right to equality under Article 14, the Constitution secures to all citizens a freedom from discrimination on grounds of religion, race and caste. In the specific application of this equality guarantee, the state is further forbidden to discriminate against any citizen on grounds of place of birth, residence, descent, class, language and sex.[8] Untouchability has been abolished and the citizens are protected against discrimination even on the part of the private persons and institutions.[9] The Constitution after guaranteeing the general right to equality under Article 14 defines equality in terms of justice by non-discrimination provisions contained in Articles 15(1) and 16(1) and proceeds to incorporate provisions of preferential treatment so as to permit the state to achieve equality to disadvantaged sections by giving them preferential treatment in all its dealings and particularly in the area of public employment. While Article 16(1) guarantees equality of opportunity for all citizens in matters of employment or appointment to any office under the state, Article 16(2) provides that no citizen shall on grounds only of religion, race, caste, sex, descent, place of birth, residence or any of them, be ineligible for or discriminated against in respect of any employment or office under the state. And Article 16(4) which provides for the protective measure of reservations of seats in government employment lays down that nothing in this Article shall prevent the state from making any provision for reservation of appointments or posts in favour of any backward class of citizens which in the opinion of the state is not adequately represented in the services under the state.

Provisions for reservations in educational institutions to deprived sections of scheduled castes and scheduled tribes have been secured under Article 15(4), and special provisions for women and children under Article 15(3). Article 15(1) specifically bars the state from discriminating against any citizen, race, caste, sex, and place of birth or any of them. Article 15(3), on the other hand, lays down that the state is not prevented from making any special provision for the women and children. The expression "making any special provision" is evidently an open-ended provision and the government can really go on providing a whole array of facilities for promoting the interests of socially and educationally backward classes, for example, waiver of fees, waiver of age requirements, special coaching, scholarships, grants, loans, etc.

What is needed to be understood by the above account of affirmative action programme in India is that the concept lies at the root of the principle of 'equality of opportunity' which is the basis of true democracy. Affirmative action is needed to equalise the opportunities among the people who are endowed differently. Even in United States, affirmative action programmes have actively promoted rights since 1974. The Indian Constitution provides one of the most comprehensive schemes of affirmative action programmes, barely available anywhere in the world. The Affirmative Action Programmes as has been delineated above are available to the disadvantaged sections of society, namely, SCs and STs, etc., and it is on these lines that women's reservations is also being talked about as one of the measures of affirmative action programmes which is in consonance with the democratic norms accepted all over the world. Some other programmes in the name of affirmative action programme in India being run by the state are Integrated Child Development Services (ICDS), mid-day meal schemes, targeted public distribution system, Antyodaya Anna Yojana, national maternity benefit scheme, national family benefit scheme, NREGA, and now the union government is mulling over Right to Food (RTF) scheme to be administered under a legislation that is already in the draft stage.

The author intends to make two points by this account of array of affirmative action programmes in India. The first is about a new kind of classification of affirmative action programmes where all these provisions can be subsumed, and the second is the critique of women's reservation bill and a possible way out to streamline women's representation in legislative bodies in India.

Hard and Soft Affirmative Actions

A new kind of a classification is derived from the basic classification of Prof. Davis Banjamin Oppenhiemer, who puts various types of affirmative action programmes into 'hard' and 'soft' law categories. Under the Indian Constitution as well the whole array of affirmative action programmes are divisible into hard and soft law categories. Articles 330 to 334, 340-342 and 15 and 16 can be categorised as 'hard' law approaches as they prescribe certain legal norms whereby the historical injustices have sought to be done away with or provided with some kind of reparation element by way of protective action or affirmative action. These provisions have already been talked about. Article 15 states preferences in resources distribution and amelioration programmes that are divisible into 'soft' law category affirmative action programmes for the following reasons:

> First, the expression under Article 15(3) "Any special provision for women and children" is an open ended and very wide provision. This particular provision can be used both as a 'hard' as well as 'soft' law affirmative action programme. It is unfortunate that it has not been utilised adequately in 'soft law' way for other purposes. It cannot be said that there are no other methods to consider by which that status of women can not be improved because to say this is to overlook the wide scope of Article 15(3). The language of Article 15(3) shows first that reservations as such are not expressly mentioned in Article 15(3), but fall within the wide expression "special provisions for women and children."

Unfortunately it is overlooked that special provisions include every kind of assistance which can be given to women and children to make them stand on their feet or, as is commonly said, to bring them into the mainstream of national life. Illustratively those measures would include empowerment by granting of property rights, which may include grant of land either free or on nominal cost. These measures would also include schemes for training the women to pursue trades or small business which would fetch a reasonable income. In relation to education itself, under Article 15(3) the state can give free education, free textbooks, free uniforms and subsistence allowance, merit scholarships and the like, starting from the stage of primary education and going right up to university and postgraduate education. Once this is realised, how vast and varied are the powers at the disposal of the state if it really takes care to improve the lot of women in the real sense of the term. The controversies of reservations, which more often than not are accused to be governed by political considerations, lose much of the shine of affirmative action programmes.

WOMEN'S RESERVATION BILL: A CRITIQUE

The 81st Constitutional Amendment Bill, popularly known as the Women's Reservation Bill (WRB), was introduced in the parliament in 1996. The Bill provides for as nearly as may be one-third of all seats in the Lok Sabha and state legislative assemblies shall be reserved for women; that reservation shall apply in case of seats reserved for scheduled castes (SCs) and scheduled tribes (STs) as well; that seats to be reserved in rotation will be determined by draw of lots in such a way that a seat shall be reserved only once in three consecutive general elections.

The most serious flaw in the Bill as indicated by the critics is the rotational reservation of one-third seats. This would result in denial of pre-election nursing of a Lok Sabha or state assembly constituency which involves a very heavy investment on the part of political parties and individual aspirants. This clause of 'rotation of seats' is seen by the opponents of Bill to 'strike at the very heart of democracy and democratic values' as, according to their logic, the representative will not get a chance to nurture his constituency nor the electorate will get a chance to reward or punish their representative, as a corollary to it hardly any ties would be established between the two.

It must be appreciated that rotational reservation of one-third of the seats exclusively for women would lead to a grave uncertainty for sitting male MPs, eroding their meticulously developed political base and leaving them no scope to pursue politics as a lifelong mission or career. We must understand that passing the Bill in the current format would mean political suicide for the sitting male members of parliament and state legislative assemblies. The refusal of the women's organisations to negotiate this despite a lot of drawbacks in the scheme as has been demonstrated in the working of a similar rotation scheme in panchayati raj bodies is one of the most important stumbling blocks of women's reservation bill. This is going to cause enormous harm for the political career of existing individual politician as well as for the process of the development of national level leaders with towering personalities.

An important impact this would have on the political system as a whole is that this would dwarf the popularly elected political leadership and strengthen the bureaucracy. We must understand the enormous loss it may cause to the fledgling democratic system in this country. Bureaucracy, which is already too entrenched in the system and has been proving to be a hurdle in the process of democratic consolidation by way of a variety of measures that the system has been trying to usher into, have been blocked by the bureaucracy.

One of the main reasons for the failure of democratic experiment in local self-government has been an over-weaning influence of the bureaucracy over the system at the grassroots level, either in panchayati raj bodies or urban local bodies. They consider the emergence of local leaders as their competitors eroding their power base and therefore they do everything to halt the emergence of popular leaders at the grassroots level. The interests of political leaders at the higher levels of political system and the bureaucracy coincide here, and they connive to keep the emergence of local leaders in these bodies so as to prevent the erosion of their political and financial power base. It is anybody's imagination as to what would happen if the same process is somehow allowed to be replicated at the apex of the political system. A proposal emphasizing nomination of 33 per cent women candidates instead of reserving the constituencies for women has been advocated by a senior feminist activist scholar, Madhu Kishwar.[10] The proposal is aimed at amending the Representation of People's Act 1951, to compel political parties to nominate women for one-third of their seats or lose recognition. This, according to Rajindar Sachar, former Chief Justice of Delhi High Court, is flawed, as it would violate the Constitution of India, which guarantees its citizens the right to form association under Article 19(1)(c) as a fundamental right. Reasonable restrictions on this right to form associations can be imposed on in the interest of sovereignty and integrity of India or public order or morality, and such an amendment would not obviously fall within the permissible reasonable restrictions on fundamental rights of the citizens.

Apart from this, as justice Rajinder Sachar argues, this alternative, will not achieve the objective behind the Amendment Bill, because even if a third of women candidates are put up by political parties, there is no guarantee that the same member will get elected, or even winnable seats by the political parties would be allotted to the women candidates. The political parties will tend to allow women candidates to fight elections from their weak constituencies. This is obvious for it is freely admitted by all across the political party spectrum that due to the inbuilt prejudice against women, male candidates will have an unfair advantage in elections.

It has been taken note of that women's reservation is a way of seeking women's emancipation by way of state intervention, i.e., affecting social reform by the instrumentality of the political system. It has been argued that this measure for women's upliftment is neither sufficient nor purposive but is merely a political face-wash. There is nothing to suggest that bringing 181 women in the parliament might benefit the women in general. Studies have compelling evidence to suggest that ascendancy of women to political eminence does not necessarily lead to the beneficial deal in favour of women. Rajasthan and U.P. where women chief ministers have ruled for substantial period of time have not changed power equations in favour of women. Indira Gandhi was at the apex of Indian political scene for almost two decades. Mrs. Bhandaranaike and then her daughter Chandrika Kumaratunge had dominated the political scene of Srilanka, and the political scene of both Pakistan and Bangladesh had been dominated by women politicians until recently. Benazir Bhutto, Begum Zia and Shiekh Hasina Wajed have been the names that have dominated the political scene of Pakistan and Bangladesh. One may meaningfully raise a question whether this has brought in any significant change in the lot of South Asian women. The answer is categorically a big NO.

Added to it is the fact that women political leaders, even if at the apex of political/state organisation, would not necessarily favour women-centric policies for the dynamic of power structure is different. The reason for the low influence of women-centric policies in the formal political structures and decision-making levels seems to lie in the compulsions of competitive elections and the quest for power by the political parties in a multiparty democracy. Increasingly, the compulsions of the political parties due to narrow majorities, precarious coalitions and hung parliaments have made the question of power rather than that of representation the determining factor. Women's issues and women's participation and representation are encouraged only within the parameters of power, and are constrained by the basic objectives and interest of the parties either to capture power or for survival, if in power.

Further, it must be understood very clearly that women's reservation may bring about a swift quantitative jump in legislatures. It is unlikely to improve the overall quality of the governance in the country and benefit the women in any significant manner. The argument that the participation of a few in the decision-making process might give a sense of participation to a large section of women presumes that the public institutions are the resources at the disposal of their members for altering the distribution of power in the directions that they consider desirable.[11] While this does not serve the purpose of empowerment any significant manner, it leads in to the displacement of objects of the institutions and wastage of public resources. This also entails the question of efficiency of the system as a whole.

It may also be noted that during the debate on women's reservations G.S. Banatwala had demanded that there should be comprehensive reservation both for men and women to give proportional representation to OBCs, dalits and minorities.[12] In fact, this was the precise language used by Jinnah during the Round Table Conference while demanding a fair representation for Muslims. One might venture to guess in which direction we are moving. One might fruitfully remind oneself that the special subcommittee of Sardar Patel, Ambedkar, Pandit Nehru, Rajendra Prasad and K.M. Munshi formed on minority problems had rejected both separate electorate and reservation, saying these might disrupt the whole conception.[13] Patel wrote, "Although the abolition of separate electorate had removed much of the poison from the body politic, the reservation seats for religious communities it is felt, leads to a certain degree of separatism and was to that extent contrary and exception to a secular and democratic state."[14] Needless to say that this would also go against the secularism that has been emphasized so much by political parties all over the country, as one of the basic values of our Constitutional system.

Concluding Remarks

The morales of the story is that there is no consensus emerging on the point of women's reservations. The democratic system being run on the basis of democratic values has to evolve a consensus, it has to resolve itself in practice into a continuous search for agreement through discussions, and compromise and action on the basis of which maximum measure of agreements is obtainable. While in terms of principle women's reservations as one of the methods of affirmative action programme cannot be denied to the women, bringing it without removing the variety of lacunae indicated above would amount to an undemocratic exercise and would smack of politicking on a point of very basic value of democratic systems. What should be true positioning of justice in the dynamically changing society? Amartya Sen[15] argues that in a society which is always on the move, the entity that keeps the cohesiveness in the society cannot be made fixed. Nobody would doubt that the current time for Indian polity is one of the most dynamic and crucial time in the history of the democratisation process, fixing things on an issue which is potentially so divisive, would amount to atrophying one of essential processes of democratic politics.

There have been alternative proposals, which go beyond partition politics. One important method that was sought to be worked out was in 2003, when the then speaker of Lok Sabha, Manohar Joshi, convened the meeting of major political parties to evolve some kind of a consensus. The proposal that was evolved in this meeting was later taken up by the BJP in its national executive meet, and a resolution was passed to that effect that called upon the government to bring a Constitutional Amendment to convert one-third of Lok Sabha constituencies into dual-member constituencies.[16]

The proposal mooted was to group the current 543 Lok Sabha constituencies into three groups of 181 each. In each election, one of these groups would be converted into dual-member constituencies, each electing two members of parliament - a male and a female. This would increase the number of elected Lok Sabha members to 724 (362 + 181 + 181) from 543 Lok Sabha constituencies.[17] This dual-membership would rotate after each election to the next group of 181 constituencies. The proposal would also apply to state assemblies and to SC and ST constituencies. This proposal would provide a solution to the issue of women's reservation in legislative bodies by providing greater representation to women without depriving men of their existing representation. This would not rupture the process of leadership development, which is a huge risk, and as has been discussed above, involved in the Women's Reservation Bill.

Nobody would dispute that if the country is to march confidently into a new era of equality and prosperity and take long strides in the matter of development, the lot of women has got to be improved. There is certainly a need for women's more effective role in decision-making processes for the democratic and Constitutional assurances of equal citizenship and rights in the Indian Constitution to become a reality at the operational level. After all, citizenship is linked to political participation and representation. How the goal of emancipation of women is to be achieved is a matter on which there has to be a thorough debate. It must be recognised that boosting women's political participation needs to go beyond raw numbers to encompass the complex relationship between power, poverty and participation. Women want and need to be able to participate in the decisions that affect them, their families and communities.

It needs to understand that mere reservations *per se* would not guarantee effective and meaningful participation of women in the political process; rather additional supportive measures, what the author proposes as 'soft law' approach in affirmative action programmes, must be initiated in order to make women's representation sustainable and palatable to the entire political class. It should be made obligatory for all the political parties to provide a definite number of organisational representation of women without violating the constitutional norms as Justice Rajinder Sachar puts it. This representation should be encouraged right from the enrolment of members to the national executives and parliamentary boards which would go a long way in increasing the pool of eligible women candidates helping the evolution of robust political leadership amongst women as well. This is also likely to reduce the element of proxies' politics that has been happening in the panchayati raj bodies right now and would eventually lead to much higher representation of women even from open electoral constituencies.

References

1. V.D. Mahajan, *Indian Democracy and Governance,* Asia Publishing House, Bombay, 1988.
2. Jed Rubenfeld, "Affirmative Action," 107, Yale L.J. 427, 1997.
3. Ibid., 1407.
4. Marc Gallanter, *Law and Society in Modern India,* Oxford University Press, New Delhi, 1990, p.185.
5. Ibid.
6. Indian Parliament is a Bicameral Legislature. Rajya Sabha is the upper chamber of the Parliament having 250 members elected indirectly for six years. Lok Sabha is the lower chamber, consisting of 544 members elected directly for five years.
7. V.N. Shukla, *Constitutional Law of India,* Eastern Book Company Lucknow, 1990.
8. Article 15 (1), and 15 (2) of Indian Constitution.
9. Article 17 of the Indian Constitution, also see the Protection of Civil Rights Act 1957.
10. "The Alternate Bill," *Manushi* No. 116, 2000.
11. Andre Betielle, "Power and Authority," *Times of India,* New Delhi, 19 April 1994.

12. Zafar Agha, "Pulled and Pushed," *Hindustan Times*, New Delhi, 19 July 1998.
13. B. Shiva Rao, *The Framing of India's Constitution*, Select Documents (Govt of India Press 1968).
14. Ibid.
15. *The Idea of Justice*, Oxford University Press, London, 2009.
16. *The Hindu*, New Delhi, July 20, 2003.
17. Lok Sabha has 545 members of which 543 are elected and the President nominates two members from the Anglo-Indian community.

12

Enhancing Political Participation through Women Empowerment: Role of Legislature

— *Abhilasha Kataria, Saumya Sharma & Prateek Bhattacharya*

Introduction

> Women have no money. What money they get becomes the property of the husband, the moment they acquire it. Women are bought and sold, and are on a level with chattels.
>
> —*Jaimini*[1]

Men have dominated women within the household and even beyond the household for centuries. Political participation that was earlier limited to males of the society has been extended to women through key ingredients of democracy such as universal adult franchise and equality for all. Political participation requires a woman to make decision with respect to the polity. However due to the strongly patriarchal society in India the decision-making power of a woman in her own household is very limited.[2] This makes us sceptical of the autonomy in decision-making power that she exercises beyond the level of her family. Until and unless a woman at the level of her household is not given freedom in decisionmaking, the level to which she will act as an autonomous political actor, which is essential for political participation, will be limited.

Political participation may be in the form of voting, campaigning for election, funding a political party, rallying, listening to political speeches, etc. On the election front, to increase political participation, the 73rd and 74th Constitutional

Amendments have been brought forward by the government to provide 33 per cent reservation for women at the level of village panchayats.[3] This paper, on the basis of various studies, tries to highlight that even though such type of provisions have been a success in bringing about a numerical increase in women at the decision-making level, many of these women, due to lack of decision-making power, fail to act as active political actors who bring about a change in government policy. Part I of the paper explains political participation and the level of political participation as conceived by Lester Milbrath. It then tries to find a corelation between decision-making powers of a woman at the level of her household. Part II of the paper talks about household empowerment approach towards political participation of women and how it influences political participation in the form of contesting elections, voting, attending a political rally, etc.

The decisionmaking power of a woman in the household influences her political participation. In order to give a woman more decision-making powers with respect to her position in the family the parliament has come up with good governance legislations in matters of dowry, domestic violence, abortion, etc. The intention with which these legislations were passed was undoubtedly that of women empowerment; however these legislations have certain inherent flaws which, when combined with a general lack of execution and implementation, fail to ensure that women are on an equal status with men. Part III of the paper deals with the effects brought about by, and the subsequent flaws in, various women-related laws in our country.

PART I

What is Political Participation?

Political participation in layman's terms means to play a role in the policy-making process in a democracy through the exercise of political rights such as universal adult franchise or being a part of a pressure group buffeting the government for change in the policy framework. The varying degrees and extent of political participation have been explained by Lester Milbrath through his hierarchical framework of political participation.[4] Political participation varies with the extent to which a citizen affects or can affect the decisionmaking of the government. Milbrath classified activities of citizens with respect to its influence on decision-making and political participation. He classified the activities into gladiator activities, transitional activities and spectator activities.[5] Spectator activities include holding an office, being a candidate for an office, contributing to a political campaign, etc. Transitional activities include attending a political rally, donating money to a political party, etc. *Gladiator activities* include trying to talk to someone into voting a certain way, political discussions, voting, etc. Hence the level of decisionmaking and political participation increases on moving from the Spectator activity to the Gladiator activity.

Women and the inter-relation between decision-making and political participation

While there have been different interpretations of the origin and dynamics of subordination of women, family has been viewed as the major site of women's oppression by the feminist writers.[6] Aristotle in his book *Politics* writes that the household consists of free men, women, children and slaves.[7] According to him, unlike men, women should not be given the privilege of participation in the political activities of the state since the soul of a woman is to be governed by man for her own good.

Progressive revolutionary movements have attempted to elicit condemnation by society for such misplaced and archaic notions. Sadly, society's predefined role of a woman as a good mother, a dutiful wife and an obedient daughter in the household remains unchanged.

The existing power structure in the institution of family needs to be reformed to encourage independent decision making amongst women.[8] The ability to make decisions that affect her own life gives a woman the confidence to consider possibilities beyond her household, which include stepping into the political field, which is considered to be a predominantly male arena.

PART II

Household Empowerment Approach towards Political Participation of Women

The level of political participation of a woman increases in ascending order when she is casting her vote, attending a political rally and standing for an election. The more and more a woman steps out of the private domain into the public domain the more empowered she is to be considered.[9] The more the participation of a woman in the public domain, the more empowered she is considered to be.[10] One of the key features of empowerment for a woman is the ability to make decisions independently.[11] Hence the greater the level of political participation, the greater the decision making power (with respect to policy making) which is vested in women. Hence they step out of their households into the public arena and become more empowered, and when they are more empowered they have more freedom to make decisions for themselves. Before women step out into the public arena they need to negotiate space for themselves in the household itself, and until they are able to do so their political participation will be lower than that of men due to male dominance in their lives.[12]

Table 1

Gender and the Influence of Elections on the Government[13]

Issue	*Women Answering Yes*	*Men Answering Yes*
Do you have a say in government?	23	39
Do elections influence the government?	32	53
Does voting have an effect on government action?	38	59

According to a post-election survey done by the Centre for Developing Studies it was found that:

i) Lesser number of women as compared to men believed that their political participation was likely to have an influence on the government.

ii) This lower level of belief (as compared to men) that their political participation is not likely to change the government process is mostly the result of a process of socialisation that leads them to view their political activity in a different way than men do.[14]

Voting is the simplest way of political participation in a democracy. Therefore the societal structure of family, which is responsible for the process of socialisation is to an extent responsible for the way in which women view political activity. This strongly patriarchal family structure which subordinates women[15] combined with its effect on an individual in society[16] results in the social conditioning of women over the years leading to an acceptance of the cultural discrimination as a part of tradition itself.[17] Therefore practices such as dowry, female foeticide, etc., are looked upon as tradition. Due to lack of decision making at the level of the household, women will never be able to look at themselves as autonomous political actors, and will therefore remain less politically active as compared to men.

In 1992 the government passed the 73rd and 74th Constitutional Amendments, which provided for one-third reservation for women at the panchayat level. This is one of the steps to attain the critical mass for good governance that has been talked about by Kofi Annan[18]. Moreover reservation helps to achieve the higher levels of political empowerment discussed in the Lester Milbrath Model. However we need to look at the political empowerment and participation beyond mere numerical values. Reservation is a progressive step toward political empowerment but if women are not empowered to make decisions for themselves at the basic level of the household itself, the point of such reservation fails entirely. There are several instances where men use women as proxies to further their own political purpose. In a 1998 Survey of Women and Political Participation in Haryana it was found that 60 per cent women believe that men will never let women enjoy the same status as men, and 56 per cent believed that a lack of cooperation from men hinders their development.[19] The existing power structure at the level of the household hinders active participation of women in politics in the following ways:

1. Women are met with resistance that obstructs their political participation since men feel that women will oppose their decisions;[20]
2. Women can participate in panchayat meetings only with the permission of their husbands;[21]
3. Sometimes men use them as proxies in panchayat election;[22]
4. Men also believe that women are good only for "kitchen talk" and not for political discussions.[23] It is notions like these that make women believe that reservation is just a sham since men will never treat women as their equal.[24]

The household is the logical start of the existing discrepancy in the power structures in society since it is the family environment, which enables or constrains the participation of its members in society.[25] To provide an enabling environment for political participation through increased decision-making, the status of women at the level of the family needs to be raised.

Part III

The Indian society is primarily patriarchal in nature. As such, in order to enforce the Constitutional right of equality of men and women, the upliftment of women from a history of degradation and humiliation was essential. In furtherance of this objective, various legislations have been introduced, passed and amended over the last half century for the purpose of empowering women. However, this has done little to improve the status of women in Indian society. The incidence of rape has increased exponentially from 2,487 in 1971 to 20,737 in 2007, cruelty by husband or relatives has increased from 28,579 in 1995 to 75,930 in 2007, and the number of dowry deaths has risen from 4,648 in 1995 to 8,093 in 2007.[26] This is the case despite the enactment and enforcement of several legislations empowering women. The reason for this is the inherent drawbacks and defects of various Acts of Parliament. The shortcomings of the 73rd and 74th Constitutional Amendments have already been discussed. The other acts and legislations are discussed below.

The Dowry Prohibition Act, 1961

The Dowry Prohibition Act was enforced on July 1, 1961.[27] As per the Act:

1. A person who gives or takes, or helps in the giving or taking of dowry can be sentenced to jail for five years and fined Rs.15,000/- or the amount of the value of dowry, whichever is more.[28]
2. To give or to agree to give, directly or indirectly, any property or valuable security, in connection with a marriage is prohibited. The giving of or agreeing to the giving of any amount either in cash of kind, jewellry, articles, properties, etc. in respect of a marriage is absolutely prohibited by the Dowry Prohibition Act.
3. The making of a demand for dowry also is now prohibited and it is punishable with imprisonment up to two years and a fine of Rs.10,000/-.[29]
4. Nobody can advertise to give money or share in his property as a consideration for the marriage.[30]
5. An Agreement between the parties, to give or to take dowry, is considered as void and cannot be enforced in law and the person who has received dowry is liable to return it to the wife.[31]
6. Genuine presents offered to the bride or to the bridegroom, at the time of the marriage, are however not prohibited by this Act. The giving of such presents however must be customary. The value of such presents, however, should not be excessive, compared to the financial status of the parties giving such presents. A list of such presents is also required to be maintained wherein the name of the person who has given the present, his relationship with the bride or bridegroom, description of the presents given and the value of the presents is to be mentioned and that list has to be signed by both the bride and the bridegroom.[32]

Over the next few decades, however, several defects and shortcomings were noticed in the legislation, leading to the appointment of a Joint Committee of both houses of parliament on whose recommendations the Dowry Prohibition (Amendment) Acts of 1984 and 1986 were passed in order to revise the Act and give it more teeth, thus ensuring better efficacy. That was two decades ago. In the last 20 years, however, there has been no significant drop in the number of dowry deaths; suffering and ill-treated women are still helpless at the hands of their in-laws; and India is no closer towards the eradication of this menace than it is now.

The Dowry Prohibition Act still faces the following shortcomings:

1) The 1984 Amendment substituted the words "as consideration for marriage" with the words "in connection with the marriage" in Section 2 of the Act. This widened the meaning of dowry but retained the essential character of dowry. The Amendment Act of 1986 further widened this meaning.

   Dowry is generally defined as the money, goods, or estate that a wife brings to her husband at marriage.[33] The 91st Report of the Law Commission of India recommended the following definition of dowry:

   > Dowry means money, or other thing estimable in terms of money, demanded from the wife or her parents or other relative by the husband or his parents or other relatives, where such a demand is not properly referable to any legally recognised claim and is relatable only to the wife's having married into the husband's family.

   But Parliament has failed to accept this definition.[34] The more wide and accommodating the definition is, the greater the probability of surer convictions under the Act.

2) Under Section 7(2) and Section 8A of the Punjab Act of 1976, no court shall take cognisance of any offence except

upon a complaint made within one year from the date of the offence.[35] These provisions are still present in the Amendment made by the State of Punjab to the Dowry Prohibition Act. The problem with the provision is that it describes a strict time limit for the enforcement of the provision of the Act and does not recognise any offence after this one-year duration is complete. In a household scenario where a wife is tortured and tormented for years, and where, considering the social stigma attached, a substantial amount of fortitude and moral fibre is required to make such a complaint, the wife often takes a large amount of time before she can sum up the courage to do so.

3) There is a contradiction between Section 3 and Section 7(3) of the Act. Section 3 states that the giving or taking dowry is a punishable offence. This means that even the bride's parents or relatives who were forced to accept the demands of the bridegroom's family are punishable under the Act. The Act, however, simultaneously, under Section 7(3) states, "Notwithstanding anything contained in any law for the time being in force, a statement made by the person aggrieved by the offence shall not subject such person to a prosecution under this Act." Therefore, while the aggrieved person is guaranteed immunity for making a complaint, he is, at the same time guilty for having given dowry. The giver of the dowry is a mere victim rather than a criminal. The parents do not give dowry out of their free will but are compelled to do so. When both the giver and the taker are punishable, no giver can be expected to come forward to make a complaint.[36]

The Act is therefore rendered toothless by glaring defects and inadequacies in its provisions and the failure of the legislature in taking appropriate action for correction of the same. Due to such loopholes, the Act fails towards empowerment of women.

The protection of women from domestic violence act, 2005

The purpose of this Act is to provide for more effective protection of the rights of women guaranteed under the Constitution who are victims of violence of any kind occurring within the family and for matters connected therewith or incidental thereto. The highlights of this Act are as follows:

1. Any harm, injury to health, safety, life, limb or well-being or any other act threatening or coercion, etc., by any adult member of the family, constitutes domestic violence.[37]
2. Any woman who is, or has been in a domestic or family relationship, and is subjected to any act of domestic violence is competent to make a complaint.[38]
3. The aggrieved or affected woman can complain to the concerned Protection Officer, Police Officer, Service Provider or Magistrate.[39]
4. The aggrieved woman has the right to be informed about the available services and free legal services, from the Protection Officer, etc.[40]
5. Shelter homes and medical facilities can be provided to the aggrieved woman.[41]
6. Interim compensation can be made available to the aggrieved woman.[42]
7. Proceedings of the complaint can be held *in camera*.[43]
8. Every aggrieved woman has the right to reside in a shared household.[44]
9. Protection order by Magistrate can be given in favour of the aggrieved woman.[45]
10. Monetary relief can be given to the aggrieved woman to meet expenses or losses.[46]
11. An appeal can be made to the Sessions Court within 30 days from the date of issue of the order of the concerned Magistrate.[47]
12. Imprisonment up to one year or a fine up to Rs.20,000 or both may be awarded for breach of a protection order by the opposite party.[48]

13. The Protection Officer can be prosecuted, up to one-year imprisonment or with a fine up to Rs.20,000 or both for the failure of his duties.[49]

The inherent defects in the PWDVA are as follows:

1) Section 16 of the Act allows the magistrate to hold proceeding *in camera* if he deems it necessary. Sometimes *in camera* proceedings can protect the aggrieved woman to a great extent from a lot of humiliation and shame, especially when explicit acts of sexual abuse and violence are being discussed. But sometimes, *in camera* proceedings only intimidate the aggrieved in favour of the respondent. This is especially so when the aggrieved is the only woman in the court, facing a completely male- dominated room of hostile, sneering magistrates, lawyers, officials, police, the male respondent, etc. The solution is to amend this section to only allow for *in camera* proceedings not when either party so desires but only if the aggrieved party so desires. Also, the aggrieved party should be allowed to be accompanied by any relative/woman social worker, etc., of her choice for moral support.[50]

2) The Act is very ambiguous with reference to the provision for service providers under Section 10. "This is the first act that is encouraging NGOs and social workers to become service providers but neither is there mention of the eligibility or the procedure for applications to be made in this regard."[51]

3) With reference to the appointment of Protection Officers under Section 8 of the Act, there is no mention of how many officers are to be employed and at what levels.[52]

4) Another drawback on the part of the government in introducing the Act is inadequate budgetary allocation and lack of proper infrastructure for the implementation of the PWDVA. These have emerged as areas of concern, both in the Lawyers Collective Women's Rights Initiative Report and in the observations of women activists.[53] As a result it becomes difficult to appoint new Protection Officers or provide infrastructure, and existing government officials

and infrastructure have to be given this additional responsibility or utilised respectively, thus reducing effectiveness.[54]

Despite the good intention behind the provisions of this Act, it is obvious that such provisions are incomplete. Where they provide a good and valid idea, they fail to identify the means of implementation of the same, nor are the ideas thought through to the end.

The Medical Termination of Pregnancy Act (MTP), 1971

The Medical Termination of Pregnancy Act (MTP), 1971 was drafted in order to give women key decision-making power with respect to their pregnancy. Its provisions require the satisfaction of certain prerequisites before a pregnancy can be terminated. These include whether the pregnancy will result in mental and/ or physical torture for the woman, the age of the foetus in terms of weeks as well as the qualifications and number of the medical practitioners required to perform the operation. On the face of it the MTP Act provides that only the consent of the woman is required.[55] Spousal consent here is irrelevant; however some doctors refuse to perform the abortion if the married woman fails to produce a document stating the consent of her husband.

In *Suman Kapur* v. *Sudhir Kapur*[56], *Sushil Kumar Verma* v. *Vsha*[57] and *Deepak Kumar Arora* v. *Sampuran Arora*[58] the court has held that that obtaining abortion by the wife without consent or even knowledge of the husband is in the nature of mental cruelty. Therefore this has created a loophole wherein even though on paper a woman doesn't require the consent of her husband, in reality if the husband's consent is absent it can be a ground for obtaining divorce.

Thereafter at the level of the family, in actuality a woman cannot make an independent decision with respect to her abortion. So in reality, due to the perverse interpretation of the MTP Act by the Courts, the decision-making power of women is curtailed. According to Raghunath Karve, "Unless a woman acquires complete right to decide on the pregnancy, any talk of empowerment of women would be shallow."

Marital Rape

Rape is seen as an act striking at the core of the family unit, which is essential for stability and progression of society.[59] Yet, under the exception to Section 375 of the Indian Penal Code sexual intercourse by a husband with his wife shall not be considered as rape. Women, hence, are left with no option but to live with their abusive husbands where they are reminded of the abuse that they have had to go through day and night.[60] The idea of a husband being immune from prosecution of rape of his wife[61] is contrary to the civilised concept of marriage.[62] In the United Kingdom[63] and the United States of America[64] the exemption on marital rape can no longer be claimed. The existing law in India which presupposes women as chattel of men[65] requires to be amended so as to provide women with the same status and natural rights that men[66] enjoy in the household. If this is not done, women shall continue to be second-class citizens, dominated by their husband with little or no freedom to speak out against the atrocities committed on them at home.

Conclusion

The issue that is being dealt with is very specific. There is an urgent need to increase the participation of women in politics. The ratio of the number of women electors who were eligible to vote with respect to the number of actual women voters in the last Lok Sabha General Election in 2004 was 321,997,066: 172,714,226.[67] And this was merely participation as voters. As has been mentioned above there are several forms of political participation. And the only manner in which there is going to be a greater participation on the part of women is by liberating them at home first. Women at home first need to be able to make household decisions themselves in order to take the next step of making political decisions. However, as long as the very laws, which are meant to empower women and provide them with protection and assurance of their equal status in the household, are riddled with ambiguity, unenforceability and half-hearted measures, women shall forever remain the subordinate sex in the arena of politics.

In order to prevent such happening it is essential that these loopholes identified above be plugged. There may be many other provisions of different legislations that are disempowering for women, and until and unless they are all changed, women will never be treated as equals.

It is absurd and ridiculous to treat women as mere property, ridding them of their rights and liberties in the contemporary society. Indian society has progressed to a great extent since independence. If the status of women in Indian society is not brought on par with that of men, and with as much expediency as possible, it will only serve as a hindrance to the advancement of India. A country can never progress by wasting the talent of half its population. Political participation can be made meaningful only when the woman is provided her due space within the household.

References

1. K.L Sarkar, *Mimansa Rules of Interpretation,* Allahabad: Modern Law Publications, 2008, 2nd Ed., p.139.
2. Sadhna Arya, *Women, Gender Equality and the State,* New Delhi: Deep and Deep Publications Pvt. Ltd., 2002, p. 8.
3. The Constitution (Seventy-Fourth Amendment) Act, 1992.
4. D. Ruedin, *Testing Milbrath's 1965 Framework of Political Participation: Institution and Social Capital,*

   http://journal.ciiss.net/index.php/ciiss/article/viewFile/43/50 last visited January 19, 2009.
5. Ibid.
6. Sadhna Arya, *Women, Gender Equality and the State,* New Delhi: Deep and Deep Publications Pvt. Ltd., 2002, p. 5.
7. Aristotle, *The Politics,* Translated by T. A. Sinclair, London: Penguin Books, 1992, p.57.
8. Srilatha Batliwala, *Putting power back into empowerment,*

   http://www.opendemocracy.net/article/putting_power_back_into_empowerment_0 last visited January 22, 2009.
9. Rosalind Eyben and Rebecca Napier Moore, *Conceptualising Women's Empowerment in International Development Agencies,* http://www.pathwaysofempowerment.org/International_

Development_Agencies_working_paper_draft.pdf, last visited January 2, 2009.

10. Bilkis Vissandjee and others, *Empowerment Beyond Numbers: Substantiating Women's Political Participation,*

    http://www.bridgew.edu/SoAS/JIWS/Nov05V2/India.pdf. last visited January 19, 2009.

11. Ibid, n 9.

12. UNDP, *Women's Political Participation and Good Governance: 21st Century Challenges,*

    htt p://www.undp.org/governance/docs/Gender-Pub-21stcentury.pdf last visited January 23, 2009.

    http://www.worldvaluessurvey.org/Upload/5_india-gender_2.pdf last visited January 24, 2009.

13. 1971 Centre for Developing Studies Post-election Survey as cited from Pradeep Chhibber, Why Are Women Politically Active? *The Household, Public Space, and Political Participation in India,* p. 1.

14. Ibid., p.1.

15. Lalitha Sridhar, *Treating infanticide as homicide is inhuman,*

    http://infochangeindia.org/20040817165/Women/Features/-Treating-infanticide-as-homicide-is-inhuman.html last visited November 3, 2008.

16. Graziella Bertocchi, *Women and Politics,*

    http://www.voxeu.org/index.php?q=node/418#fn2 published on July 30, 2007.

17. *Patriarchy,* http://en.wikipedia.org/wiki/Patriarchy last visited January 26, 2009.

18. Sri Lanka: Women, Political Empowerment And Concerns, *Daily Mirror,* taken from

    http://www.peacewomen.org/news/SouthAsia/Sept08/SriLankaPolitical.html published on September 4, 2008.

19. Pradeep Chibber, op.cit.

20. Sara Anderson and others, *Women's Political Participation in Kerala, South India*– A case of based on obstacles met when entering the political sphere,

    http://www.niaslinc.dk/gateway_to_asia/nordic_webpublications/x483469067.pdf last visited January 18, 2009, p.51.

21. Ibid , p.48.
22. Pradeep Chibber, op.cit.
23. Ibid., p.51.
24. Ibid.
25. Sara Anderson and others, *op.cit,* p. 42.
26. *Incidence Of Cognisable Crimes (IPC) Under Different Crime Heads During 1953 To 2007,* National Crime Records Bureau,

    http://ncrb.nic.in/cii2007/cii-2007/1953-2007.pdf published on November 7, 2008.
27. Roma Mukherjee, *Legal Status and Remedies for Women in India,* New Delhi: Deep & Deep Publications, 1998, 1st Ed., p.119.
28. Section 3(1) of the Dowry Prohibition Act, 1961.
29. Section 4 of the Dowry Prohibition Act, 1961.
30. Section 4-A of the Dowry Prohibition Act, 1961.
31. Section 5 of the Dowry Prohibition Act, 1961.
32. Section 3(2) of the Dowry Prohibition Act.
33. Dictionary.com,

    http://dictionary.reference.com/browse/dowry.
34. Mohd. Umar, *Bride Burning in India* (A Socio-Legal Study), Google Book Search, http://books.google.co.in/books?id=xGeaOVxSFIs C&pg=PA167&lpg=PA167& dq= history +of+ the+ Dowry+Prohibition+ Act+1961&source= bi&ots =dydV7o HbP2&sig=tvVw03-rEZgOxWlnSI942 mXv_44&hl =en& sa=X&oi= book_result&resnum=9&ct=result#PPP16, M1, p. 167-169.
35. Roma Mukkerjee, op.cit, p.141.
36. Ibid., pp.143-144.
37. Section 3 of the Domestic Violence Act.
38. Provisio to Section 2(q) of the Domestic Violence Act.
39. Section 5 of the Domestic Violence Act.
40. Section 5(b) of the Domestic Violence Act.
41. Sections 6, 7 of the Domestic Violence Act.
42. Sections 2(k), 12(2) of the Domestic Violence Act.
43. Section 16 of the Domestic Violence Act.

44. Section 17 of the Domestic Violence Act.
45. Section 18 of the Domestic Violence Act.
46. Sections 2(k), 20 of the Domestic Violence Act.
47. Section 29 of the Domestic Violence Act.
48. Section 31 of the Domestic Violence Act.
49. Section 33 of the Domestic Violence Act.
50. Srilata Swaminathan, *On the Protection of Women from Domestic Violence Act,*

    http://www.cpiml.org/liberation/year_2005/october05/domestic_voilence_act.htm last visited on January 28, 2009.
51. Madhuri Sumant, Counselor, Susamvad (NGO), taken from Kalindi Kokal, *Domestic Violence still a concern, Pune Newsline,*

    http://cities.expressindia.com/fullstory.php?newsid=225498, last updated on March 8, 2007.
52. Ibid.
53. *Womens Feature Service, Two Years On: Are Women Staying Alive?*

    http://newsblaze.com/story/20090106055647iwfs.nb/topstory.html published on January 6, 2009.
54. One World South Asia, *Study highlights loopholes in India's domestic violence law,* http://southasia.oneworld.net/todaysheadlines/study-highlights-loopholes-in-india-domestic-violence-law published on January 14, 2009.
55. Section 3(4) of Medical Termination of Pregnancy Act 1971.
56. MANU/SC/4705/2008.
57. AIR 1987 (Del) 86.
58. 1 (1983) D.M.C. 182.
59. David J. Giacopassi and Karen R. Wilkinson, Rape and the Devalued Victim, 367, *Law and Human Behavior,* 1985.
60. Sallee Fry Waterman, *For Better or Worse: Marital Rape,* 15 N. Ky. L. Rev. 611 (1988).
61. *Udday v. State of Karnataka,* AIR 2003 SC 1639.
62. *SW v. United Kingdom* 21 EHRR 363.

63. R v. R [1991] 4 All E.R. 481.
64. Libertas case 64 N.Y.2d 152 (1984).
65. K.L. Sarkar, op.cit.
66. Rebecca M. Ryan, The Sex Right: A Legal History of Marital rape Exemption, 20 L. & *Soc. Inquiry* 941 (1995).
67. *Statistical Report on General Elections, 2004 to the 14th Lok Sabha,* Volume I (National and State Abstracts & Detailed Results), Election Commission of India, New Delhi, p.167.

13

Legislature as a Tool to Enhance Women's Participation: Need to Rethink Proper Implementation

—Geetanjali Sharma & Pradnya Satish Talekar Patil

Compared to countries like Sweden and Canada which have 47 per cent and 21 per cent of women legislators in union legislatures, India has a pitiable 9 per cent. Though this paper would not delve into the intricacies of the reasons of such low percentage of women participation, there is an interesting observation to share. Most of us believe that education is the solution to all problems but it has failed us in this case as is brought forth by the statistics. There seems to be no direct correlation with literacy and the level of political participation of women or at least political support to women candidates. A comparison between the states of Kerala and Rajasthan, whose literacy rates are at opposite ends of the spectrum, demonstrates this clearly. In Kerala, the women literacy rate is reportedly 86 per cent. By contrast, in Rajasthan, female literacy is a mere 20 per cent, and only 12 per cent of females are literate in rural areas. But surprisingly the political participation in both the states is a mere 8 per cent. Some political parties find the solution for this in reservation of seats which is a greater evil in disguise.

The Reservation Bill being the controversy of the day has been getting massive media attention, and rightly so because it is being promoted as a political manoeuvre even though it is replete with flaws. Not only is it undemocratic but also instead of raising participation of women in the political process of the nation it will ghettoise the women and also it will lead to proxy candidates tarnishing the picture of the largest democracy of the world which has a record of being one of the first countries to give franchise to women. This paper seeks to provide feasible alternatives to the Women Reservation Bill which would have a closer nexus with the object of enhancing women participation in the democratic process, than the concept of reservation.

Alternatives to the Bill

Dual Member Constituency

On July 15, 2003, Manohar Joshi, then Speaker of Lok Sabha, convened a four-party[1] meeting to discuss a proposal of dual-member constituencies. Afterwards on July 19, 2003 at the National Executive meeting at Raipur the Bharatiya Janata Party (BJP) passed a resolution to that effect and called upon the government to bring a Constitutional Amendment, to convert one-third of the Lok Sabha constituencies into dual-member constituencies.[2] The highlights of this proposal are:

> The current 543 Lok Sabha constituencies would be grouped into three lots of 181 each. In each election, one of these lots would be converted into dual-member constituencies, each electing two members of parliament - a male and a female. This would increase the number of elected Lok Sabha members[3] to 724 (362 + 181 + 181) from 543 Lok Sabha constituencies. The dual-membership would rotate after each election to the next lot of 181 constituencies. The proposal would also apply to state assemblies and to SC and ST constituencies.

Strengths of the proposal

1. Without lifting the current freeze on delimitation of constituencies it will be possible to create wider opportunities to address the needs of representation of people, who have grown in numbers from 300 million to

over 1,080 million without an increase in the number of representatives.

2. It proposes a win-win solution to the issue of women's quota by providing greater representation to women without depriving men of their existing representation.
3. It will not rupture the process of leadership development, which is a risk involved in the Women's Reservation Bill (WRB).
4. Dual-member constituencies do not undermine the importance of the members. The autonomy of each member in dual-member constituencies can be guaranteed by ensuring the same MP Local Area Development Fund[4] for each of them. This would also mean that the dual-member constituencies would get double development fund than single-member constituencies, for one term.

The proposal of dual-member constituencies makes up only to 25 per cent as opposed to the 33 per cent promise of the WRB. This reduction from 33 per cent to 25 per cent can be compensated by way of women's reservation in Rajya Sabha and legislative council.

But one major drawback of this would be that rotation of the dual constituencies means rotation of those reserved seats for women. Though this does away with the provision of destabilising male candidates it still keeps the situation the same for female candidates for whom the dual constituencies would change every election. In a full circle we come back to the flaws of the present Bill itself. Also there are chances that women become add-ons in a new constituency which has been a battleground for the persisting male candidate for years.

Reservation in Political Parties

The important provisions of the proposed Alternative Bills are as follows:

1. A law should be enacted amending The Representation of the People Act, 1951, to make it mandatory for every

recognised political party to nominate women candidates for election in one-third of the constituencies.

2. Each party can choose where it wishes to nominate women candidates, duly taking local political and social factors into account.
3. Among seats reserved for SCs and STs also, one-third of the candidates nominated by recognised parties shall be women.
4. To prevent a party from nominating women candidates only in states or constituencies where the party's chances of winning election are weak, and to ensure an even spread of women candidates, the unit for consideration (the unit in which at least one out of three party candidates shall be a woman) for the Lok Sabha shall be a state or union territory; for the state legislative assembly, the unit shall be a cluster of three contiguous Lok Sabha constituencies.
5. In the event of any recognised party failing to nominate one-third women candidates, for the shortfall of every single woman candidate, two male candidates of the party shall lose the party symbol and affiliation and all the recognition-related advantages.
6. A law amending Articles 80 and 171 of the Constitution should be enacted providing for women's reservation of one-third of the seats, elected or nominated, to Rajya Sabha or legislative councils. Corresponding amendments need to be made in the Fourth Schedule of the Constitution and, the Representation of the People Act, 1950.

Advantages of this model

1. Parties will be free to choose their female candidates and constituencies depending on local political and social factors. They will nurture women candidates where they can offer a good fight rather than in pre-fixed lottery based constituencies, where they may or may not have viable women candidates. Thus there is flexibility and promotion of natural leadership.

2. A woman candidate will be contesting both against female and/or male candidates of rival parties. Therefore, the democratic choice of voters is not restricted to compulsorily electing only women candidates. Also as women members are elected in competition with other candidates – without reserving seats – they will be seen as legitimate representatives in the eyes of the public and not just beneficiaries of charitable measures.
3. A winning woman candidate will have been elected on her own strength, backed by party support. She will not be a mere proxy or political lightweight.
4. There will be no need for rotation of reservation. Therefore the elected women and men can nurture their constituencies and emerge as major political figures in their own right, with an independent power base.
5. Parties will be able to nominate women from backward castes (BCs), minorities and other communities for elective office in areas where there is electoral advantage to them. This obviates the need for a quota within quotas, an issue which has blocked the existing bill. Those who are concerned about BC representation need not settle merely for one-third quota for BC women within the 33 per cent women's quota as they are demanding now. They can field as many BC or minority women as they think appropriate.
6. This method is most likely to find favour with political parties and incumbent legislators, as there will be no fear of being uprooted at short notice by draw of lots. Both compulsory reservation and regular rotation are avoided.
7. Unlike with the lottery system of reserved constituencies, in which women's presence is likely to get ossified at 33 per cent since there would be resistance to letting women contest from non-reserved constituencies, this model allows for far greater flexibility in the number and proportion of women being elected to legislatures. If women are candidates for one-third of all seats contested by each party, theoretically they could even win the vast majority of seats—all on merit.

8. This model also provides for reservation of seats for women in the upper houses.

However, given the present state of affairs, it is likely that, to begin with, about one-third of the contested seats will be won by women. But this percentage is likely to grow over time as women gain more confidence and strength. It also ensures that their presence in legislatures more nearly reflects their actual electoral strength so that they are not seen as mere recipients of charitable measures. But with this are attached quite a few disadvantages as well, which are as follows:

1. There is no guarantee that a significant number of women would get elected.
2. Political parties may assign women candidates to constituencies where they are weak.
3. This might lead to resentment if a woman is accommodated to the disadvantage of a stronger male candidate.
4. The most important disadvantage is that it would be totally undemocratic and unconstitutional to make it compulsory for the political parties to reserve seats for women, as it *ipso facto* violates the Article 19(1)(c) which reads as the right to freedom to form an association or union.

Another innovative proposal was put forth by Shetkari Sangathan of Maharashtra in its Aurangabad conference of 1993 on seat reservation for women which seems to be more promising than the mechanical, rotating, quota system being currently proposed in the parliament. This proposal was formulated after the Sangathan carried out a review of the results of the one-third reservation quota for women at the panchayat and zilla parishad levels.

The proposal advocates the creation of multi-seat constituencies, with one-third of the seats reserved for women. For instance, three constituencies could be clubbed together to make one and these clubbed constituencies can be represented by three people, one of whom must be a woman. The third seat will go to the woman who has secured the highest number of votes amongst other women candidates. This can further be extended to 50 per cent reservation by making a two-member constituency. This system of representation can be followed in our "first-past-the-post" system, or even if we adopt the proportional system in the future. The advantages of this system can be outlined as follows:

- Representation will not be frozen at 33 per cent only as women can win the general seat as well besides the reserved one. Moreover this system is to be followed in all the constituencies, hence the scope of participation widens.
- All the voters in every constituency will get to vote for women as opposed to the present Bill which proposes only one-third constituencies to vote for women.
- Women would be able to opt for constituency where they have built support rather than shunted around from one constituency to another.
- Men would not feel forced out of their nursed constituencies, but simply asked to spare space with women. All candidates, regardless of sex, would have an opportunity to win one of the first two seats if they are able to garner enough votes. If a party does not wish to field women candidates, it could choose to put up only one or two male candidates. It would not have to draw a total blank in a constituency simply because it did not have eligible women or simply did not want to put up women candidates.
- Women will not be fighting only against women, but would compete with men as well. They would also get an opportunity to team up with male colleagues to cover their joint constituency on behalf of their party, so they would not in any way be confined to the *zenana dabbas*.

In multi-seat constituencies, voters will have the choice to elect leaders from more than one party. If the three (or one of the two) winning candidates are from different parties, they are likely to act as a check on their colleagues and compete with each other in serving the constituency.

An opposition to the model could be that clubbed constituencies might prove unduly large and unwieldy. But then three candidates of the same party are required to campaign and serve it jointly. This may promote a measure of team spirit. Moreover, a big constituency is a disadvantage for only those who step in the electoral fray at the last minute. But those who have nurtured their constituencies by prior hard work would not feel handicapped.

Hence these changes ought to be simultaneously accompanied by other electoral reforms with well-defined rules that allow for public monitoring. However the real cleansing of our politics will take place when the government dismantles the 'license-permit-kickback raj.' Only then would the citizens be free and participate in the governance of the country.

It is thus clear that women's political participation is premised on three fundamental and non-negotiable principles of:

- The equality between men and women;
- Right to full development of women's potentials;
- Right to self-representation and self-determination.

Any step taken to recognise women's voice in our democratic set-up should keep in mind the following points and give them enough "power" to "access," "control" and make "informed choices." By reviewing thoroughly the issues of political mobilisation of women, representation, power distribution and implementing a well-defined, democratic policy to bring the women to the forefront, our country would witness an era of complete liberation and empowerment of women. This is the need for the hour because it is aptly said:

> As a global trend, rising number of women in politics will indicate that human beings are making progress towards a more humane world— not because women are necessarily more humane than men, but because any society that categorically excludes half of its members from the process by which it rules itself will be ruled in a way that is less than fully human.

Works Cited

Alida, Brill, *A Rising Public Voice: Women in Politics Worldwide,* New York, N.Y.: The Feminist Press, 2000, p.1.

Georgina, Ashworth, Gendered Governance: An Agenda for Change, UNDP: Gender in Development, Monograph Series # 3, *Bureau for Development Policy,* March 1996, p.5.

Hamadeh-Banerjee Lina and Paul Oquist, "Women's Political Participation and Good Governance: 21st Century Challenges," *Women's Political Participation and Good Governance: 21st Century Challenges,* UNDP, 2000, p.2.

Isham, Jonathan, D. Narayan and L. Pritchett (1995)."Does Participation Improve Performance? Establishing Causality with Subjective Data," *The World Bank Economic Review,* Vol. 9, No. 2, May.

Menon, Nivedita (2000), "Elusive Women: Feminsim and Women's reservation bill, *Economic and Political Weekly* , vol. 35, Nos. 43, 44, Oct 28, pp.35-42

Raman, Vasanthi, 2003, "The Implementation of Quotas for Women: The Indian Experience." *The Implementation of Quotas: Asian Experiences.* Quota Workshops Report Series No.1, International Institute for Democracy and Electoral Assistance.

Richard L., Johnson Gandhi's soul politics: The liberation of women and men in India, *Gandhi Marg,* Vol XXI, No.1, April-June, 1999.

Sharma, Kumud, "Grassroot Organisations and Women's Empowerment": Some Issues in the contemporary debate, in Samya Shakti, *Centre for Women's Development studies,* New-Delhi, vol. VI, 1991-92, p.29

_____________ 2000, "Power and Representation: Reservation for Women in India," *Asian Journal of Women's Studies. 6* (1).

"The Best Man for the Job? The Selection of Women Parliamentary Candidates," *Finding of the Fawcett Society,* February, 1997, Presented at Listen to Women's Vote, 1998, p.19.

UNIFEM, *Progress of the World's Women 2000: UNIFEM Biennial Report,* New York, N.Y.: UNIFEM, 2000, p.9.

UN Economic and Social Council, *Review and Appraisal of the Implementation of the Beijing Platform for Action,* January 2000, pp.71-72.

14

Growth of Women Organisations in Villages: Its Impact on Political Consciousness and Participation

— Aman

Then let our strengths fuse
With that of our million sisters,
And surge to the moment of change
Moving always towards,
Another time
Another Place,
Of our own making

(Esther Ramani)

Active participation of people in the political activities and not just political participation in the context of decision making from portfolio positions, or being a part of the elections within a democratic set-up does justice to the term that has been coined for such a political system. Ideally, this participation should permeate to all sections of the society.

Political participation needs to be defined far more liberally. It must go beyond the politics seen at the legislative and the executive levels. Sidney Verba defines the same as, "Acts by those who are not formally empowered to make decisions—the acts being those intended to influence the behaviour of those who have such decisional powers."[1] Myron Wiener reciprocates the idea in another way saying that "political participation refers to any voluntary action, successful or unsuccessful, organised or unorganised, episodic or continuous, employing legitimate or illegitimate methods intended to influence the choice of public policies."[2] Both the definitions have something in common, a presumption that there is political consciousness among the participants who influence the people who have the decision making power. Hence to enhance the participation and make democracy more effective, the prerequisite is capacity-building.

It is redundant to elaborate the evident fact that the Indian democratic set-up lacks this basic consciousness at the very roots. However democracy in the modern times has witnessed the emergence of many apolitical organisations which act as vents for the voice of those who have been oppressed through ages. These organisations, apolitical (in the narrow sense) at many times have gone a long way to educate people to form an organised forum to voice their demands. The emergence of these non-state actors has given a new meaning to democracy and political participation which the paper wishes to explore.

The paper wishes to assess the promising nature of these organisations as an instrumental tool to increase the political consciousness of women, who, when compared to the others have been shamelessly secluded from the political process. Putting a thought in this direction would not only lead to better governance by politically empowered women but would also lead to a general rise in the level of consciousness owing to the upper hand women have in reaching out to the other members in the family, especially the growing children. The first part of the paper deals with the rise of politics beyond the state organisations. The second part is why such non-state instruments would help in the enhancement of the political participation of the women. The third section deals with the real life examples of grassroots level women organisations that have shown the rise of political consciousness among the women and Part four concludes the paper.

The Rise of Grassroots Organisations

The growth of the grassroots organisations is a response to the crisis caused by the striking governmental inaction and the rise in the number of people being marginalised. New types of movements have emerged at various levels showing the need of new instruments of political action.[3] Rajni Kothari points out that "This transformation should be understood as a part of a wide range of attempts at redefining the content of politics by the marginalised and the oppressed sections of the society. They need to be seen as a stirring of consciousness engulfing large mass of people."[4] Invigorated by new visions, there is an upsurge in the consciousness among various grassroots organisations functioning all over India. Fighting from structures existing outside the existing structures, they not only define the concept and the structure of politics but go a long way to empower the people.[5] This has given a fresh expression to people's movements which must be preserved to make these "creative impulses," the harbingers of a revolutionary change.[6]

The biased development has created a disorganisation among the masses and the growth of such organised political groups needs to be complimented in this context. Other than emancipation and furtherance of effective democracy, they also come up with the local solutions to many problems and hence have a great utility value.[7]

Women and Grassroots Organisations

The rise of grassroots organisations of women is natural and predictable. Women have been shockingly secluded from the political arena, owing to various reasons. The emergence of such groups among the womenfolk who have been marginalised indicates that they have come out of the cocoon to openly fight for their rights. It is the failure of the established institutions to hear their cause that acts as a major spur for this form of political establishment. The situation is comparable to the emergence of the regional parties in India who came to put forth the interests of the regions in a far more effective manner.[8]

These women organisations go a long way to spread consciousness about the rights and duties. Beyond the struggle, they have a huge contribution in helping women; who have always spent their life in subjugation and oppression, economic dependence, high levels of illiteracy, proclivity of getting misled, low level of public life and prone to character assassination; to make politically sound decisions.[9]At times, people from such organisations go on to contest elections as well.[10] Hence it helps a lot in capacity building.[11] For participation in active politics, women need to break free from the habit of being influenced and must be driven and inspired by issues, specially the ones related to them. Mere reservation would not suffice[12] as numerical equality would not enhance political participation[13] and would just create "Alices in Wonderland."

Women can do many things if they are united as illustrated in the next section which deals entirely with the stories of success of these groups at the grassroots level. Women's unions in villages has made women more "issue oriented" with regards to their political life and have been successful on many accounts in wielding influence in politics, administration and social activities.[14] These things have been tried successfully in Bangladesh and other neighbouring countries where they have voter education, leadership training programmes and political empowerment programmes that have been carried on by the NGO's. [15] Back home even the government has taken some actions to that regard in states like Kerela.[16]

Malaysia's Neelen Heyger defines empowerment by its four components: internal strength; confidence to face life; right to determine choice; and the power to control their life in and outside.[17] It is quite obvious that one of the outcomes of such political consciousness leads a woman to empowerment. It is said that a woman must not only create space but also expand it. The only possible way to achieve so is to be politically more conscious. And this has been seen to rise with these organisations coming into the picture which have been expanding their base; consequently a rise in "quality participation" is witnessed.

South Asian women have borne the greatest burden of poverty, deprivation, illiteracy and morbidity. They have also been the major victims of violence. Yet, contradictorily enough, it is also South Asia that has mobilised thousands of women through grassroots initiatives in rural areas, as in the example of the Grameen Bank project in Bangladesh [18] indicating that the model can very well work to increase the political participation in India as well.

Grassroots Organisations and Their Achievements

In the national movement women carved out a very significant political role for themselves and contributed in nation building so much that Gandhi described them as the best soldier for non-violence and peace. Women equalled men in the revolutionary movement. The consciousness was lost with the disentrenchment of the state from the people.[19] It is only now that after being marginalised for so long that people have come up to form organised groups to be a part of the "politics" of the nation. Some of them have been talked about in this study.

The Government of Rajasthan brought a very revolutionary system to achieve the development of women under the Women's Development Programme where they instituted 800 Sathins in 800 remote villages which created a wave against social justice in the villages. The name of the group became *Sathino ke Karyakarme* owing to the popularity of the entire endeavour.[20] They brought a serious decline in the rate of child marriages in Rajasthan. The Sathins have been very successful in finding solutions for their local problems. In various instances, they have achieved their objectives against the interests of the upper classes and the government at times. Women in Datan village got two hand-pumps installed in the lower caste villages against the upper class resistance.[21] Sathins of Kalsera village forced the mate to re-institute 11 female workers he had arbitrarily dismissed from the famine works.[22] In Malwa Chora, the women were involved in the shutting down of the illicit distillation of liquor which was the reason for alcoholism and beating of the wives.[23] However, being a government-based body, it faced resistance when it went against the interests of the government.[24] But the Sathins have become quite popular and an entity independent of the government. They have done full justice in "empowering the women through communication of information, education and training to enable them to recognise and improve their social and economic status; in rediscovering the self confidence and faith in themselves."[25] Women like Bhanwari Bai who, in spite of facing a horrific thing like a rape, have continued their fight against child marriages.[26] Many sub-groups have also been formed under the umbrella of this group, and they work as independent grassroots organisations towards the emancipation of women.[27] Many of the Sathins are now a part of the active governance of the village from elected positions.[28]

"Gulabi Gang," another apolitical organisation, is fighting for women's rights in Banda, which is at the heart of the blighted region of Bundelkhand. To make things worse, it is a highly caste-ridden, male-dominated society, and Sampat Lal Devi and her "Gang for Justice" tries to go against this very set-up. They are a women's vigilante group aiming to root out the corrupt, and be self-reliant. They claim they have returned 11 girls who were thrown out of their homes to their spouses.[29]

Instances of "collective authority of power" of women are seen widely in Uttarakhand where owing to the lower employment opportunities, men migrate leaving the women to deal with the callous administration.[30] The women in Chamaila (Tehri Garhwal) are fighting corruption at the grassroots level with the assistance of Chetna Andolan, and have made their Employment Assurance Scheme successful.[31] It was only because of the informal organisation of women in Almora in 1980 that the hill could be saved from the onslaught of the mine that was built on the top of the hill. It was the concerted efforts of the women that led to the cancellation of the mining lease.

Scattered efforts have been taken in many villages by women's organisations without any external supports to fight the Anti-alcohol addiction movements. Such movements have been a huge success in various parts of the country: Meira Palbis of Manipur, Shramik Sangathan in Orissa, movements by grassroots women's organisations that began in Debagatta village, Nellore, Andhra Pradesh.[32]

Radhika Devi of the Chakdalar Group in the village by the same name in Uttaranchal is illiterate but when it comes to discussing issues that affect society actually doing something about it, and she never steps back. The women in her group are planning something about education. In Andhra Pradesh, Satyavathi, who is part of a women's self-help group, spearheads the movement in her village to solve issues of land to the poor.[33]

With the aid of Non-Governmental Organisations too, many local organisations have been formed. With the assistance of Jagori, an NGO based in Delhi, samitis have been formed in Bawana to see the proper functioning of the Public Distribution System.[34]

Most examples show that these organisations are in a very nascent stage. Very little is thought about them in the academic sphere as well. To give a boost to these organisations would help in managing many problems that the state faces today.

CONCLUSION

Political participation as discussed earlier has to be liberally defined in a democratic set-up. It would be a significant enhancement in participation and consciousness if more people can express their opinions in the governmental process. The rise of the grassroots organisations have given a platform and voice to all those who were least conscious and the most oppressed sections of the society, thereby paving a way towards qualitative involvement from these people and, in the context of this paper, the women in the villages.

The success of these organisations lies not only in the results they have achieved as a consequence of their concerted actions but also evidence how the women in villages organise and express themselves on problems that exist in the society. Such form of activism by the women organisations is a logical corollary of the enhancement of political consciousness and effective participation in the political process. In most villages, the rise of movements by the women is a commendable achievement in terms of the political emancipation when seen against the traditional seclusion of women in the socio-political context.

However the rise in these civil society organisations might be a threat to the country as well if there is an unchecked growth of such groups,[35] and hence the government should step in and promote such multifaceted approach towards democracy. They should, in a way, regulate their sphere of activities without compromising on the quintessential bit of allowing these organisations to find local solutions and make democracy at the grassroots more effective.

We can neither be sure of the outcome of such an emergence nor can we be optimistic about the same. But we need to recognise that the consciousness that is emerging is serious and genuine. It may still be weak, fragmented, lacking in resources and influenced by all kinds of organisational and theoretical crisis[36] but it is a must that such a genuine and emerging consciousness be encouraged by all parts of the society, and thought be put in the same regard so that the end result of the enhancement of the political participation of the women is in a far more qualitative way.

References

1. K.A. Kunjakkan, *Feminism and Indian Realities,* New Delhi: Mittal Publications, 2002, p.378.
2. Ibid. p.378.
3. Rajni Kothari, *Rethinking Democracy,* Haingatnagar: Orient Longman, 2005, p.136.
4. Ibid. p.139.
5. Ibid. p.140.
6. Ibid. p.141.
7. Ibid. p.137.
8. Ibid.
9. *Ibid.* n.1, p.380; Farah Kabir, "Political Participation of Women in South Asia" retrieved from << http://www.nwmindia.org/resources/research/links.htm >>.
10. An example of this would be Bhanwari Bai, a Dalit woman of a remote village Bhattri in Bassi Tehsil in Rajasthan joined the Sathin Samoh.
11. K.A., Kunjakkan, op.cit., p.378.
12. Ibid. p.388.
13. Ibid. p.388.
14. Ibid. p.402.

15. Farah Kabir, op.cit.
16. In the state of Kerala systematic gender training programmes for women in panchayats have been conducted and technical training on gender-budgeting of projects imparted by the government.
17. K.A., Kunjakkan, op.cit.,
18. Farah Kabir, op.cit.
19. Rajni Kothari, *op.cit.*, pp. 45-54.
20. Manimala, "Bhanwari Bai's brave struggle for Justice" retrieved from << http://www.pucl.org/from-archives/Dalit-tribal/bhanwari-bai.htm>>.
21. "Development for whom ?-A critique on the Women's Development Programme" (October, 1991)

    <<http://74.125.153.132/search?q=cache:RrYhZtzcY-QJ:cssh.unipune.ernet.in/HumanRights/07%2520STATE%2520AND%2520GENDER/09.pdf+"Mahila+Samooh+Kekri"&cd=1&hl=en&ct=clnk&gl=in >>.
22. Ibid.
23. Ibid.
24. Ibid.
25. Sharada Jain et. al., "Exploring Possibilities: A review of the Women's Development Programme", Jaipur:Institute of Development Studies, 1987, pp. 13-15.
26. Manimala, op.cit.
27. An example of this is the Mahila Samoh Kekri, a local women's group in the nine villages of the Kekri Panchayat Samiti that has stemmed from the Sathin Samooh.
28. Development for whom?, op.cit.
29. Soutik Biswas, "India's 'Pink' Vigilante Group," BBC News, Banda, November 26, 2007 retrieved from << http://news.bbc.co.uk/2/hi/south_asia/7068875.stm>>.
30. "Mobilising them against a callous administration," retrieved from << http://uttarakhand.prayaga.org/news-1997-1.html>>.
31. Ibid.

32. Nitin Sethi, "Tiny steps to a women's march," *The Times of India,* March 8, 2007 retrieved from << http://timesofindia.indiatimes.com/India/Tiny_steps_to_a_womens_march/articleshow/1733700.cms>>.
33. Azera Rahman, "Winds of change blow among rural Indian women," *Thaiindian News,* March 7, 2008 as read from << http://www.thaindian.com/newsportal/uncategorised/winds-of-change-blow-among-rural-indian-women_10024879.html>>.
34. "For a handful of Rice", retrieved from<<http://jagori.org/wp-content/uploads/2006/10/for-a-handful-of-rice.pdf>>.
35. Jeff Haynes, *Democracy in the Developing World,* London: Blackwell Publications, 2001, p. 122.
36. Rajni Kothari, op.cit., p.137.

15

Political Participation of Women in India

—Kamala Kumari

> You can tell the condition of a nation by looking at the status of its women.
>
> *—Jawaharlal Nehru*

Patriarchy and the obvious gendered notions of what a woman's place should be sometimes have specific agencies that contrive to keep women tied down to what are considered traditional roles. In India the continuing patriarchal, caste and religious structures hinder women's emancipation. Despite continued lip-service to the ideal of political and social equality for women, things have not moved forward as much as the women themselves would like. In this context it is important to study the reactions that women have had to their continued lack of representation in the political arena, the kind of initiatives that they have taken and the consequences. This paper critically analyses the participation of women in the political process in India on the basis of the 2004 general elections and recently held elections in five state assemblies.

Ever since India got independence, politics in the country has been male-dominated. Indian women are barely present in political process as well as the internal organisation of political parties. Even if they get some ranks in any party, their role generally remains confined to women or to the issues surrounding women. Thus it can be said that political participation of women in India is inadequate. The paper attempts to bring forth key reasons for the lack of political participation of women duly endorsed by facts and figures. Traditionally in India, women were never a part of decision making barring a few exceptions. These practices are still prevalent in several parts of India. Lack of opportunities and absence of education are two key factors responsible for their awareness level. Although there are several bodies dealing with women related issues, yet they are not always effective.

Marginalisation of women and insincere efforts of mainstreaming them into the political process play a detrimental role in their current level of political participation. It remains difficult for any women coming from an average household to climb up the political ladder. There is no doubt that there are several women holding key positions at various political levels, but given the size of their share in the electorate and population, their political participation is not encouraging. Women cannot exercise their rights and enjoy liberties till they are given their due share. This is the reason why their presence is hardly felt when important decisions for the countries or for women welfare are made.

There is no denying that India figures among the first few states in the world to have a woman as head of the government and head of the state.[1] Indian women got the right to equal political participation, including their right to vote, much earlier than most of the Western countries.[2] In the regional political scenario there are few women who have become prominent centres of power in their respective states, for instance, Mayawati in Uttar Pradesh, Jayalalitha in Tamil Nadu or Mamata Banerjee in West Bengal. They also have got significant influence on the national politics. However, it should also be kept in mind that these women entered politics and rose to glory because of their proximity to male leaders. Excepting a few women, politics in India is still a male bastion.

For sustainable economic and social development in any country, it is necessary that people participate in the political process. It is not possible to assume that all sections of the population take part effectively in the political and democratic processes of society. There are many reasons why people may not participate – from apathy to a sense of helplessness – and women are particularly vulnerable to falling into this category.

India is a society noted for its contradictory nature, segmentation, and ideological and political diversity. Despite several socio-political changes in post-independence India, the country continues to be driven by caste and religious violence that have affected the political and civil rights of its citizens. Democratic institutions, in spite of years of operation, are often weak and corrupt. And following the beginning of the liberalisation process of the economy in the 1990s, socio-economic conditions too have changed immensely altering the structure of society-state interactions. In the socio-economic realm, the development of private initiative and globalisation have resulted in better standards of living and a quality of life for the vast majority of people which fall far short of what can be considered adequate.

Women in India are not free from the impact of globalisation. Due to information technology revolution and journalistic and judicial activism, women issues have received considerable attention. As a result, political participation of women has certainly increased. But it has been noticed that on the whole the advantages of a liberalised economy and globalisation have accrued more to women of the higher strata of society rather than those from the lower rungs. The latter in fact, have faced greater problems in certain instances, particularly in the rural sector where crop failures have led to a spate of farmers' suicides, and the breakdown of the public distribution system has led to starvation deaths.

One of the key findings of the papers is that unless women get adequate political representation, their problems will remain unheard. Socio-economic and cultural factors are also responsible for the lack of representation and should be addressed. In spite of the fact that India has a long list of laws to protect the rights of women, including the Prevention of Immoral Traffic, the Sati (widow burning) Act, and the Dowry Prevention Act, and also that women have figured prominently in the government's agenda of social reforms and initiatives, the condition of women in India is not really encouraging.

Constitutional Provisions

According to Article 14 of the Constitution of India, all citizens are equal. In practice, we are not. It is evident in day-to-day life that despite almost equal to men in terms of numbers, women are a neglected lot, particularly in politics. Women in Indian politics are marginally represented.[3] As evident from the facts discussed below, like the developed countries, women in India need emancipation.

The Constitution of India makes the gender equality mandatory. In reality, the equality cannot be achieved unless women have adequate representation in the law-making bodies. Women are getting representation, but in terms of percentage, it is negligible. It is an established fact that India promises more theoretically than it actually offers to women. While women were granted equal rights to men the actual state of affairs belied the spirit of these laws. Women in India are under-represented in almost all the sectors including the political sphere. As far as statistical figures of the Election Commission of India are concerned, women participation has remained considerably low. Despite the fact that India figures among the first few countries to have women holding the topmost posts including that of the Prime Minister, the President, Governors and even several Chief Ministers, the country does not have proportionate political representation for women. Women in India constitute almost 50 per cent of the electorate, however the proportion of women parliamentarians has not exceeded 10 per cent of the total elected candidates.

Therefore, a complete overhauling of the system is the need of the hour. To put in the words of Devaki Jain, "The quest for equity cannot come about without wider representation of all groups, especially those currently denied access to power, and the presentation of all points of view in the process of decision-making. Revision of the current administrative and political structures, and their rules, is necessary in order to facilitate this broader representation and its translation into political power for those who are currently marginalised."[4]

Actual State of Affairs

Given the socio-cultural and agrarian background of the country, women representation in India can be ensured through reservation of women in legislatures. Despite years of deliberations and bickering in the political circles, ironically, the Women's Reservation Bill still has to see the light of day. Paradoxically, the ruling coalition, UPA has Sonia Gandhi, as its chairperson, but none of the constituents of the coalition government has reserved seats for women either in party organisation, in the assembly or parliamentary elections. BJP is the only party so far to announce 33 per cent of seats reserved for women in its party organisation. But when it comes to actual power sharing, women remain a neglected lot excepting few.

Within different political parties, the women members are generally marginalised as far as actual decision-making bodies are concerned, and seldom influence the important party policies. They are confined to the "women's cells" of the party and are supposed to take care of specific "women's issues" such as dowry and rape cases. Ironically women protests are also limited to domestic and kitchen related issues like inflation and domestic violence.

All this goes against the spirit of the Constitution and the commitments of the politicians. Whatever said and done, the fact remains that the importance of women in the politics or nation building cannot be overlooked. Women occupy a significant portion in all walks of life and deserve a fair deal of representation both at the national as well as the regional levels. Looking at the achievement of the women leaders in India, most of them have dynastic advantage, including UPA chairperson Sonia Gandhi. But her achievements as a woman leader are commendable. Jayalalitha and Mayawati initially may have risen in politics because of their proximity to or support from male leaders, but they exercise a considerable degree of influence on their own parties as well as national politics. Mamata Banerjee fought her way to glory through several odds and she could rise to the elite political circles on her own. Sheila Dikshit has carved a niche for herself and can be termed as one of the most successful Chief Ministers in India. Although she maintains a low political profile and has become an important woman leader in the present times by leading her party to a third consecutive victory in the Delhi Legislative Assembly, ironically, other than herself, she has only two women ministers in her council of ministers.[5] Vasundhara Raje is yet another example though not very successful as compared to other female leaders. Ironically, the number of these women leaders is very low, and despite their key positions and long tenures in power, they have not done anything substantial to improve the representation of women either in the organisational structure of their own parties or otherwise. Under the present set of conditions, it has been proved that women leaders are neither worse nor better than their male counterparts. Even the strongest woman in the independent India's history, Mrs Indira Gandhi, was also not an exception to this rule.

Moreover, women's representation in national legislative bodies, while important on the ground of social justice and legitimacy of the political system, does not easily translate into improved representation of women's interests. Indeed, despite, the best of intentions, the Women's Reservation Bill introduced in 1998, ended up on the side of controversy and was eventually buried in the flux of the Indian male-ordered politics.

India has passed laws that make it mandatory for local governments to include women. These laws do not apply to state and national level legislatures. One-third of the seats in local bodies – gram or village panchayats, municipalities, city corporations and district bodies – are reserved for women. It would be an exaggeration to say that women got empowered with the Panchayati Raj Act and by giving positions in the panchayats. In practice, their political significance is mostly symbolic. Their caste, class, and religious identities in the society run deeper than their gender identity. In case of a conflict between any of the two identities, the obvious preference will be religion, caste, class and then the gender – the first in order is the first in preference. The biggest drawback of this kind of reservation is that it leads to "proxy" representation, where women legislators run as "fronts" for their husbands or other male interests. Jane S. Jaquette contests that "In India... there are many anecdotal cases of this phenomenon."[6]

There is a strong need to draw a line between women who come from a political background and women who have somehow got the opportunity to contest owing to the 73rd Amendment. It is painful to observe that the Women's Reservation Bill is still awaiting political consensus among different parties. This reflects the hypocrisy of the politicians and the lack of support for issues related to women.

There is a substantial history of women's political rights in India. However, as has been seen the world over, rights on paper did not automatically translate into power, in the hands of women in practice. India is emerging as an economic power and compared to other developed countries has better track record as far as democracy and other human rights related issues are concerned. It is imperative on India to improve its image in ensuring equality to all its citizens irrespective of gender. In this regard, India can set Scandinavian countries as a benchmark. These countries have the highest percentage of women representatives. Moreover, with the increased political participation of women in India, the democracy will further deepen as well as grow stronger. The Women's Reservation Bill, if passed, will be instrumental in supplementing the positive results of the panchayati raj legislation.

International Situation

The international situation as far as political representation of women in the world is concerned is also not very encouraging for women. There are 8,028 women parliamentarians constituting 15.38 per cent as compared to 44,170 men in the national parliaments which is 84.62 per cent of the total.[7]

India ranks 107 as far as the percentage of women in the country's parliament is concerned.[8] According to the Inter-Parliamentary Union (IPU), India has 49 (9.1 per cent) women representative in Lok Sabha out of 541 and 24 (9.9) women representatives in Rajya Sabha out of 243. India stands at number 68 as far as its ranking in giving the number of ministerial berths to women is concerned. In India, out of a total 39 ministerial positions, only four are given to (10.3 per cent) women representatives.[9] The only place where India could perform fairly well is the position of the head of the state. India figures among the top seven (4.7 per cent) countries out of 150 to have a woman as the head of the state. The world average of women in parliament is 17.7 per cent and the Asian average is 16.7 per cent while India's average representation is less than 10 per cent.[10]

Women in Indian Politics

Women are as ever under-represented in the election fray and in party structures, but in many ways, they have never been as important as they are today. It is been observed that during the elections, the issue of providing one-third reservation for women in legislative bodies including the parliament gains more importance. After the elections are over nobody pays any heed to it barring a few women activists and women NGOs. The issue of reservation for women has gained a little momentum when all the women legislators across the party line came together in its support, but getting it approved in the parliament still remains a distant dream.

Women's Political Representation in India

Table 1: Women's Representation in Parliament

Year	*Total* Seats	*Lok* Sabha	*Percent-* age	*Total* Seats	*Rajya* Sabh*a*	*Percent-* *age*
1952	499	22	4.4	219	16	7.3
1957	500	27	5.4	237	18	7.5
1962	503	34	6.8	238	18	7.6
1967	523	31	5.9	240	20	8.3
1971	521	22	4.2	243	17	7.0
1977	544	19	3.4	244	25	10.2
1980	544	28	7.9	244	24	9.8
1984	544	44	8.1	244	28	11.4
1989	517	27	5.3	245	24	9.7
1991	544	39	7.2	245	38	15.5
1996	543	39	7.2	223	20	9.0
1998	543	43	7.9	245	15	6.1
1999	543	49	9.0	245	19	7.8
2004	539	44	8.2	245	28	11.4

Source: *http://www.indiastat.com/*

Table 1 shows that the percentage of women in Lok Sabha was the highest in 1999 when it touched the 9 per cent mark. In the Rajya Sabha of the parliament, it never exceeded more than 11.4 per cent.

Political Parties and Women

Let's examine the policy documents of few of these parties and statements made by the leaders on women-related issues. One of the policy documents of the BJP clearly says that the party is committed to women's all-round empowerment; the BJP is ready to back any consensus formula to ensure early legislation for women's reservation in parliament and state legislatures. It further says, "The BJP is committed to gender equality and justice. We consider educational, social, economic and political empowerment of women to be one of the preconditions for making India a Developed Nation. ...In the 21st century, it is once again necessary for men to play a constructive role in establishing gender equality. They can play an especially crucial role in ensuring dignity of women and eliminating violence against them. Ours was the first party to raise the demand for 33 per cent reservation for women in Parliament and State legislatures. We remain committed to this goal. ...The BJP is prepared to support any alternative proposal for women's reservation, on which broad consensus can be forged."[11] However, it remains difficult to digest that the same party could not offer more than 11 per cent of seats to women in the recently held elections.[12]

The Constitution of INC makes it mandatory to reserve not less than 33 per cent seats for women at the different levels in the organisational structure but it contradicts the party's stand when it comes to sharing power at the policy making level. Among the 39 cabinet ministers including the Prime Minister, there are only two women cabinet ministers. Among eight Minister of State (Independent Charge), only two are women and six women state ministers out of 40.[13] The present state of affairs is also not very encouraging in any of the states, be it led by the INC, the BJP or any other political party. Any analysis of the candidates fielded by the various political parties will show that women account for a non-significant percentage of all candidates across parties and regions. Same is true for the party being led by women leaders, be it the congress, the Trinamul Congress or the BSP. This trend has remained almost unchanged since independence.

In the last general elections the most audacious supporters of Women's Reservation Bill did not field enough women candidates. In no case the number of women candidates was more than 10 per cent of the total candidates launched by any national political party. Table 2 shows that all six major national political parties including the Bharatiya Janata Party (BJP), the Bahujan Samajwadi Party (BSP), the Communist Party of India (CPI), the Communist Party Marxist (CPM), the Indian National Congress (INC) and the National Congress Party (NCP), altogether fielded 110 women candidates out of which only 30 could manage to win. Altogether 355 women were in the election fray, including state/regional parties; out of them only 45 women candidates were elected.[14] There is no denying that among those who finally contested and won the elections were the most influential women who also have strongholds in the inner party structures. Therefore, it is proved that women, by and large, are less represented in all the parties and in all parts of the country.[15]

Assembly Elections in Five States: Performance of Women Candidates

In sum, the BJP fielded only 76 female candidates out of its total list of 653 in all the six states which amounts to 11 per cent of the total. The BSP launched 39 women candidates out of 670, nearly six per cent of the total. The more progressive parties like the CPI just have four women candidates in all the six states out of its total list of 140 candidates which is close to 3 per cent. The CPM could not find any suitable female candidate in all the six states, however the party had a total of 66 candidates contesting elections in these six states which underwent democratic process of elections recently. The INC remained quite close to the BJP and had given its election tickets to 75 women candidates out of its staggering total of 703 and thus had slightly more than 10 per cent of women candidates. The NCP could only find and launch three women candidates out of their total of 86 candidates, i.e., 3.5 per cent of its total number of candidates. With the BJP and Congress being exceptions, no other national party could cross the 10 per cent. Satirically, we find the strongest advocates of adequate representation to women at all political level through Women Reservation Bill or otherwise. Out of total 2,328 candidates launched by these national parties, only 197 were women.

Table 2

Number of Contestants State-Wise: Assembly Elections 2008

Parties	*States*	*J&K*	*MP*	*Mizo-ram*	*Rajas-than*	*Chattis-garh*	*Delhi*
BJP	Male	59	205	7	161	80	65
	Female	5	23	2	32	10	4
	Total	64	228	9	193	90	69
BSP	Male	79	215	0	187	82	68
	Female	4	13	0	12	8	2
	Total	83	228	0	199	90	70
CPI	Male	7	21	0	20	20	68
	Female	0	0	0	1	1	2
	Total	7	21	0	21	21	70
CPM	Male	8	12	0	34	8	4
	Female	0	0	0	0	0	0
	Total	8	12	0	34	8	4
INC	Male	74	199	39	177	77	62
	Female	4	29	1	23	10	8
	Total	78	228	40	200	87	70
NCP	Male	18	3	6	37	3	16
	Female	1	0	0	2	0	0
	Total	19	3	6	39	3	16

Source: Election Commission of India, http://eci.nic.in/

Conclusion

The Indian political scene is gradually changing as more women are entering into politics across the country irrespective of their educational, regional, socio-economic background. Panchayati raj institutions have played a vital role in empowering rural women to a considerable level. Still much remains to be done. There also exists a view that says ensuring women's representation through quotas may change the nature of political competition and thus have direct effects as it has been proved that both men and women have different preferences in terms of developmental works.[16]

The Women's Reservation Bill optimises the promises made to women by various political parties and leaders. However, the bill is still pending in the Parliament. There is a need to think out of the box and go for effective and instantaneous solutions. Otherwise, following the examples of the West, Indian women may have to resort to options like having their own political parties. This may not work for long but will definitely draw the attention of the larger Indian community towards women issues. In an unequal society, women have a long winding path to scale before they can command the same respect that a male politician does.

In particular, unless specific conditions are met, women face multiple hurdles and find it difficult to participate in the political process that has hitherto been a male bastion. The reasons for this are gender specific. Women are less mobile than men are. They have domestic responsibilities, which puts limits on the time they can spend in such processes. And then there are historical prejudices. Besides, until the establishment of equality in employment and income, equality of social rights will only accentuate the actual inequality between men and women.

Two facts are clear from the wider political picture in India; first, Indians are not averse to having women leaders but the overall system will be governed and run by the menfolk, and the second is that women leaders themselves are not very keen on the question of women's political emancipation. Women leaders are acceptable in the political system but at the same time the voices of ordinary women or even those of party workers remain unheard. Media also plays a significant role in projecting these women leaders as the women heroines but do not question their accountability and commitment as far as Women issues are concerned. A majority of the Indian women have confined themselves to traditional patriarchal notions of femininity and do not fight for their basic rights including political participation and representation.

The lack of inner party democracy and almost opaque functioning of Indian political parties can also be held accountable for not giving women a fair chance to excel politically. Party hierarchy is usually determined by the number of years of service to that particular political party. For most women it is highly unlikely to spend their entire lifetime in the party like their male counterparts. This suggests that the political empowerment cannot be achieved without active political awareness and participation. Women are to be made to lead the society and hence the country from the front. The fact of the matter is that women have a long way to go. To put it in the words of Jayati Ghosh, "this is not to say that the electoral representation of women is unimportant, but rather that it needs to be both deeper and wider than its current manifestation in the form of the prominence of a few conspicuous women leaders."[17]

REFERENCES

1. "Women in Politics 2008," as on January 2009. Data based on the report of Inter-Parliamentary Union (IPU) http://www.ipu.org/wmn-e/world.htm
2. Before independence also there were several influential women organisations such as the All India Women's Conference and National Council for Women and women leaders like Annie Besant and Sarojini Naidu, who fought for women's rights. Due to their efforts, around 10 lakh women got right to vote as early as 1919 under the Montaague-Chelmsford Reforms. Women were even allowed to contest and they were elected as the public representatives. Women's political rights were gradually enhanced in subsequent Government of India Acts and by the time of independence, all women were given equal rights and liberties without any discrimination. See R. Letha Kumari, *Women in Politics: Participation and Governance*, Delhi: Authorspress, 2006, p. 9.
3. Madhavi Lakshmi Kondreddy, "Construction of Gender: Deprivation of Women from Politics in India" in Kiran Saksena, (ed.), *Women in Politics*, New Delhi: Gyan Publishing House, 2000, p. 33.
4. Devaki Jain (September 1996), "Panchayat Raj: Women Changing Governance," As read on http://www.onlinewomeninpolitics.org/india/1996_undp_panchayat.htm
5. See Delhi Government's Official website for more information, http://delhigovt.nic.in/cabn/welcome.html.
6. Jane S. Jaquette, "Women in Power: From Tokenism to Critical Mass," *Foreign Policy*, No. 108 (Autumn, 1997), p. 33.
7. Women in Politics: 2008, As on January 2009, http://www.bgipu.org.
8. This calculation is based on the number of women in both houses (wherever applicable, otherwise unicameral legislatures are also counted) of parliaments of all the countries of the world. The data is updated till 1 January 2009 and published by the Inter-Parliamentary Union (IPU) and the United Nations Division for

the Advancement of Women, February 2008.

9. The total includes Deputy Prime Ministers and Ministers. Prime Ministers were also included when they held ministerial portfolios. Vice-Presidents and heads of governmental or public agencies have not been included.
10. Women in Politics 2008, op.cit.
11. See the official website of the Bharatiya Janata Party for more details. http://www.bjp.org/
12. See Table 2.
13. Figures based on the official website of the government of India, http://india.gov.in/govt/cabinet.php#cab.
14. Performance of Women in National Parties vis-à-vis others, Election Commission of India, 2004 (14th Lok Sabha)
15. All India Anna Dravida Munnetra Kazhagam (AIADMK) has been making conscious efforts to bring more number of women into higher echelons within the party remains an exception. Jayati Ghosh, "Women in Indian Politics," *Frontline,* Vol. 16, No. 20, September 25-October 08, 1999.
16. In their study Raghabendra Chattopadhyay and Esther Duflo have found that women representatives, in few of the places, tend to invest more on the programmes which are directly related to their welfare. If these findings are to be generalised then more women representatives in Central and state level will ensure more women-oriented policies. Raghabendra Chattopadhyay and Esther Duflo, "Women as Policy Makers: Evidence From A Randomised Policy Experiment In India," *Econometrica,* Vol. 72, No. 5 (September, 2004), pp. 1409-1443.
17. Jayati Ghosh, "Women in Indian Politics," *Frontline,* op.cit.

16

Institutional Mechanisms to Enhance Women's Political Participation in India

— *Nayanthika R. & Shreya Garg*

Introduction

There is no paucity of mechanisms, institutional or otherwise to increase the representation of women in politics, but before that the question that really needs to be answered is whether there is need for such a thing to achieve the logical end, that is, improve the status of the women in the country. The authors' contention is that only when the society's male chauvinists realise that contesting in elections is not their God-given right, can a woman truly be empowered? It is absolutely true that women are capable of being elected without help from any external mechanism. However, given the prevailing incidence of corruption and power politics, it is extremely rare and increasingly difficult for a woman to be awarded the necessary opportunities to realise her true potential. Therefore we propose the readers to have a look at the below mentioned mechanisms that have been implemented in countries across the world.

Enough time has been wasted, sitting on the issue, in the hope that the representation of women will occur through natural changes. It is not necessary that these mechanisms be made mandatory, but political parties should become aware of the need for increasing the number of women in their parties. If this objective is achieved, they would adopt these on a voluntary basis from time to time to ensure that there is no drop in the number of women. After an analysis of these suggestions probably, the Indian legislature will decide that it is high time that the Indian woman be given her slice of political power, to ensure justice and fairness and to fulfil the commitment to eliminate discrimination against women and achieve gender parity.

WHAT ARE INSTITUTIONAL MECHANISMS?

Institutional mechanisms for the advancement of women is a more inclusive term than merely the infrastructure created by the government[1], and it includes mechanisms and strategies to increase political participation of women. To elaborate, it includes reservations, government structures with a mandate for women, government-sponsored agencies devoted to women's issues, parliamentary committees, local government institutions, mechanisms and plan like gender budgets and component plans, women's bodies and groups, federations, unions and cooperations.[2]

Countries around the world have taken many steps towards the cause of political empowerment of women and various agencies working towards this cause have suggested numerous measures that if adopted, have the potential to enhance the political participation of women exponentially. The paper discusses various kinds of such institutional measures.

Reservation

Reservation is a method where a certain percentage of seats in the legislature are reserved for a particular section of the society. It is provided to that section of the society that have been left behind in the process of socio-economic development; and social and political modernisation. Sometimes the seats in the legislatures are reserved in proportion to the population of that section in the country.

This mechanism is also executed through providing reservation to that section of the population within the registered political parties when they field their candidates at the time of contesting in elections for legislature. Thus, it is mandatory for the political parties that are allowed to contest elections under a common allotted party symbol to reserve the fixed number of tickets to contest for that particular section of the society.

Reservation in Indian politics has been a much awaited, much deliberated upon issue on which no action has been taken so far despite political parties, which, over the years have at the time of their political manifesto made promises of providing reservation for women in the parliament. The concept of reservation proposed in India had its origin in the 81st Amendment Bill that proposes to reserve 33 per cent of seats in the parliament for women. The concept of reservation, interestingly, was initially discarded by the constituent assembly as the women representatives were of the opinion that since ours is a democracy; there would be adequate representation of all sections of the society. In reality however, women especially hailing from the rural areas continued to be largely under represented and their needs were very rarely taken into consideration. Once the women realised this, they started pushing for reservation, akin to the one already in place for minorities.

Research studies have indicated that the presence of women in the parliament would make a huge difference to the whole society and not just the womenfolk. In support of this, an article[3] cites the example of Rwanda where a much-needed legislation on rape and sexual abuse was passed only after women were given seats in the Parliament as men considered the issue a taboo. Till date, though the need for this is very clearly established, there has been hullabaloo surrounding the issue and no legislation has been enacted.

In India the present representation of women in the parliament and state legislative assemblies reveal the stark reality that even after 60 years of independence, women still find themselves unable to compete with men as equals even if they are as qualified because of the sexist approach steeped in the political system. Those who have argued for reservation have put forth arguments that centre on gender balanced representation thereby culminating in better and more beneficial perspectives for development.

The oft quoted argument against providing reservation for women would be Nehru's quote that reservation for any caste, clan or sex is undemocratic and leads to "inefficiency and second-rate standards." However all propounders of this argument seem to have missed the differences between the two terms: distinction and affirmative action. Providing reservation for women will redress and help put women on their own feet. It is next to impossible for a nation to progress and be efficient where nearly half the talent is wasted and is confined within the four walls of the house. The number of women in decision making does not seem to have gone up very sharply, thereby forcing us to face the woeful situation that at the current rate of progress gender parity will remain a dream for a long time to come.

Another bone of contention seems to be that the women so elected through reservation of seats will function as mere puppets and there will be no meaningful participation, reducing the democratic system to a mockery. However when a woman is elected, she will have to perform her allocated duties, attend parliament and cannot be permitted to appoint a non-elected member to do her work for her. She will have to think for herself and if every piece of beneficial legislation is so questioned and its implementation impeded then there will be no piece of welfare legislation in the nation.

Electoral Methods

Apart from the most popular measure to increase women's participation, there are also other mechanisms that can be used to increase the representation of women at the party level. Some of these have been discussed below:

Zipping System

This was a method that was introduced in 1993 in Sweden. According to this system, men and women are alternated on the party list. This is also referred to as the sandwich nomination lists.[4] This system is the reason why Sweden has the highest proportion of women legislators in the developed world.[5] This system was also used in the United Kingdom prior to the 1999 elections to the European parliament. They had lists of candidates for each of the 10 regions of the UK. The first name on the five lists was a woman, with a man in second place; the other five lists were headed by a man, with a woman second. As a result, they had five women and five men elected as Members of European Parliament (MEPs). The greatest disadvantage to the use of this system is that it only works in small constituencies each with several elected representatives, i.e., appropriate for a multi-member constituency. Therefore it becomes a little complex to be applied to the Indian legislatures.

2.2 Twinning System

A modification of this system, known as the *twinning* system, is being used in Wales. In this system, a party pairs two constituencies and ensures that one fields a woman and the other a man.[6] Or another form of this method is where two local parties select their candidates jointly, with a requirement that one man and one woman are selected. This again can be put into work, only in countries/areas divided into small constituencies and where, unlike in India, the political parties can reach a consensus on the candidates. This will be a cumbersome and fruitless exercise in a country like India.

All Women Shortlists (AWS)

All Women Shortlists, or AWS as they are commonly known, has been hailed as the only significant mechanism that has helped boost the number of women representatives in the House of Commons in a short span of time. This method seeks to increase the number of women by allowing only women to stand in particular constituencies.[7] This has been introduced to allow political parties to use all-women shortlists to select candidates for parliamentary elections; elections to the European parliament; elections to the Scottish parliament; elections to the National assembly for Wales; and most local government elections.[8] The hindrance in the working of these systems is that it will be violation of the Constitutional principle of equality as men are altogether debarred from contesting in the election in a certain constituency. This is why it has been introduced with a 'sunset' clause in the United Kingdom. This system, though widely criticised, has been of immense use in bringing women to the forefront of politics.

OTHER MECHANISMS

Trust Funds for Women in Political Parties

Another institutional mechanism is the establishment of trust funds for women within all the political parties. A specified percentage of the party resources should be allocated for this fund, as women face more obstacles than men in raising funds for political campaigning. The advantage of creating such funds is that it will push the political parties towards inducting female candidates and encourage them in making special efforts to do so as a certain portion of their resources will necessarily be reserved for women. Even if no female candidate is contesting, this fund should be employed for media campaigning to encourage female candidates to come forward and participate in the political process for instance, which would help in increasing the political participation of women and will also enhance the image of the political party, and prevent the fund from becoming redundant. This fund should be used exclusively for female candidates.

The roadblock to this mechanism could be the high level of corruption prevalent in the Indian political party system where such funds can be easily misused for purposes other than the specified ones and hence a strong execution mechanism needs to be developed to safeguard this measure and help in its successful implementation.

Amendment to the Companies Act, 1956

Private companies that fund the political parties should be encouraged to incorporate a criteria to the effect that "the party will take substantive steps to increase participation of women in the political party by specific measures," in their mandate that lists the criteria for corporate funding, in pursuance of the concept of corporate social responsibility (CSR).

Until 1969 a company in India was permitted, under Section 293A of the Companies Act, 1956 to contribute a certain amount of money to political parties provided its memorandum of association authorised such contributions. In 1960, the Companies Act was amended to provide a ceiling for donations to political parties.

The intention behind corporate funding is mainly protection of the domestic companies from the entry of multinational corporations[9] and introducing an element of CSR gives a three tier advantage as it works in favour of the company, the political party and, of course, the women.

Strategies

Sandwich Strategy

The sandwich strategy has been very successful in central and eastern Europe, and is oft quoted as the primary reason for the enhancement of political participation of women. The basic premise of the strategy is the establishment of a planned coalition between civil society organisations and international organisations. There is pressure both from below (bottom-up approach from local women's organisations) and from above (top-down approach from the international community such as the UN)[10] to encourage participation of women in politics. The top-down pressure consists of funding and knowhow whereas the bottom-up pressure is used to build up regionally connected and extensive coalitional movements cutting across gender disparity. The two pressures have an effect on the national government and the leaders of the political parties, propelling them to focus on equality issues, specifically political empowerment of women.[11] This strategy, if adopted in India, can increase the political participation of women manifold, it being a signatory to various international conventions on women's rights and the role of local organisations in political empowerment being indispensable.

Parallel Electoral Campaigns

These electoral campaigns are conducted by civil society organisations and women organisations with the support of the government to ensure that women are aware of their political rights and that the voters are aware of the credentials of the female candidates contesting the elections. The role of the organisations in such parallel measures is that of a watchdog of women's rights and freedoms. They are called 'parallel' electoral campaigns as they are conducted simultaneously with the electoral campaigns carried out by candidates of all the political parties. Some of the elements of such an electoral campaign are:

- Encouraging political parties to incorporate gender aspects in their party manifesto;
- Lobbying for the rule that women are given the first or second place on the party list;
- Newsletters, street actions, public debates, media campaign encouraging people to vote for female candidates.

For instance, the parallel electoral campaign for women candidates in Slovenian European elections in 2009 conducted by an NGO lobbied for a rule that in every election, the top of the list should be given to the candidate of the gender, which came second at the former election.[12] Such campaigns are desperately needed for the enhancement of the participation of women in India. It will bring the issue of women political participation in the mainstream electoral campaign and encourage voters and party leaders to discard their bias against female candidates.

Conclusion

After a comprehensive understanding of the above stated mechanisms, it becomes very apparent that the mechanisms adopted in the Western countries cannot be adopted *prima facie* without suitable modifications to suit the Indian political climate. Among the mechanisms, the easiest to adopt one, is easily the system of reservation that is being pressed for by various support groups. So, the legislature should expedite the matter and pass the proposed Amendment without much ado. The other mechanisms of Twinning and Zipping can possible be considered once the corruption level comes down from its current abysmal high. The adoption of trust funds for women by political parties can possibly be made a voluntary resort giving parties that adopt it incentives to continue with the funds. They can be allowed to campaign till 24 hours prior to the election unlike other parties that needs to stop campaigning activities 48 hours prior to the election. The Amendment to the Companies Act will serve the twin purpose of adding to the corpcrate social responsibility of companies as well as enhancing awareness about need for women's participation. The sandwich strategy should be the basic premise for the majority of the strategies directed at women's political participation henceforth. The idea of parallel electoral campaigns should be popularised. Thus, it is not only necessary that the government acts upon this urgent need to increase women's participation but also the women themselves utilise the opportunities provided to them without squandering the resources.

REFERENCES

1. http://www.un.int/india/ind125.htm (Visited on February 2, 2010).
2. Women Group Report on Empowerment of Women for the XI Plan, Ministry of Women and Child Development,

   <http://wcd.nic.in/ > (Visited on February 2, 2010)
3. http://economictimes.indiatimes.com/opinion/columnists/mythili-bhusnurmath/Women-demand-one-third-reservation-in-Parliament/articleshow/4949634.cms (Visited on February 4, 2010)
4. http://www.db-decision.de/CoRe/Sweden.htm (Visited on February 5, 2010).
5. McSmith, Andy (23 August 2006)" The Big Question: Are all-women shortlists the best way to achieve equality in Parliament?"

   <http://www.independent.co.uk/news/uk/politics/the-big-question-are-allwomen-shortlists-the-best-way-to-achieve-equality-in-parliament-412987.html> (Visited on February 4, 2010).
6. http://www.hinduonnet.com/thehindu/mag/2003/05/18/stories/2003051800650300.htm (Visited on February 5, 2010)
7. Ibid.
8. Section 1 (Chapter 2), *Sex Discrimination (Election Candidates) Act 2002.*
9. V. Venkatesan, *Chequered Relations,* Vol.16, n.16,

   http://www.hinduonnet.com/fline/fl1616/16160100.htm (Visited on February 3, 2010).
10. http://www.quotaproject.org/faq.cfm (Visited on February 4, 2010)
11. Drude Dahlerup, *Women, Quota and Politics,* Routledge, Francis & Taylor Group, p.146.
12. http://www.iknowpolitics.org/files/Parallel_NGO_Campaign_Slovenia_Report.pdf (Visited on February 4, 2010).

Annexure – I

Women in National Parliaments Situation as of 31st May 2009

The data in the table below has been compiled by the Inter-Parliamentary Union on the basis of information provided by National Parliaments by 31 May 2009; 187 countries are classified in descending order of the percentage of women in the lower or single house.

Rank	*Country*	*Lower or single House*				*Upper House or Senate*			
		Elections	*Seats**	*Women*	*%W*	*Elections*	*Seats**	*Women*	*%W*
1	Rwanda	9 2008	80	45	56.3	10 2003	26	9	34.6
2	Sweden	9 2006	349	164	47.0	—	—	—	—
3	South Africa	4 2009	400	174	43.5	4 2009	54	16	29.6
4	Cuba	1 2008	614	265	43.2	—	—	—	—
5	Iceland	4 2009	63	27	42.9	—	—	—	—
6	Finland	3 2007	200	83	41.5	—	—	—	—
7	Netherlands	11 2006	150	62	41.3	5 2007	75	26	34.7

(Contd...)

(Contd...)

8	Argentina	10 2007	255	102	40.0	10 2007	72	28	38.9
9	Denmark	11 2007	179	68	38.0	—	—	—	—
10	Angola	9 2008	220	82	37.3	—	—	—	—
11	Costa Rica	2 2006	57	21	36.8	—	—	—	—
12	Spain	3 2008	350	127	36.3	3 2008	263	79	30.0
13	Norway	9 2005	169	61	36.1	—	—	—	—
14	Belgium	6 2007	150	53	35.3	6 2007	71	27	38.0
15	Mozambique	12 2004	250	87	34.8	—	—	—	—
16	New Zealand	11 2008	122	41	33.6	—	—	—	—
17	Nepal	4 2008	594	197	33.2	—	—	—	—
18	Germany	9 2005	612	197	32.2	N.A.	69	15	21.7
19	Andorra	4 2009	28	9	32.1	—	—	—	—
20	Belarus	9 2008	110	35	31.8	7 2008	56	19	33.9
21	Uganda	2 2006	332	102	30.7	—	—	—	—
22	Burundi	7 2005	118	36	30.5	7 2005	49	17	34.7
23	United Republic of Tanzania	12 2005	319	97	30.4	—	—	—	—
24	Guyana	8 2006	70	21	30.0	—	—	—	—
25	Timor-Leste	6 2007	65	9	29.2	—	—	—	—
26	Switzerland	10 2007	200	57	28.5	10 2007	46	10	21.7

(Contd...)

(Contd...)

27	Portugal	2 2005	230	65	28.3	—	—	—	—
27	The F.Y.R. of Macedonia	6 2008	120	34	28.3	—	—	—	—
28	Austria	9 2008	183	51	27.9	N.A.	61	15	24.6
29	Afghanistan	9 2005	242	67	27.7	9 2005	102	22	21.6
30	Peru	4 2006	120	33	27.5	—	—	—	—
31	Namibia	11 2004	78	21	26.9	11 2004	26	7	26.9
32	Trinidad and Tobago	11 2007	41	11	26.8	12 2007	31	13	41.9
33	Australia	11 2007	150	40	26.7	11 2007	76	27	35.5
34	Viet Nam	5 2007	493	127	25.8	—	—	—	—
35	Kyrgyzstan	12 2007	90	23	25.6	—	—	—	—
36	Iraq	12 2005	275	70	25.5	—	—	—	—
36	Suriname	5 2005	51	13	25.5	—	—	—	—
37	Lao People's Democratic Republic	4 2006	115	29	25.2	—	—	—	—
38	Lesotho	2 2007	120	30	25.0	3 2007	31	9	29.0
38	Monaco	2 2008	24	6	25.0	—	—	—	—
39	Singapore	5 2006	94	23	24.5	—	—	—	—

(Contd...)

(Contd...)

40	Liechtenstein	2 2009	25	6	24.0	—	—	—	—
41	Republic of Moldova	4 2009	101	24	23.8	—	—	—	—
42	Seychelles	5 2007	34	8	23.5	—	—	—	—
43	Honduras	11 2005	128	30	23.4	—	—	—	—
44	Luxembourg	6 2004	60	14	23.3	—	—	—	—
45	Mexico	7 2006	500	116	23.2	7 2006	128	23	18.0
46	Tunisia	10 2004	189	43	22.8	8 2008	112	17	15.2
47	Pakistan	2 2008	338	76	22.5	3 2009	100	17	17.0
47	United Arab Emirates	12 2006	40	9	22.5	—	—	—	—
48	Canada	10 2008	308	68	22.1	N.A.	93	32	34.4
48	Mauritania	11 2006	95	21	22.1	1 2007	56	9	16.1
49	Eritrea	2 1994	150	33	22.0	—	—	—	—
49	Senegal	6 2007	150	33	22.0	8 2007	100	40	40.0
50	Ethiopia	5 2005	529	116	21.9	10 2005	112	21	18.8
51	Bulgaria	6 2005	240	52	21.7	—	—	—	—
52	Serbia	5 2008	250	54	21.6	—	—	—	—
53	China	3 2008	2987	637	21.3	—	—	—	—
53	Italy	4 2008	630	134	21.3	4 2008	322	58	18.0

(Contd...)

(Contd...)

54	Croatia	11 2007	153	32	20.9	—	—	—	—
55	Estonia	3 2007	101	21	20.8	—	—	—	—
56	Philippines	5 2007	239	49	20.5	5 2007	23	4	17.4
57	Poland	10 2007	460	93	20.2	10 2007	100	8	8.0
58	Latvia	10 2006	100	20	20.0	—	—	—	—
59	Dominican Republic	5 2006	178	35	19.7	5 2006	32	1	3.1
60	United Kingdom	5 2005	646	126	19.5	N.A.	746	147	19.7
61	Slovakia	6 2006	150	29	19.3	—	—	—	—
62	El Salvador	1 2009	84	16	19.0	—	—	—	—
63	Dominica	5 2005	32	6	18.8	—	—	—	—
64	Bangladesh	12 2008	345	64	18.6	—	—	—	—
64	Venezuela	12 2005	167	31	18.6	—	—	—	—
65	Nicaragua	11 2006	92	17	18.5	—	—	—	—
66	France	6 2007	577	105	18.2	9 2008	343	75	21.9
66	Saint Vincent & the Grenadines	12 2005	22	4	18.2	—	—	—	—
67	Cape Verde	1 2006	72	13	18.1	—	—	—	—
67	Sudan	8 2005	443	80	18.1	8 2005	50	3	6.0
68	Lithuania	10 2008	141	25	17.7	—	—	—	—

(Contd...)

(Contd...)

69	Israel	2 2009	120	21	17.5	—	—	—	—
69	Tajikistan	2 2005	63	11	17.5	3 2005	34	8	23.5
69	Uzbekistan	12 2004	120	21	17.5	1 2005	100	15	15.0
70	Mauritius	7 2005	70	12	17.1	—	—	—	—
71	Bolivia	12 2005	130	22	16.9	12 2005	27	1	3.7
72	Turkmenistan	12 2008	125	21	16.8	—	—	—	—
72	United States of America	11 2008	435	73	16.8	11 2008	98	15	15.3
73	Gabon	1 2009	120	20	16.7	1 2009	102	18	17.6
74	Indonesia	4 2009	560	93	16.6	—	—	—	—
75	Cambodia	7 2008	123	20	16.3	1 2006	61	9	14.8
76	Kazakhstan	8 2007	107	17	15.9	10 2008	47	2	4.3
77	Democratic People's Republic of Korea	3 2009	687	107	15.6	—	—	—	—
78	Czech Republic	6 2006	200	31	15.5	10 2008	81	14	17.3
79	Burkina Faso	5 2007	111	17	15.3	—	—	—	—
80	Zambia	9 2006	158	24	15.2	—	—	—	—
80	Zimbabwe	3 2008	210	32	15.2	3 2008	93	23	24.7
81	Chile	12 2005	120	18	15.0	12 2005	38	2	5.3

(Contd...)

(Contd...)

81	San Marino	11 2008	60	9	15.0	—	—	—	—
82	Greece	9 2007	300	44	14.7	—	—	—	—
83	Cyprus	5 2006	56	8	14.3	—	—	—	—
84	Russian Federation	12 2007	450	63	14.0	N.A.	169	8	4.7
85	Cameroon	7 2007	180	25	13.9	—	—	—	—
86	Djibouti	2 2008	65	9	13.8	—	—	—	—
86	Swaziland	9 2008	65	9	13.8	10 2008	30	12	40.0
87	Republic of Korea	4 2008	299	41	13.7	—	—	—	—
88	Grenada	7 2008	15	2	13.3	8 2008	13	4	30.8
88	Ireland	5 2007	166	22	13.3	7 2007	60	13	21.7
88	Jamaica	9 2007	60	8	13.3	9 2007	21	3	14.3
88	Slovenia	9 2008	90	12	13.3	11 2007	40	1	2.5
89	Sierra Leone	8 2007	121	16	13.2	—	—	—	—
90	Liberia	10 2005	64	8	12.5	10 2005	30	5	16.7
90	Paraguay	4 2008	80	10	12.5	4 2008	45	7	15.6
91	Niger	12 2004	113	14	12.4	—	—	—	—
91	Syrian Arab Republic	4 2007	250	31	12.4	—	—	—	—
92	Bahamas	5 2007	41	5	12.2	5 2007	15	9	60.0

(Contd...)

(Contd...)

93	Uruguay	10 2004	99	12	12.1	10 2004	31	4	12.9
94	Guatemala	9 2007	158	19	12.0	—	—	—	—
95	Bosnia & Herzegovina	10 2006	42	5	11.9	3 2007	15	2	13.3
96	Thailand	12 2007	480	56	11.7	3 2008	150	24	16.0
97	Azerbaijan	11 2005	123	14	11.4	—	—	—	—
97	Romania	11 2008	334	38	11.4	11 2008	137	8	5.8
98	Botswana	10 2004	63	7	11.1	—	—	—	—
98	Hungry	4 2006	386	43	11.1	—	—	—	—
98	Saint Lucia	12 2006	18	2	11.1	1 2007	11	3	27.3
98	Togo	10 2007	81	9	11.1	—	—	—	—
99	India	4 2009	543	59	10.9	7 2008	243	23	9.5
100	Benin	3 2003	83	9	10.8	—	—	—	—
100	Malaysia	3 2008	222	24	10.8	N.A.	59	17	28.8
101	Antigua & Barbuda	3 2009	19	2	10.5	4 2009	17	5	29.4
101	Central African Republic	3 2005	105	11	10.5	—	—	—	—
101	Morocco	9 2007	325	34	10.5	9 2006	270	3	1.1

(Contd...)

(Contd...)

102	Mali	7 2007	147	15	10.2	—	—	—	—
103	Barbados	1 2008	30	3	10.0	2 2008	21	4	19.0
103	Equatorial Guinea	5 2008	100	10	10.0	—	—	—	—
103	Guinea-Bissau	11 2008	100	10	10.0	—	—	—	—
104	Kenya	12 2007	224	22	9.8	—	—	—	—
105	Gambia	1 2002	53	5	9.4	—	—	—	—
105	Japan	9 2005	480	45	9.4	7 2007	242	44	18.2
106	Turkey	7 2007	549	50	9.1	—	—	—	—
107	Brazil	10 2006	513	46	9.0	10 2006	81	10	12.3
108	Cote d'Ivoire	12 2000	203	18	8.9	—	—	—	—
109	Malta	3 2008	69	6	8.7	—	—	—	—
110	Bhutan	3 2008	47	4	8.5	12 2007	25	6	24.0
110	Panama	5 2009	71	6	8.5	—	—	—	—
111	Armenia	5 2007	131	11	8.4	—	—	—	—
111	Colombia	3 2006	166	14	8.4	3 2006	102	12	11.8
111	Democratic Republic of the Congo	7 2006	500	42	8.4	1 2007	108	5	4.6
112	Samoa	3 2006	49	4	8.2	—	—	—	—

(Contd...)

(Contd...)

112	Ukraine	9 2007	450	37	8.2	—	—	—	—
113	Ghana	12 2004	228	18	7.9	—	—	—	—
114	Algeria	5 2007	389	30	7.7	12 2006	136	4	2.9
114	Kuwait	5 2008	65	5	7.7	—	—	—	—
114	Libyan Arab Jamahiriya	3 2009	468	36	7.7	—	—	—	—
115	Congo	6 2007	137	10	7.3	8 2008	70	9	12.9
115	Sao Tome and Principe	3 2006	55	4	7.3	—	—	—	—
116	Albania	7 2005	140	10	7.1	—	—	—	—
117	Nigeria	4 2007	358	25	7.0	4 2007	109	9	8.3
118	Saint Kitts & Nevis	10 2004	15	1	6.7	—	—	—	—
119	Maldives	5 2009	76	5	6.6	—	—	—	—
120	Jordan	11 2007	110	7	6.4	11 2007	55	7	12.7
121	Montenegro	3 2009	81	5	6.2	—	—	—	—
122	Georgia	5 2008	150	9	6.0	—	—	—	—
123	Somalia	8 2004	523	31	5.9	—	—	—	—
124	Sri Lanka	4 2004	225	13	5.8	—	—	—	—

(Contd...)

(Contd...)

125	Chad	4 2002	155	8	5.2	—	—	—	—
126	Lebanon	5 2005	128	6	4.7	—	—	—	—
127	Kiribati	8 2007	46	2	4.3	—	—	—	—
128	Haiti	2 2006	98	4	4.1	4 2009	18	?	?
128	Mongolia	6 2008	74	3	4.1	—	—	—	—
129	Vanuatu	9 2008	52	2	3.8	—	—	—	—
130	Tonga	4 2008	32	1	3.1	—	—	—	—
131	Comoros	4 2004	33	1	3.0	—	—	—	—
131	Marshall Islands	11 2007	33	1	3.0	—	—	—	—
132	Iran (Islamic Republic of)	3 2008	286	8	2.8	—	—	—	—
133	Bahrain	11 2006	40	1	2.5	12 2006	40	10	25.0
134	Egypt	11 2005	442	8	1.8	6 2007	264	18	6.8
135	Papua New Guinea	6 2007	109	1	0.9	—	—	—	—
136	Yemen	4 2003	301	1	0.3	4 2001	111	2	1.8
137	Belize	2 2008	32	0	0.0	3 2008	13	5	38.5
137	Micronesia (Federated States of)	3 2009	14	0	0.0	—	—	—	—

(Contd...)

(Contd...)

137	Nauru	4 2008	18	0	0.0	—	—	—	—
137	Oman	10 2007	84	0	0.0	11 2007	70	14	20.0
137	Palau	11 2008	16	0	0.0	11 2008	13	2	15.4
137	Qatar	7 2008	35	0	0.0	—	—	—	—
137	Saudi Arabia	2 2009	150	0	0.0	—	—	—	—
137	Solomon Islands	4 2006	50	0	0.0	—	—	—	—
137	Tuvalu	8 2006	15	0	0.0	—	—	—	—
138	Ecuador	4 2009	124	?	?	—	—	—	—
138	Malawi	5 2009	193	?	?	—	—	—	—

*Figures correspond to the number of seats currently filled in parliament

Guinea: The parliament was dissolved following the December 2008 coup.

1. *South Africa:* The figures on the distribution of seats do not include the 36 special rotating delegates appointed on an ad hoc basic, and all percentages given are therefore calculated on the basis of the 54 permanent seats.
2. *United States of America:* The total refers to all voting members of the House.
3. *Tonga:* No women were elected in 2008, however one woman was appointed to the Cabinet. As cabinet ministers also sit in parliament, there is one woman ou

Compiled by OM Prakash

Annexure – II

Chronology of Events (Modern World)
Women's political participation, voting rights, Head of the States

Sr. No.	*Year/s*	*Event*
1.	1756	Lydia Chapin Taft became the first legal woman voter in America. She voted in three town hall meetings with the consent of the electorate.
2.	1788	United States of America granted women the right to stand for election.
3.	1869	Wyoming became the first sub-national territory to grant women the right to vote, followed by Utah (1870, lost in 1887, restored in 1895), Colorado (1893), Arizona (1912), Oregon (1912), Illinios (1913) and Montana (1914).
4.	1872	Susan B. Anthony was the first US woman to vote in a presidential election; subsequently, she was arrested for having voted illegally. However, her trial provided her with a much more public platform to spread her message. She never paid the fine imposed upon her as punishment for voting.
5.	1881	The Isle of Man gave property-owning unmarried women and widows the right to vote, becoming the first nation to do so.
6.	1882	Aletta Jacobs was the first woman in the Netherlands to attempt to register to vote; her application was denied.

(Contd...)

(Contd...)

7.	1893	New Zealand granted all women the right to vote; however, New Zealand was not a sovereign nation at this time but a self-governing colony of the British Empire. Regardless, New Zealand is often credited today for being the first nation to grant all women the right to vote.
8.	1902	Australia granted, the right to vote subject to conditions or restrictions.
9.	1906-07	Finland became the first European nation to give women the vote, and 19 women were elected to the Finnish parliament.
10.	1907	Norway provided women right to stand for election subject to conditions and restrictions.
11.	1911	The International Women's Day was first celebrated in 1911 by a few countries.
12.	1913	Norway provided women the right to vote.
13.	1915	Denmark and Iceland provided women the right to vote.
14.	1916	Jeanette Rankin of Montana became the first woman elected to the U.S. House of Representatives.
15.	1917	Netherlands provided women the right to stand for election.
16.	1918	Canada, Ireland, United Kingdom provided women the right to vote to women with certain conditions and restrictions.
17.	1918	Estonia, Austria, Georgia, Germany, Hungary, Kyrgyzstan, Latvia, Poland, Russian Federation provided women the right to vote.

(Contd...)

(Contd...)

18.	1919	Belarus, Luxembourg, Ukraine, Netherlands gave women the right to vote.
19.	1919	Belgium, Sweden provided women the right to vote with certain conditions.
20.	1919	Women gained the right to stand for office in New Zealand.
21.	1920	American women obtained full electoral citizenship with the ratification of the Nineteenth Amendment, which enfranchised women.
22.	1920	Albania, Canada gave women the right to stand for election subject to conditions.
23.	1920	Czech Republic, Slovakia, gave women the right to vote.
24.	1921	Armenia, Azerbaijan, Belgium provided women the right to stand for election subject to conditions.
25.	1921	Georgia and Lithuania provided women the right to vote.
26.	1921	Sweden provided the women full right to vote.
27.	1924	Kazakhstan, Mongolia, Saint Lucia and Tajikistan provided women the right to vote.
28.	1927	Turkmenistan provided women the right to vote.
29.	1928	Ireland provided women the full right to vote.
30.	1928	Women ages 21 to 29 in Britain were made able to vote for the first time, as women's suffrage got reduced from age 30 to 21.
31.	1929	Ecuador, Romania provided women the right to vote with certain conditions.
32.	1930	South Africa gave white women the right to vote; Turkey also provided women the right to vote.

(Contd...)

(Contd...)

33.	1930	Alexandra Kollontai was appointed Ambassador from the Soviet Union to Sweden, became the first woman Ambassador in modern history.
34.	1931	Chile, and Portugal provided women the right to vote with certain condition while Spain and Sri Lanka gave women the right to vote.
35.	1932	Maldives, Thailand and Uruguay provided women the right to vote.
36.	1933	Frances Perkins, the first U.S. female Cabinet member, was appointed Secretary of Labor.
37.	1934	Brazil and Cuba provided women the right to vote.
38.	1934	Portugal provided women the right to vote with certain conditions.
39.	1934	Turkey provided women the right to stand for election.
40.	1935	Myanmar provided women the right to vote.
41.	1937	Philippines provided women the right to vote.
42.	1938	Bolivia provided women the right to vote subject to conditions; Uzbekistan provided right to vote.
43.	1939	El Salvado provided women the right to vote.
44.	1941	Panama provided women the right to vote subject to conditions.
45.	1944	Bulgaria, France, Jamaica provided women the right to vote.
46.	1945	Croatia, Guyana provided women the right to stand for election, while Indonesia, Italy, Japan, Senegal, Slovenia, Togo provided right to vote.

(Contd...)

(Contd...)

47.	1946	Women voted and stood for election to the House of Representatives for the first time in Japan. Of the 79 women running for office, 39 got elected.
48.	1946	Cameroon, D.P.R. of Korea, Djibouti provided women the right to vote; Guatemala, Liberia, Myanmar gave women the right to stand for election; Panama, Macedonia, Trinidad and Tobago, Venezuela, Vietnam, Yugoslavia and Romania gave women full right to vote.
49.	1947	Argentina, Japan, Malta, Mexico, Pakistan, Singapore provided women the right to vote.
50.	1948	Belgium, Israel, Niger, Republic of Korea, Seychelles, Suriname provided women the right to vote.
51.	1949	Bosnia and Herzegovina, Chile, China, Costa Rica provided women the right to vote.
52.	1950	Barbados, Canada, Haiti, India provided women the right to vote.
53.	1951	Antigua and Barbuda, Dominica, Grenada, Nepal, Saint Kitts and Nevis, Saint Vincent and the Grenadines provided women the right to vote.
54.	Since 1952	Elizabeth II or Elizabeth Alexandra Mary is the Queen of the United Kingdom of Great Britain and Northern Ireland (and nominal head of State for 15 Commonwealth countries) since 6 Feb 1952 in the death of her father, King George VI. She is currently the longest-time woman ruler in the world.
55.	1952	Bolivia, Greece, Lebanon provided women the right to vote.
56.	1953	Bhutan, Guyana provided women the right to vote; Mexico provided women the right to stand for election.

(Contd...)

(Contd...)

57.	1954	Belize, Colombia, Ghana gave women the right to vote.
58.	1953-54	Sühbaataryn Yanjmaa was first Deputy Chairman of the Presidium of the People's Great Khural of Mongolia and acted as Chairman of the Presidium i.e., head of the State.
59.	1955	Cambodia, Eritrea, Ethiopia, Honduras, Nicaragua, Peru provided women the right to vote.
60.	1956	Benin, Comoros, Egypt, Gabon, Mali, Mauritius, Somalia provided women the right to vote.
61.	1957	Egypt elected the first Arab woman to parliament.
62.	1957	Malaysia, Zimbabwe provided women the right to vote.
63.	1958	Burkina Faso, Chad, Guinea, Lao P.D.R., Nigeria provided women the right to vote.
64.	1959	Madagascar, San Marino, Tunisia, United Republic of Tanzania provided women the right to vote.
65.	1960	Canada provided women the right to stand for election; Cyprus, Gambia, Tonga provided women the right to vote.
66.	1960	Nakayama Masa was appointed Minister of Health and Welfare in Japan, became Japan's first female cabinet member.

(Contd...)

(Contd...)

67.	1960-65;1970-77; 1994-2000	Sirimavo Bandaranaike was Prime minister of Sri Lanka thrice. She was the first woman prime minister in world history and probably the oldest female political leader in active politics by the time of her demise.
68.	1961	Bahamas provided women the right to vote subject to conditions; Burundi, El Salvador, Malawi, Mauritania, Paraguay, Rwanda, Sierra Leone provided women the right to stand for election.
69.	1962	Algeria, Australia, Monaco, Uganda, Zambia provided women the right to vote.
70.	1963	Congo, Equatorial Guinea, Fiji, Iran, Kenya, Morocco provided women the right to vote, Papua New Guinea provided women the right to stand for election.
71.	1964	Bahamas, Libya, Sudan, Papua New Guinea provided women the full right to vote.
72.	1965	Afghanistan, Bostwana, Lesotho gave women the right to vote.
73.	1966-77; 1980-84	Indira Gandhi served as Prime minister of India twice.
74.	1968	Soong Ching-ling was named Co-Chair woman of the People's Republic of China, became the first non-royal woman to lead the state of China.
75.	1969-74	Golda Meir was Prime Minister of Israel and third women in the world to reach that post behind Sri Lanka's Sirimavo Bandaranaike (1960) and India's Indira Gandhi (1966).
76.	1971	Switzerland provided women the right to vote.

(Contd...)

(Contd...)

77.	1972	Bangladesh provided women the right to vote.
78.	1974	Maria Estela (Isabela) Martinez de Peron succeeds her husband and becomes the first woman President of Argentina and the first female head of state in the Americas.
79.	1974-76	María Estela Martínez de Perón Served as president of Argentina. She was the first woman who became president, both in America and in the world. And also was the first one ousted in a military coup.
80.	1975-76	Elisabeth Domitien was Africa's first woman prime minister and the first black woman ruler of an independent State. She was Prime Minister of the Central African Republic.
81.	1979	Lidia Geiler is the first woman elected President of Bolivia.
82.	1979	Simone Weil of France is the first woman elected President of the European Parliament.
83.	1979-80	Maria de Lourdes Pintasilgo was Prime Minister of Portugal.
84.	1979-90	Margaret Thatcher was Prime Minister of the United Kingdom and first woman elected ruler in Europe.
85.	1980	Song Qingling was elected "Honorary President" of the People's Republic of China shortly before her death.
86.	1980	Vigdis Finnbogadottir is the first woman elected President of Iceland.

(Contd...)

(Contd...)

87.	1980	Jeanne Sauve is the first woman appointed Speaker of the House of Commons of Canada.
88.		Since1980 Beatrix Wilhelmina Armgard is the Queen of the Netherlands since 1980.
89.	1980-95	Mary Eugenia Charles served as Prime minister of Dominica. She was the first Caribbean female premier and the third American female ruler.
90.	1980-96	Vigdís Finnbogadóttir became President of Iceland and is the first woman President in Europe, the first one elected directly by the people in the world and when quitting in 1996 was the female political ruler longest-time in office in the world, as well as the doyen among all European non-monarch rulers.
91.	1981	Maria Lea Pedini-Angelini became head of State and Government of San Marino.
92.	1981-86; 1989-90	Gro Harlem Brundtland was Prime minister of Norway twice. She is the first woman to become Prime Minister of Norway. She currently serves as chief of the World Health Organisation (WHO).
93.	1982	Eugenia Charles, Doinica, is the first woman to become Prime Minister in the Caribbean.
94.	1982-86	Milka Planinc was Prime Minister of former Socialist Yugoslavia, the only woman premier of a communist country in history.
95.	1982-87	Agatha Barbara became elected President of Malta. She was the second woman President in Europe behind Vigdís Finnbogadóttir.

(Contd...)

(Contd...)

96.	1984	Geraldine Ferraro is the first woman nominated for Vice-President by either major political party in the United States.
97.	1984;1989-90	Gloriana Ranocchini served as head of State and Government of San Marino.
98.	1984	Carmen Pereira was acting President of Guinea Bissau in the capacity of chairman of the National People's Assembly.
99.	1985	Maria Liberia-Peters is the first woman to become Prime Minister of the Netherlands Antilles.
100.	1986-92	Corazon Aquino served as President of the Philippines, was Asia's first woman President.
101.	1988-90;1993-96	Benazir Bhutto served as Prime minister Pakistan twice. She was the first woman Prime Minister of a muslim country; she was assassinated in Rawalpindi on 27 Dec 2007.
102.	1989	Violeta Barrios de Chamorro got elected as President of Nicagagua.
103.	1990	Sabine Bergmann Pohl Chairman of the *Volkskammer* of the late German Democratic Republic was the last head of State before the unification. She was the only female head of State in former communist East Europe.
104.	1990-97	Mary Robinson is the first elected woman President of Ireland.
105.	1990	Ertha Pascal-Trouillot is the first woman elected President of Haiti.
106.	1990	Carmen Lawrence is Australia's first female Premier.
107.	1990-91	Kazimiera Danutë Prunskienë was Prime Minister of Lithuania.

(Contd...)

(Contd...)

108.	1991	Edith Cresson is the first woman elected Prime Minister of France.
109.	1991	Rita Johnston is Canada's first female Premier.
110.	1991-92	Edda Ceccoli served as head of State and Government of San Marino.
111.	1992	California elected two women, Dianne Feinstein and Barbara Boxer, to the U.S. Senate.
112.	1992	Betty Boothroyd the first woman chosen to be Speaker of the House of Commons in Great Britain.
113.	1992	Hanna Suchocka is the first woman to become Prime Minister of Poland.
114.	1993	Kim Campbell served as Prime minister of Canada. She was first woman ruler in North America.
115.	1993	Patricia Busignani was Head of State and Government of San Marino in 1993.
116.	1993	Toujan Faisal is the first woman elected to the Parliament of Jordan.
117.	1993	Tansu Ciller is the first woman elected Prime Minister of Turkey.
118.	1993	Agathe Uwilingiyimana is the first woman to become Prime Minister of Rwanda, though she was officially relieved of her position eighteen days later. She remained in the position however in a "caretaker capacity" until her assassination in 1994 at the beginning of the Rawandan Genocide.
119.	1993	Anson Chan is the first woman, also the first Chinese person, to be appointed Chief Secretary, the number two position in Hong Kong.

(Contd...)

(Contd...)

120.	1993	Sylvie Kinigi is the first woman to become Prime Minister of Burundi.
121.	1993-94	Sylvie Kinigi was Acting President of Burundi.
122.	1993-96	Tansu Çiller was Prime minister of Turkey. She belongs to the notable women rulers in Muslim countries, along with Pakistan's Benazir Bhutto, Bangladesh' Hasina Wajed and Khaleda Zia, and Indonesia's Megawati Sukarnoputri.
123.	1993-94.	Sylvie Kinigi was Prime Minister of Burundi.
124.	1993-94	Agathe Uwilingiyimana was Prime minister of Rwanda.
125.	1994	Chandrika Kumaratunga served as Prime Minister of Sri Lanka.
126.	1994-95	Reneta Indzhova was interim Prime Minister of Bulgaria.
127.	1994-2005	Chandrika Kumaratunga served as President of Sri Lanka.
128.	1995	Two women ran for President and 8 for Vice President of Peru, the first time women have been candidates for these offices.
129.	1995-96	Claudette Werleigh was Prime Minister of Haiti.
130.	1996-97	Ruth Perry Chairman of the Council of State of the National Transitional Government of Liberia.
131.	1996- 2001; since Jan 2009	Sheikh Hasina Wajed served as Prime Minister of Bangladesh twice.
132.	1997-99	Janet Jagan served as Prime Minister of Guyana.
133.	1997	Mary McAleese has been President of Ireland since 1997. She is the first woman President having succeeded another one, Mary Robinson, in history.

(Contd...)

(Contd...)

134.	1997-99	Jenny Shipley was Prime Minister of New Zealand. Shipley was not only the first woman ruler in New Zealand.
135.	1999	Vaira Vike-Freiberga elected to President of Latvia. She is the first woman President of a country in Eastern Europe of the former Soviet Union.
136.	1999	Mireya Elisa Moscoso de Arias becomes first female President of Panama.
137.	1999	Helen Clark got elected as Prime Minister of New Zealand.
138.	1999	Irena Degutienë acted as Prime Minister of Lithuania twice.
139.	1999	Nyam-Osoriyn Tuyaa was acting Prime Minister of Mongolia.
140.	1999	Rosa Zafferani became head of State and Government of San Marino twice, from 1 Apr to 1 October 1999 and from 1 April to 1 October 2008.
141.	1999-2000	Ruth Dreifuss was the first female Swiss head of State as President of the Confederation. Dreifuss was elected by the Federal Assembly to serve as president of Switzerland.
142.	1999-2004	Mireya Elisa Moscoso de Arias was the first woman President of Panama..
143.	1999-2007	Vaira Vike-Freiberga was the first woman to be President of a country in East/Central Europe or came out with the former Soviet Union, was elected by the Parliament of Latvia on 17 Jun 1999 for a four-year term, starting on July 8. After winning a second and final term in 2004, she left the office on July 8, 2007.
144.	1999-2008	Helen Elizabeth Clark became the second consecutive woman Prime Minister of New Zealand, succeeding Jenny Shipley.

(Contd...)

(Contd...)

145.	2000	Maria Domenica Michelotti Co-captain regent of San Marino.
146.	2000-06	Tarja Kaarina Halonen served as Finland's first woman President.
147.	2001	Maria Gloria Macapagal Arroyo elected President of the Phillippines.
148.	2001-04	Megawati Sukarnoputri elected as the first woman President of the Republic of Indonesia
149.	2001-02.	Mame Madior Boye Prime Minister of Senegal.
150.	2002	Nancy Pelosi sworn in as the House Democratic Whip - the highest-ranking leadership position ever held by a women in the United States Congress at that time. She was later named Minority Leader.
151.	2002-2003	Maria das Neves Ceita Baptista de Sousa served Prime Minister of São Tomé and Príncipe.
152.	2003	Anneli Tuulikki Jäätteenmäki, Prime Minister of Finland was country's first woman premier.
153.	2003	Beatriz Merino was elected as Prime Minister of Peru, became the first woman to hold the position.
154.	2003	Since 2003 Egypt has seen its first female judge, a female university President, and several female cabinet ministers. All were appointed by President Hoshni Mubarak in an effort to push women's political participation.
155.	2003-04	Valeria Ciavatta Co-captain regent of San Marino.
156.	2003-04;2007-08	Nino Burdzhanadze was Acting President of Georgia twice.
157.	2004	Luisa Diogo got elected as Prime Minister of Mozambique.

(Contd...)

(Contd...)

158.	2004-05	Yulia Tymoshenko helps lead the Ukrainian Orange Revolution and is named Prime Minister by her "Orange Partner" President Viktor Yushenko.
159.	2005	Fausta Simona Morganti Co-captain regent of San Marino.
160.	2005	Ellen Sirleaf-Johnson got elected as Africa's first female President as Liberia's head-of-state in November.
161.	2005-2006	Maria do Carmo Silveira served as Prime minister of São Tomé and Príncipe.
162.	2005	Angela Merkel was Federal Chancellor of Germany.
163.	2006	Democrats takes control of the United States Congress and Nancy Pelosi was elevated to the position of Speaker of the House. She is the third highest ranking official in the United States government and the highest ranking female in US political history.
164.	2006	Michelle Bachelet got elected as President of Chile.
165.	2006	UAE held their first elections for both men and women in Mid-December 2006. However, they may only vote for 20 seats in the UAE Federal National Council which serves only an advisory purpose. No elected officials have actual political power.
166.	2006	Portia Simpson Miller elected first Prime Minister of Jamaica.
167.	Since 2006	Ellen Johnson-Sirleaf is President of Liberia. She is Africa's first elected woman President.
168.	Since 2006	Michelle Bachelet Jeria served as President of Chile.
169.	2006-2007	Portia Simpson-Miller was Prime Minister of Jamaica.
170.	2006-07	Han Myung Sook was Prime Minister of South Korea.

(Contd...)

(Contd...)

171.	2007	Dalia Itzik being the Speaker of the Knesset, ruled in 2007 as acting President of the State of Israel till the inauguration of Shimon Peres.
172.	2007	Senator Hillary Clinton is the first woman to ever be considered as a top candidate for the US Presidency. However, she eventually loses the Democratic Party Nomination to Senator Barack Obama of Illinois in the Primary race in US history.
173.	Since 2007	Cristina Fernández de Kirchner got elected as President of Argentina.
174.	2007	Pratibha Patil was elected President of India.
175.	2007-08	Micheline Calmy-Rey became President of the Swiss Confederation.
176.	2008.	Michèle Pierre-Louis was Prime Minister of Haiti.
177.	2008	Zinaida Greceanîi was elected Prime Minister of Moldova.
178.	2008- 09	Assunta Meloni became Co-Captain-regent (head of State and Government) of San Marino.
179.	2009	Jóhanna Sigurdardóttir was made Prime Minister of Iceland.
180.	2009	Jadranka Kosor became Prime Minister of Croatia.
181.	2009	Saudia Arabia will establish first co-ed university in Riyadh.
182.		Since 2009 Dalia Grybauskaite is President of Lithuania.
183.	2010	United Arab Emirate will provide full voting right to women.

Compiled by OM Prakash

(Contd...)

Annexure – III

Chronology of Events (India) Women's Movements, Empowerment, Assertion of Their Rights and Legislations

Sr. No.	*Year/s*	*Event*
1.	1500-1000 BC	During Rig Vedic Period women had significant rights and privilege in society. Their political participation was confined to Vidatha, the folk assembly.
2.	1000 BC	In post-Vedic period women got deprived of all the political as well as social privilege and rights.
3.	1236-40 AD	Razia Sultana ruled over Delhi Sultanate
4.	1795	Infanticide was declared as murder by Bengal Regulation XXI in Bengal Presidency.
5.	1804	Infanticide was declared illegal throughout the British territory in India.
6.	1819	Calcutta Female Juvenile Society was established by Christian Missionaries for the purpose of education in India.
7.	1829	Regulation of 1829 declared Sati System illegal in India.
8.	1854	Charles Wood's dispatch gave first time much emphasis on women's education.

(Contd...)

(Contd...)

9.	1856	Passage of a Bill which allowed widow remarriage.
10.	1861	Widow Marriage Association was established.
11.	1870	More laws against female infanticide were passed by Lord Mayo.
12.	1886	Swarna Kumari Debi started the women's organisation Sakhi Samiti in 1886 for widows.
13.	1891	Age of Consent Bill, 1891 raised the marriageable age of Girls to 12.
14.	1899	D. K. Karve established a Widow's Home in Poona.
15.	1900	Sister Nivedita, a disciple of Swami Vivekanand became a member of the National Revolutionary Council and in that capacity, organised women for nationalist activities.
16.	1905-08	The *Swadeshi* movement in Bengal (1905-8) marked the beginning of women's participation in nationalist activities.
17.	1907	Madame Cama, a Parsi nationalist, persuaded the International Socialist Congress at Stuttgart to support the Indian Independence Movement and also began a monthly journal called *Vande Mataram* towards this end.
18.	1916	Formation of Home Rule League by Annie Besant.
19.	1916	First Indian Women's University was established by D. K. Karve.
20.	1917	Annie Besant became President of Indian National Congress.
21.	1917	Annie Besant and few other women met Mr. Montague to demand voting rights for Indian women.

(Contd...)

(Contd...)

22.	1917	Annie Besant, Dorothy Jinarajadasa, Malathi Patvardhan, Ammu Swaminathan, Mrs. Dadabhoy and Mrs. Ambujamal founded the Women's Indian Association, described as the first truly feminist organisation.
23.	1925	The first Indian women President of Indian National Congress, Sarojini Naidu addressed the Kanpur Session.
24.	1926	The All India Women's Conference was formed and became extremely active on the question of women's suffrage, labour issues, relief and nationalist work.
25.	1929	Sarda Act raised the marriage age of the girl to 14.
26.	1929-30	Aruna Asaf Ali's first major political involvement was in the salt march at which she was arrested and prosecuted. She was also active in the Quit India movement, edited *Inquilab* magazine of the Congress and established the National Federation of Indian Women.
27.	1947	Constitution based on the principles of equality guaranteed equal rights to suffrage for women.
28.	1947-49	Sarojini Naidu Became Governor of Uttar Pradesh
29.	1955	Hindu Marriage Act, 1955 raised the marriage age of girls to 15 years.
30.	1956	Hindu Succession Act, 1956 made the daughter an equal co-heir with the son.
31.	1961	The Dowry Prohibition Act, 1961 was passed.
32.	1961	The Maternity Benefits Act, 1961 was passed.
33.	1966	Mrs. Indira Gandhi became the first woman Prime Minister of the country.
34.	1972	Anti-Liquor Campaign by Women in Maharashtra

(Contd...)

(Contd...)

35.	1974	Women have been actively involved in the Chipko Movement since 1974.
36.	1974	Progressive Women's Organisation was established in Osmania University in Hyderabad which was influenced by Maoism and became one of the important feminist organisation in the country.
37.	1975	Stree Mukti Sangathan was established in Bombay which was also influenced by Maoism.
38.	1975	United Nations declared International Women's Year and 8 March as International Women's Day for an intensified action to promote gender equality and women's role in national development.
39.	1976	Equal Remuneration Act, 1976 were to provide for the payment of equal remuneration to men and women workers and for the prevention of discrimination on the ground of sex and against women in the matter of employment.
40.	1978	Child Marriage Restraint Act, 1978 increased the age of marriage for girls to 18 years.
41.	1981	All Indian Democratic Women's Association was formed which main agenda was to launch a campaign against bride burning and dowry death.
42.	1983	Karnataka which provided reservation for women in its three tier panchayati raj system.
43.	1985	Shah Bano Case

(Contd...)

(Contd...)

44.	1988	The draft recommendations of the Government of India's National Perspective Plan (NPP) for Women 1988, acknowledged the problem of under-representation and recommended 30 per cent reservation for women in local governance, panchayat, zilla and in local municipal bodies.
45.	1991	The Janata Party Government in Karnataka in 1991 passed a Bill to implement 25 per cent reservation for women in local elections.
46.	1991	National Plan of Action for the Girl Child 1991-2000 was launched.
47.	1992	The 73rd Constitutional Amendment Act introduced not less than 33 per cent reservation for women in the panchayat raj institutions in the rural areas.
48.	1992	74th Constitutional Amendment Act introduced similar reservation for women in nagara palika and municipalities in towns and urban areas.
49.	1992	Induction of women in the armed forces. The first batch had joined in 1992.
50.	1992	The National Commission for Women was set up as statutory body in January 1992 under the National Commission for Women Act, 1990 (Act No. 20 of 1990 of Government of India) to review the Constitutional and Legal safeguards for women; recommend remedial legislative measures; facilitate redressal of grievances and advise the Government on all policy matters affecting women.
51.	1995	The United Nations Economic and Social Council endorsed a target of 30 per cent women at all levels by 1995.

(Contd...)

(Contd...)

52.	1996	In September 1996, a private member's bill was moved, introducing reservations for women, a day before the closing of the monsoon session of the parliament. However it was this move that subsequently led to the introduction of the present Reservation Bill.
53.	1999	Constitution (85th Amendment) Bill 1999, popularly known as Women's Reservation Bill, was introduced on December 23, 1999. On December 22, 2000, it was once again shelved.
54.	2000	The coalition government of the United Front introduced the 81st (Constitutional) Amendment also known as the Women's Reservation Bill.
55.	2008	Mrs. Pratibha Singh Patil became the first women President of the country.
56.	2009	Ms. Meera Kumar became the first women Speaker of the Lok Sabha.

Compiled by OM Prakash

Bibliography

UN Reports

Achieving Good Governance: the Essential Participation of Women, UNIFEM: Accountability to the World's Women: Review and Renewal of Commitments to Gender Equality Through Beijing+5 and Dakar+5 Processes, 1999 ECA/ACW 40th Anniversary Conference Outputs.

Gender Balance in the United Nations Common System: Progress, Prognosis, Prescriptions, UN International Civil Service Commission (ICSA), December 1998.

Mid-term Review of the Implementation of the System-Wide Medium-Term Plan for the Advancement of Women, United Nations, Economic and Social Council E/CN.6/1998/3, Commission on the Status of Women (1996-2001), January 6, 1998.

UNIFEM and Gender Equality, UN Newsletter, February 24-March 2, 2001, vol. 26 no.8., United Nations Information Centre, New-Delhi.

Women 2000: Women and Decision Making, United Nations Division for the Advancement of Women (UNDAW), Department of Economic and Social Affairs, 1997, New York.

Women 2002: Gender Equality and the Millennium Development Goals, United Nations Development Fund for Women, Volume 2, New York.

Women in Politics and Decision Making in the Late Twentieth Century: A United Nations Study, 1992, Boston: Martinus Nijhoff Publishers.

Books

Andrews, Peggy, *Sisters Listening to Sisters: Women of the World Share Stories of Personal Empowerment,* South Hadley, MA.: Bergin and Garvey, 1996.

Ashworth, G., *Gendered Governance: An Agenda for Change: UNDP Gender Monograph Series No. 3*, New York, UNDP, March 1996.

Awkward, Michael *Negotiating Difference: Race, Gender, and the Politics of Positionality*, Chicago, University of Chicago Press, 1995.

Bannerji, Himani, *Returning the Gaze: Essays on Racism, Feminism, and Politics*, Sister Vision Press, 1993.

Thinking Through: Essays on Feminism, Marxism, and Anti-Racism. Minnesota, Women's Press, 1995.

Bar On, Bat-Ami, *Engendering Origins: Critical Feminist Readings in Plato and Aristotle*, New York, State University of New York Press, 1994.

Basu, Amrita, *The Challenge of Local Feminisms: Women's Movements in Global Perspective*, Boulder, San Francisco, Westview Press, 1995.

Brill, Alida, *A Rising Public Voice: Women in Politics Worldwide*, New York, The Feminist Press, 1995.

Briskin et al, *The Contemporary Women's Movement in Canada*, Toronto, Oxford University Press, 1988.

Brown, L. Susan, *The Politics of Individualism: Liberalism, Liberal Feminism and Anarchism*, London, Black Rose Books Ltd., 1993.

Butler Judith & Scott Joan W., *Feminists Theorize the Political*, New York, Routledge, 1992.

_____________ *Excitable Speech: A Politics of Performance*, London, Routledge, 1997.

_____________ *Gender Trouble: Feminism and the Subversion of Identity*, New York, Routledge, 1999.

Carver, Terrell & Veronique Mottier, *Politics of Sexuality*, New York, Routledge, 1998.

Chandra Talpade Mohanty, Ann Russo, & Lourdes Torres, *Third World Women and the Politics of Feminism*, Bloomington: Indiana University Press, 1991.

Chapman, Jennifer *Politics, Feminism and the Reformation of Gender*, New York, Routledge, 1992.

_____________ *Politics, Feminism and the Reformation of Gender*, New York, Routledge, 1993.

Connolly, William, *Identity/Difference: Democratic Negotiations of Political Paradox*, Minneapolis, University of Minnesota Press, 2002.

Coole, Diana H., *Women in Political Theory: From Ancient Misogyny to Contemporary Feminism*, Sussex, Wheatsheaf Books, 1988.

Daniels, Cynthia R., *Feminists Negotiate the State: The Politics of Domestic Violence*, USA, University Press of America, 1997.

De Mel Niloufer, *Women and Nation's Narratives: Gender and Nationalism in 20th century Sri-Lanka, Kali for Women,* New-Delhi, Oxford University Press, 2001.

Dean, Jodi, *Solidarity of Strangers: Feminism after Identity Politics,* Berkeley, University of California Press, 1996.

Deveax, Monique, *Cultural Pluralism and Dilemmas of Justice,* Ithaca, Cornell University Press, 2000.

Di Stefano, Christine, *Configurations of Masculinity: A Feminist Perspective on Modern Political Theory,* Ithaca, Cornell University Press, 1991.

Dreze, Jean and Sen, Amartya, *India: Economic Development and Social Opportunity,* New-Delhi, Oxford University Press, 1995.

Eisenberg, Avigail, & Jeff Spinner-Halev, *Minorities Within Minorities: Equality, Rights, and Diversity,* Cambridge, Cambridge University Press, 2005.

Eisenstein, Z, *Contemporary Feminist Thought,* London, Unwin Press, 1984.

Elman, R. Amy, *Sexual Politics and the European Union: The New Feminist Challenge,* New York, Berghahn Books, 1996.

Elshtain, Jean Bethke, *Meditations on Modern Political Thought: Masculine/ Feminine Themes from Luther to Arendt,* Pennyslvania, Penn State University. Press, 1992.

Firestone, Shulamith, *The Dialectic of Sex: The Case for Feminist Revolution,* New York, Morrow Press, 1970.

Flax, Jane, *Thinking Fragments: Psychoanalysis, Feminism, and Postmodernism in the Contemporary West,* Berkeley, University of California Press, 1989.

Fowlkes, Diane L., *White Political Women: Paths from Privilege to Empowerment,* Knoxville, Univ. of Tennessee Press, 1992.

Fraser, Nancy, *Justice Interruptus: Critical Reflections on the Post-socialist Condition,* New York, Routledge, 1997.

Freeland, Cynthia, *Feminist Interpretations of Aristotle,* University Park, Pennsylvania University Press, 1998.

Friedan, Betty, *The Feminine Mystique,* New York, Norton Press, 1963.

Frye, Marilyn, *The Politics of Reality: Essays in Feminist Theory,* Trumansberg, New York, The Crossing Press, 1983.

Gatens, Moira, *A Companion to Feminist Philosophy,* Cambridge, Blackwell, 1998.

Genevieve Lloyd, *Feminism and History of Philosophy,* New York, Oxford University Press, 2002.

Gottfried, Heidi, *Feminism and Social Change: Bridging Theory and Practice,* Illinois, University of Illinois Press, 1996.

Gould, Carol C, *Beyond Domination: New Perspectives on Women and Philosophy,* New Jersey, Rowman & Allanheld, 1983.

Hackett, Elizabeth & Haslanger, Sally, *Theorising Feminisms,* Oxford, Oxford University Press, 2005.

Hacking, Ian, *The Social Construction of What?,* Cambridge, MA, Harvard University Press, 1999.

Hartsock, Nancy C. M., *The Feminist Standpoint Revisited and Other Essays,* Boulder, Westview Press, 1998.

Heyes, Cressida J., *Line Drawings: Defining Women through Feminist Practice,* Ithaca, New York, Cornell University Press, 2000.

Hughes-Freeland, Felicia & Nickie Charles, *Practising Feminism: Identity, Difference and Power,* New York, Routledge, 1996.

Hust Evelyn, *Women's Political Representation and Empowerment in India: A Million Indira's Now?,* New-Delhi, Manohar Publishers, 2005.

Jaggar, Alison & Rothenberg, Paula, *Feminist Frameworks: Alternative Theoretical Accounts of the Relations between Women and Men,* New York, McGraw-Hill, 1993.

_____________ *Feminist Politics and Human Nature,* Lanham, MD & London, UK, Rowman & Littlefield, 1983.

_____________ James P. Sterba, Milton Fisk, William A. Galston, Carol C. Gould, Tibor Machan & Robert Solomon, *Morality and Social Justice: Point Counterpoint,* Lanham, MD & London, UK, Rowman & Littlefield, 1995.

_____________ M., *Feminist Politics and Human Nature,* Lanham, MD & London, UK, Rowman & Littlefield, 1983.

Jain, Devaki, *Panchayat Raj: Women Changing Governance* Gender in Development Monograph Series No. 5, New York, UNDP, 1996.

Jenefsky, Cindy & Ann Russo, *Without Apology: Andrea Dworkin's Art and Politics,* Boulder San Francisco, Westview Press, 1997.

Jensen, Pamela Grande, *Finding a New Feminism: Rethinking the Woman Question for Liberal Democracy,* Lanham, MD & London, UK, Rowman & Littlefield, 1996.

Jocabson, Doranne & Wadley, S. Susan, *Women in India: Two Perspectives,* New-Delhi, Manohar Publishing House, 1977.

Jones, Kathleen B. & Anna G. Jónasdóttir, *The Political Interests of Gender: Developing Theory and Research with a Feminist Face,* Newbury Park, CA, Sage, 1988.

_____________ *Citizenship in Feminism: Identity, Action, and Locale,* Bloomington, Indiana University Press, 1998.

Kaplan, Temma, *Crazy for Democracy: Women in Grassroots Movements,* New York, Routledge, 1997.

Karam, A., *Women in Parliament: Beyond Numbers,* Stockholm, Handbook Series, International Institute for Democracy and Electoral Assistance, 1998.

Kenney, Sally J. & Kinsella Helen, *Politics and Feminist Standpoint Theories,* London, Haworth Press, 1997.

King, Elizabeth M. & M. Anne Hill. *Women's Education in Developing Countries: Barriers, Benefits, and Policies,* Baltimore, Johns Hopkins University, 1993.

King, Katie, *Theory in Its Feminist Travels: Conversations in U.S. Women's Movements* , Indiana, Indiana University Press, 1994.

Kruks, Sonia, *Retrieving Experience: Subjectivity and Recognition in Feminist Politics,* Ithaca, New York, Cornell University Press, 2000.

Leacock, E, *Women and National Development: The Complexity of Change,* Chicago, University of Chicago Press, 1977.

Lombardo Harding, Sandra, *Feminism and Methodology,* Bloomington, Indiana University Press and Open University, 1987.

Marshall, Barbara L., *Engendering Modernity: Feminism, Social Theory, and Social Change,* New England, Northeastern Univ. Press, 1994.

Marshall, Catherine, *Feminist Critical Policy Analysis,* London, Falmer Press, 1997.

McDonald, Lynn, *Women Theorists on Society and Politics,* Waterloo, Wilfrid Laurier University Press, 1998.

Meehan, Elizabeth & Sevenhuijsen Selma, *Equality Politics and Gender,* Newbury Park, CA, Sage, 1991.

Meyers, Diana Tietjens, *Feminist Social Thought: A Reader,* New York, Routledge, 1997.

Mim Kelber, *Women and Government: New Ways to Political Power,* Westport and London, Praeger, 1994.

Moi, Toril, *What is a Woman? And Other Essays,* Oxford, Oxford University Press, 2000.

Monk, Janice & Maria Dolors, *Women of the European Union,* New York, Routledge, 1996.

Morales, Maria H., *Perfect Equality: John Stuart Mill on Well-Constituted Communities,* Lanham, Rowman & Littlefield, 1996.

Nancy J. Hirschmann & Kirstie Morna McClure, *Feminist Interpretations by John Locke,* University Park, Pennsylvania State University, 2007.

Naples, Nancy A., *Community Activism and Feminist Politics: Organising Across Race, Class, and Gender,* New York, Routledge, 1997.

____________ *Grassroots Warriors: Activist Mothering, Community Work, and the War on Poverty,* New York, Routledge, 1998.

Nelson, Barbara J. & N. Chowdhury, *Women and Politics Worldwide,* New Haven and London, Yale University Press, 1994.

Nelson, Hilde Lindemann, *Damaged Identities, Narrative Repair,* Ithaca, New York, Cornell University Press, 2001.

Newton, Judith, *Starting Over: Feminism and the Politics of Cultural Critique,* Michigan, University of Michigan Press, 1994.

Nicholson, Linda & Steven Seidman, *Social Postmodernism: Beyond Identity Politics,* Cambridge, Cambridge University Press, 1995.

Norris, Pippa, *Women, Media, and Politics,* Oxford, Oxford University Press, 1998.

Nussbaum, Martha C., *Women and Human Development: The Capabilities Approach,* New York, Cambridge University Press, 2000.

Okin Susan Moller, *Women in Western Political Thought,* Princeton, Princeton University Press, 1979.

Oliver, Kelly & Marilyn Pearsall, *Feminist Interpretations of Friedrich Nietzsche,* University Park, Pennsylvania State University Press, 1998.

Pateman, Carole & Elizabeth Gross, *Feminist Challenges: Social and Political Theory,* New England, Northeastern University Press, 1987.

____________ & M. Shanley, *Feminist Interpretations and Political Theory,* Malden, MA.:, Polity Press, 1991.

____________ *Participation and Democratic Theory,* London, Cambridge University Press, 1970.

____________ *The Disorder of Women: Democracy, Feminism and Political Theory,* Stanford, Stanford University Press, 1989.

____________ *The Sexual Contract,* Malden, MA.: Polity Press, 1988.

Patton, Paul, *Nietzsche, Feminism, and Political Theory,* New York, Routledge, 1993.

Pettman, Jan Jindy, *Worlding Women: A Feminist International Politics,* New York, Routledge, 1996.

Phillips Anne, *Feminism and Politics,* London, Oxford University Press, 1998.

_____________ *Democracy and Difference,* University Park, Pennsylvania State University Press, 1993.

_____________ *Engendering Democracy,* University Park, Pennsylvania State University Press, 1991.

Pyle, Andrew, *'The Subjection of Women': Contemporary Responses to John Stuart Mill,* Bristol, Thoemmes, 1995

R. Ruether, *Readings toward a Feminist Theology,* Boston, Beacon Press, 1985.

Rai M. Shirin, *International Perspective on Gender and Governance,* Great Britain, Macmillan Press, 2000.

Randall, Vicky & Waylen Georgina, *Gender, Politics and the State,* New York, Routledge, 1998.

_____________ *Women and Politics: An International Perspective,* London, Macmillan Press, 1987.

Rawls, John, *A Theory of Justice,* Cambridge, MA, Harvard University Press, 1971.

Roc. A, *Of Women Born: Motherhood as Experience and Institution,* London, Virago Press, 1977.

Sapiro,Virginia, *A Vindication of Political Virtue: The Political Theory of Mary Wollstonecraft,* Chicago, University of Chicago Press, 1992.

Sayers, Janet, Mary Evans & Nenneke Redclift, *Engels Revisited: New Feminist Essays,* London, Travistock, 1987.

Scheman, Naomi, *Engenderings: Constructions of Knowledge, Authority, and Privilege,* New York, Routledge, 1993.

Scott, Joan W., Cora Kaplan, & Debra Keates, *Transitions Environments Translations: Feminisms in International Politics,* New York, Routledge, 1997.

Sealey, Raphael, *Women and Law in Classical Greece,* Chapel Hill, The University of North Carolina Press, 1990.

Shanley, Mary Lundon and Carole Pateman, *Feminist Interpretations of Political Theory,* University Park, Pennsylvania State University Press, 1991.

Simon, Sherry, *Gender in Translation: Cultural Identity and the Politics of Transmission,* New York, Routledge, 1996.

Singer, Linda, *Erotic Welfare: Sexual Theory and Politics in the Age of Epidemic,* New York, Routledge, 1993.

Sinha Niroj, *Empowerment of Women: Through Political Participation,* New Delhi, Eastern Book Corporation, 2007.

Sperling Liz, *Women Political Philosophy*, Edinburg, Edinburg University Press Ltd., 2001.

Stanton D, *Feminist Autobiography*, Manchester, Manchester University Press, 1984.

Staudt, Kathleen, *Policies, Politics and Gender: Women Gaining Ground*, West Hartford, Kumarian Press, 1998.

____________ *Political Science and Feminisms: Integration or Transformation?*, London, Twayne/MacMillan, 1997.

____________ *Women in High-Level Political Decision-making: A Global Analysis*, Vienna, United Nations Office, Division for the Advancement of Women, 1989.

Sunstein, Cass R., *Feminism and Political Theory*, Chicago, University of Chicago Press, 1990.

Thomas, Sue & Clyde Wilcox, *Women and Elective Office*, Oxford, Oxford University Press, 1997.

____________ *How Women Legislate*, Oxford, Oxford University Press, 1994.

Tuana, Nancy, *The Feminist Interpretations of Plato*, University Park, The Pennsylvania State University Press, 1994.

____________ *The Less Noble Sex: Scientific, Religious, and Philosophical Conceptions of Woman's Nature*, Bloomington, Indiana University Press, 1993.

Varma, Sumir, *Women's Struggle for Political Space*, New Delhi, Rawat Publications, 1997.

Waring, Wendy, *By, For and About: Feminist Cultural Politics*, Minnesota, Women's Press, 1994.

Warren, Karen J. & Duane L. Cady, *Bringing Peace Home: Feminism, Violence, and Nature*, Bloomington, Indiana University Press, 1996.

Weiss, Penny A., *Conversations with Feminism: Political Theory and Practice*, Lanham, MD & London, UK, Rowman and Littlefield, 1998.

West, Lois A., *Feminist Nationalism*, New York, Routledge, 1997.

Whitworth, Sandra, *Feminism and International Relations: Towards a Political Economy of Gender in Multilateral Institutions*, New York, St. Martins Press, 1994.

Wolf, Naomi, *Fire with Fire: The New Female Power and How It Will Change the 21st Century*, Minnesota, Fawcett Books, 1993.

Young, Iris Marion, *Intersecting Voices: Dilemmas of Gender, Political Philosophy, and Policy*, Princeton, Princeton University Press, 1998.

____________ *Justice and the Politics of Difference*, Princeton, Princeton University Press, 1998.

Young, Stacey, *Changing the world: Discourse, Politics, and the Feminist Movement*, New York, Routledge, 1997.

Articles

Agnihotri, Indu & Majumdar Veena, "Changing Terms of Women's Discourse, Women's movement in India 1970s-90s," *Economic and Political Weekly* vol.30, 29, July 22, 1991, pp. 1869-79.

Aiuchi, Masako, "How Women Won or Lost in the Japanese Lower House Election: Case Studies of Women Candidates Who Ran as Challengers," *Political Science and Politics*, vol.34, no.2, 2001, pp. 221-224.

Arthur, Marilyn, "Early Greece: The Origin of the Western Attitude Toward Women" in *Women and the Ancient World: The Arethusa Paper*, J. Perradotto and J. P. Sullivan, eds., Albany: SUNY Press, 1984

Baehr, Amy R., "Toward a New Feminist Liberalism: Okin, Rawls, and Habermas," *Hypatia* vol.11, no.1, 1996, pp.49-66.

Banic-Pajnic, Erna, "Women in Renaissance Philosophy" in *Prilozi za Istrazivanje Hrvatske Filozofske Bastine*, vol.59-60, nos.1-2, 2004, pp. 69-89.

Barnes, Hazel E., "Sartre and Sexism," *Philosophy and Literature*, 1990 pp.340-347.

Bar-On, Bat Ami, "The Feminist 'Sexuality Debates' and the Transformation of the Political," *Hypatia*, vol.7, no.4, 1992, pp.45-58.

Bedi, Tarini, "The Dashing Ladies of Shiv Sena, Review of Women's Studies," *Economic and Political Weekly*, vol.42 no.17, April 28- May 4, 2007.

Bluestone, Natalie Harris, "Why Women Cannot Rule: Sexism in Plato Scholarship" in *Feminist Interpretations of Plato*, Ed. Nancy Tuana, University Park: Pennsylvania State University Press pp.109-130.

Blum, Lawrence, "Kant's and Hegel's Moral Rationalism: A Feminist Perspective," *Canadian Journal of Philosophy*, vol.12, no.2, 1982, pp.287-302.

Borresen, Kari Elisabeth, "Patristic 'Feminism': The Case of Augustine," *Augustinian Studies*, vol.25, 1994, pp.139-152.

Bradshaw, Leah, "Rousseau on Civic Virtue, Male Autonomy, and the Construction of the Divided Female" in *Feminist Interpretations of Jean-Jacques Rousseau*, Ed. Lynda Lange, University Park, Pennsylvania State University Press, 2002 pp.65-88.

Brownmiller, Susan, "Ayn Rand: A Traitor to Her Own Sex" in *Feminist Interpretations of Ayn Rand,* Eds. Mimi Reisel Gladstein and Chris Matthew Sciabarra, University Park: Pennsylvania State University Press, 1999 pp.63-66.

Burney Davis, Terri, "The Vita Femina and Truth," *History of European Ideas,* 1989, pp.841-847.

Carling, Alan, "Rational Choice Marxism and Postmodern Feminism: Towards a More Meaningful Incomprehension," in *Rational Choice Marxism* Terrell Carver, ed., University Park, Pennsylvania State University Press, 1995.

Chandrashekar, B. K., "Panchayati Raj Law in Karnataka: Janata Initiative in Decentralisation," *Economic and Political Weekly,* April, 1989.

Chiang, Lan-hung Nora "Women and Development in Taiwan," *Asian Journal of Women's Studies,* vol.4, no.4, 1998.

Christensen, Ray, "The Impact of Electoral Rules in Japan," in *Democracy and the Status of Women in East Asia.* ed. Cal Clark & Janet Clark,, Boulder, Rienner, 2000, pp.25-46.

Code, Lorraine, "Simple Equality is Not Enough," *Australasian Journal of Philosophy* Supp.64, 1986.

Deutscher, Penelope, "Is It Not Remarkable that Nietzsche...Should Have Hated Rousseau?" in *Feminism and History of Philosophy,* Ed. Genevieve Lloyd, New York, Oxford University Press, 2002 pp.322-347.

Duhan, Laura, "Feminism and Peace Theory: Women as Nurturers versus Women as Public Citizens" in *In the Interest of Peace: A Spectrum of Philosophical Views,* Wolfeboro, Longwood, 1990.

Fleming, Marie, "Women and the 'Public Use of Reason," *Social Theory and Practice* vol.19, no.1, 1993, pp.27-50.

Freeland, Cynthia, "Feminism and Ideology in Ancient Philosophy" in *Apeiron: A Journal for Ancient Philosophy and Science* vol.33, no.4, December, 2000, pp.365-406.

Froese, Katrin, "Woman's Eclipse: The Silenced Feminine in Nietzsche and Heidegger" *Philosophy and Social Criticism* vol.31, no.2, March 2005, pp.165-184.

Ghosh, Ratma & Abdulaziz Talbani, *Women, Education and Development in Asia: Cross-National Perspectives,* in ed. Grace C. L. Mak, New York, Garland Publishing, 1996 pp.165-186.

Goldstein, Leslie, "Mill, Marx, and Women's Liberation," *Journal of the History of Philosophy,* vol.XVIII, no.3, July 1980.

Gowans, Christopher W., "After Kant: Ventures in Morality Without Respect for Persons," *Social Theory and Practice,* vol.22, no.1, 1996, pp. 105-129.

Graham, Kevin M., "The Political Significance of Social Identity: A Critique of Rawls's Theory of Agency" in *Social Theory and Practice: An International and Interdisciplinary Journal of Social Philosophy,* vol. 26, no.2, September 2000, pp.201-222.

Hartel, Joseph, "The Integral Feminism of St. Thomas Aquinas," *Gregorianum,* vol.77, no.3, 1996, pp. 527-547.

Hawkesworth, Mary E., "Re/Vision: Feminist Theory Confronts the Polis," *Social Theory and Practice,* vol.13, 1987, pp.155-186.

Hickman, John C.,"The Candidacy and Election of Women in Japanese SNTV Electoral Systems" *Women and Politics,* vol.18, no.2, 1997, pp.1-26.

Holm, Elly & Paul Cilliers, "Beyond the Politics of Positionality: Deconstruction and Feminism," *South African Journal of Philosophy,* vol.17, no.4, 1998 pp.377-394.

Hoskyns, Catherine & Shirin M. Rai, "Gender, Class and Representation: India and the European Union," *The European Journal of Women's Studies,* vol.5, no.3-4, 1998, pp.345-366

Isham, Jonathan, D. Narayan & L. Pritchett, "Does Participation Improve Performance? Establishing Causality with Subjective Data," *The World Bank Economic Review,* vol.9, no.2, May, 1995.

Johnson Richard L: "Gandhi's soul politics: The Liberation of Women and Men in India," *Gandhi Marg,* vol.XXI, No.1, April-June, 1999.

Kenworthy, Lane & Melissa Malami, "Gender Inequality in Political Representation: A Worldwide Comparative Analysis," *Social Forces,* vol.78, no.1, 1999, pp.235-268.

Koikari, Mire, "Exporting Democracy? American Women, 'Feminist Reforms,' and Politics of Imperialism in the US Occupation of Japan 1945-1952," *Frontiers,* vol.23, no.1, 2002, pp.23-45.

Kruks, Sonia, "Identity Politics and Dialectical Reason: Beyond an Epistemology of Provenance" in *Feminist Interpretations of Jean-Paul Sartre,* Ed. Julien S. Murphy, University Park, Pennsylvania State University Press, 1999 pp.229-252.

Mahowald, Mary, "Freedom versus Happiness and Women's Liberation," *Journal of Social Philosophy,* vol.6, 1975, pp.10-13.

Makus, Ingrid, "The Politics of 'Feminine Concealment' and 'Masculine Openness' in Rousseau" in *Feminist Interpretations of Jean-Jacques Rousseau,* Ed. Lynda Lange, University Park, Pennsylvania State University Press, 2002 pp.187-21.

Marcil-Lacoste, L.,"The Consistency of Hume's Position Concerning Women," *Dialogue*, vol.15, no.3, 1976, pp. 425-440.

Marcuse, Herbert, "Marxism and Feminism," *Women's Studies*, vol.2, no.3, 1974, pp. 279-288.

Martin, Bill, "To the Lighthouse and the Feminist Path to Posmodernity," *Philosophy and Literature*, vol.13, 1989, pp.307-315

Matland, Richard E, "Women's Representation in National Legislatures: Developed and Developing Countries," *Legislative Studies Quarterly*, vol.23, no.1, 1998, pp.99-125.

McLaughlin, Eleanor, "Equality of Souls, Inequality of Sexes: Women in Medieval Theology," in *Religion and Sexism*, Rosemary Ruether, ed., New York, Simon & Schuster, 1974.

Meehan, Johanna,"Review Essay: Feminism, Critical Theory, and Power" *Philosophy and Social Criticism*, vol.30, no.3, May 2004, pp.375-382.

Meier, E & P, "Gender and Mainstreaming in the EU: Incorporating a Feminist Reading," *European Journal of women Studies*, vol.13, no.2, 2006, pp.151-66.

Melander, Ellinor, "Toward the Sexual and Economic Emancipation of Women: The Philosophy of Grete Meisel-Hess," *History of European Ideas*, vol.14, no.5, 1992, pp.695-713.

Menon Nivedita, "Elusive Women: Feminsim and Women's Reservation Bill," *Economic and Political Weekly*, vol.35, nos.43, 44, Oct 28, pp.35-42.

Morgenstern, Mira, "Women, Power, and the Politics of Everyday Life" in *Feminist Interpretations of Jean-Jacques Rousseau*, Ed. Lynda Lange, University Park, Pennsylvania State University Press, 2002 pp.113-143.

Nissim Sabat, Marilyn, "Freud, Feminism, and Faith," *Listening*, vol.20, 1985, pp.208-220.

Nussbaum, Martha, "Political Liberalism and Respect: A Response to Linda Barclay," *SATS: Nordic Journal of Philosophy*, vol.4, no.2, 2003, pp.25-44.

Ogai, Tokuko, "Japanese Women and Political Institutions: Why Are Women Politically Underrepresented?" *Political Science and Politics*, vol.34, no.2, 2002, pp.207-210.

Okin, Susan Moller, "Philosopher Queens and Private Wives: Plato on Women and the Family," *Philosophy and Public Affairs*, vol.6, Summer 1977.

Patton, Paul, "Nietzsche, Feminism, and Political Theory" in *New Nietzsche Studies: The Journal of the Nietzsche Society*, vol.3, nos.3-4, Summer-Fall, 1999.

Polyakov, L.V., "Women's Emancipation and the Theology of Sex in Nineteenth Century Russia," *Philosophy East and West*, vol.42, no.2, 1992, pp.297-308.

Potter, Elizabeth, "Modeling the Gender Politics in Science," *Hypatia*, vol.3, 1988, pp.19-33.

Putnam, Ruth Anna, "Democracy without Foundations" *Ethics: An International Journal of Social, Political, and Legal Philosophy*, vol.110, no.2, January 2000, pp.388-404.

Raman, Vasanthi, "The Implementation of Quotas for Women: The Indian Experience," in *The Implementation of Quotas: Asian Experiences*, Quota Workshops Report Series no.1, International Institute for Democracy and Electoral Assistance: vol.22, no.31, 2003.

Raya, Dunayevskaya, *The Power of Negativity: Selected Writings on the Dialectic in Hegel and Marx*, New York, Lexington Books, 2002.

Rule, Wilma, "Electoral Systems, Contextual Factors and Women's Opportunity for Election to Parliament in Twenty-Three Democracies," *Western Political Quarterly*, vol.40, no.2, 1987, pp.477-498.

Rumani Seth, "Contesting Indentities: Involvement of Women in the Indian National Movement," *Journal of Indian Studies*, vol.5, no.3, Nov.1996.

Schultz, Bart, "Sidgwick's Feminism" *Utilitas: A Journal of Utilitarian Studies*, vol.12, no.3, November 2000, pp.379-401.

Sen, Samita, "Toward a Feminist Politics? The Indian Women's Movement in Historical Perspective," *Policy Research Report on Gender and Development*, Working Paper Series, no. 9, 2000.

Sharma , Kumud, "Grassroot Organisations and Women's Empowerment: Some Issues in the contemporary debate," in *Samya Shakti*, Centre for Women's Development studies, New-Delhi, vol.VI, 1991-92, p.29.

Sharma, Kumud, "Power and Representation: Reservation for Women in India," *Asian Journal of Women's Studies*, vol.6, no.1, 2000, pp.65-71.

Simons, Martin, "Why Can't a Man Be More Like a Woman?, A Note on John Locke's Educational Thought," *Educational Theory*, vol.40, no.1, 1990, pp.135-145.

Smith, Dorothy, *A Feminist Sociology,* Toronto, University of Toronto Press, 1987.

Smith, Nicholas, "Plato and Aristotle on the Nature of Women," *Journal of the History of Philosophy,* vol.2, 1983, pp.467-478.

Stefano, Christine Di, "Masculinity as Ideology in Political Theory: Hobbesian Man Considered," *Women's Studies International Forum,* vol.6, no.6, 1983.

Stiehm, Judith Hicks, "The Unit of Political Analysis: Our Aristotelian Hangover," in *Discovering Reality: Feminist Perspectives on Epistemology, Metaphysics, Methodology, and Philosophy of Science,* Sandra Harding and Merrill B. Hintikka, eds., Dordrecht, Reidel, 1983.

Still, Judith, "What Foucault Fails to Acknowledge...Feminism and The History of Sexuality," *History of Human Sciences,* vol.7, no.2, 1994, pp.150-157.

Sumiko, Yazawa, "Political Participation of Japanese Women and Local Self- Governments: Its Trend and Review," *Asian Journal of Women's Studies,* vol.1, 1995, pp.98-106.

Tinker, Irene & Jane Jaquette, "UN Decade for Women: its Impact and Legacy," *World Development,* vol.15, no.3, 1987, pp.419-27.

Tinker, Irene, "Economic Development and Women," *International Encyclopedia of Social and Behavioral Sciences,* 2001.

Tinker, Irene, "The Making of a Field: Advocates, Practitioners, and Scholars" in *Persistent Inequalities: Women and World Development,* Ed. Irene Tinker, New York, Oxford University Press, 1990 pp.27-53.

Veelayudhan Meera, "Growth of Political Consciousness Among Women in Modern Kerala: Perspectives of Kerala History," *Kerala State Gazetteer* Govt. of Kerala, Tiruvananthpuram, vol.12, Part 1,, 1999, pp.486-511.

Vlastos, Gregory, "Was Plato a Feminist?" *Times Literary Supplement* 276, March 17, 1989, pp. 276, 288-289. Cited from *Studies in Greek Philosophy* ed. Daniel W. Graham, *Socrates, Plato, and Their Tradition,* Princeton: Princeton University Press, 1995 pp. 133-143.

Walker, C.,"Women, "Tradition' and Reconstruction," *Review of African Political Economy,* no.61, 1994, pp.347-58

Walsh, Sylvia, "When That Single Individual Is a Woman," *Kierkegaard Studies: Yearbook,* 2000, pp.1-18.

Weiss, Penny A, "Mary Astell: Including Women's Voices in Political Theory," *Hypatia: A Journal of Feminist Philosophy,* vol.19, no.3, Summer 2004, pp.63-84.

Whitbeck, Caroline, "Theories of Sex Difference," in *Women and Philosophy: Toward a Theory of Liberation* Carol C. Gould and Marx W. Wartofsky, eds., New York, G.P. Putnam's Sons, 1976.

Williams, Reginald M., "Affirmative Action, the May the Best Person Win Intuition, and Mill's The Subjection of Women," *Public Affairs Quarterly*, vol.19, no.1 January 2005, pp. 65-80.

Williford, Miriram, "Bentham and the Rights of Women," *Journal of the History of Ideas*, vol.36, January-March 1975.

Zack, Naomi, "Intra-Feminist Criticism and Intellectual Virtue" in *Newsletter on Feminism and Philosophy, American Philosophical Association Newsletters*, vol.2, Spring, 2000, pp.83-84.

Compiled by Geetanjali Sharma

Index